WORKING WOMEN DON'T HAVE WIVES

PROFESSIONAL SUCCESS IN THE 1990S

TERRI APTER

ST. MARTIN'S PRESS
NEW YORK

All rights reserved. For information, write:
St. Martin's Press, Inc., 175 Fifth Avenue
New York, New York 10010

First published in the United States of America in 1994

Printed in the United States of America

ISBN 0-312-09675-5

Library of Congress Cataloging-in-Publication Data

Apter, T. E.
   Working women don't have wives : professional success in the 1990s
   / Terri Apter
          p. cm.
   Includes bibliographical references and index.
   ISBN 0-312-09675-5
   1. Work and family–United States. 2. Working mothers–United
States. 3. Women in the professions–United States.   I. Title.
HD4904.25.A68 1993
331.4'4'0973–dc20
                                                93-31949
                                                    CIP

First Edition: December 1993
10 9 8 7 6 5 4 3 2

Contents

Contents

Contents

ACKNOWLEDGEMENTS

I wish to thank all the women who took time from their already time-impoverished lives to speak to me or write to me about their lives as working mothers. As they create their lives, they are creating new futures for other women and men, and therefore my tribute to them goes well beyond their generous help with this book. I have used their precise words when I have quoted from them, but I have used pseudonyms for virtually all except well-known names used only in passing, since personal revelations, however sympathetic, can, when identified by others, so easily become intrusive and further complicate already complex lives.

I wrote this book while I held the Betty Behrens Research Fellowship at Clare Hall, Cambridge. I would like to thank the President and Fellows of Clare Hall, and the executors of the Betty Behrens estate for their support. My greatest intellectual debt is to Elizabeth Garnsey at Clare Hall. It was through discussions with her that I was able to reformulate the old questions in light of a decade's research and a decade of social change.

Introduction: Why Women Still Don't Have Wives

The statement made in the title of this book is, of course, a joke. Women do not have wives because when women marry they do not have wives for spouses as men do when they marry: instead, they become wives. But the meaning of 'wife' extends beyond its specific meaning as 'female spouse', and implies, or has traditionally implied, specific roles. Men often do get, when they marry, a partner who looks after their domestic needs, cares for their children, accomodates their changing occupational needs, and puts family responsibilities first and foremost. The 'woman behind the man' is the wife who takes care of everything else, so that the man can concentrate on his career.

There must have been many jokes made by women about wives and how nice it would be to have one. A retired Cambridge lecturer is reported to have said in an interview, in reply to a question as to whether she regretted not marrying, that she would have been glad to marry, had she only found someone who would have made a good wife. Jane O'Reilly may have been the first to suggest in print that what a working woman needs is a wife,[1] though it was a wish voiced by many career-oriented women as they saw how indispensable a wife was to the colleagues with whom they worked. How nice it would be, they argued, to have someone who would organize domestic life while they attended to their work with dust-free mental furniture. They wanted to be supported, rather than burdened by the role of wife.

Yet the desire for a 'wife' was not the sort of desire women thought would be satisfied – not because it was literally impossible to do so, but because, taking the term figuratively, standing for the roles a female spouse typically fulfilled, women did not expect to reverse roles with their husbands, but merely to share them. They believed that if fathers took on half the domestic work load and took equal responsibility for the children, then each partner could live on equal terms both inside and outside the home.

Male Power versus Female Psychology

Few women in 1982, when I conducted my first study of working mothers, let alone ten years on, when I conducted the second study, would have said that this expectation of equality, either at work or at home, had been met. During the past two decades many writers in many fields have asked why this simple equation was not solved. Did the problem arise from the persistent ill-will of male partners, or the weak will of female ones? If so, then why did it persist even where men seemed so good-willed and women so strong? What was the story behind this failure – or did the failure mean that the ideal was somehow disfigured so that what we saw was not actually a failure but a sign of how things really ought to be? Or did the problem arise from a mismatch between women and the work force? Were women afraid to follow through their ambitions, afraid of being punished for deviating from traditional female roles? Were they ignorant of or ill-equipped to follow the rules for career success? Why did the same education or training that propelled men leave women stalled in their upward climb? Was it prejudice on the part of male employers, or passivity on the part of women?

The elusiveness of any single satisfactory explanation as to

2

why progress remains slow, has not been due to lack of interest. Explanations continue to proliferate. Recently discussions of women's inequality have taken one of two approaches. The first locates the causes of persistent inequality in male power. Prejudice against women sustains job segregation. Men who control the professions want to maintain their power and see women's entry as a threat. They use their power as entrenched 'owners' of jobs and arbiters of promotions either to keep women out altogether, or to prevent them from climbing the promotional ladder. They use either direct bars or informal networks of information and assistance to shore up male privilege and keep women outside the best-rewarded and most powerful positions.[2]

Male power can also be exercised in the home. As 'head of household', men may still dictate women's place.[3] They may prevent their daughters from gaining access to appropriate education or use sanctions against their wives if they seek paid employment.[4] They may use positive reinforcement, controlling as they praise their wives for staying at home with the children[5] or give them freedom to work outside the home as long as everything else at home stays the same.[6]

Male power need not be overt, but can be embodied in social structures, or patterns of interaction so stable and embedded that they are taken for granted, and not perceived as interactions of power and dependence. Explanations couched in terms of male power rest on the assumption that society is structured to support male interests. Though some feminists see the ultimate cause of gender inequality as men's malice towards women,[7] the explanations that refer to male power are generally concerned with structures, or stable patterns of interaction drawing on expectations, rules and roles. In one set of explanations, women are viewed as largely powerless when faced with such structures as the educational system and job segregation, which appear in crucial ways to embody male power.

The other type of explanation for women's lack of progress sets issues of male power to one side. Without denying that women's lives are shaped by men's wishes, these approaches find psychological reasons as to why women allow men to have their way. Women are seen as comfortable with traditional female roles, and as turning to these to escape the challenges of independence and competition.[8] Socialized to please others, they too often become the non-challenging, non-assertive homebound creatures their men want them to be[9] and avoid the sanctions which success and competition might incur.[10] Modified versions of this approach suggest that women give their permission in default of resistance: they marginalize themselves in order to avoid the sanctions that would be meted out should they voice their needs or wishes. In this modified view, men have a variety of techniques for keeping women 'in their place', while women collude in this placement either because it it too much trouble to do otherwise or because they lack the ability, in their man-made language, to name women's problems.[11]

In more positive accounts, women are seen to take a shrewd measure of the cost of success in male terms in a male world and, accordingly, choose different goals and other means of achieving them. Their priorities are different and they refuse to buy into the largely male structures of the workforce. In studying the exit of women managers from their positions, Judi Marshall has identified a resistance to the imbalance of corporate life, and to the competitive styles which are necessary to promotion.[12] Carol Gilligan has drawn attention to the different meanings which may emerge from a common male and common female perspective, wherein a woman's response is often silenced by the standards that are assumed to be objective.[13] In interpreting the observed reluctance of women to be seen to succeed,[14] Georgia Sassen suggests that women avoid achievements which are starkly competitive.[15] Though from this angle, women are seen to be justified in rejecting male terms, their complicity in their inequality is implicit.

The implied conclusion of these arguments is that if women ceased to sabotage themselves, if they learned to assert their rights and needs, then they could achieve the aims that they now fail to pursue. And if women do not succeed, the argument from female psychology suggests, this may be because they reject normal male terms of success. According to this perspective, if women freed themselves psychologically, if they changed their outlook, they could take action to remedy inequalities. Through their own agency they could free themselves of constraints which now bind them. Here constraints are seen as in part of women's making; structures reinforcing male power could crumble if recognised to be phoney obstacles which help to mislead women into believing in their own weakness.

The questions of whether constraints are imposed from within, or whether constraints are imposed from without, or how these two different forces combine and how they can be defeated, remain open. The questions about why women are not advancing at an appropriate pace in the workplace, and why women's roles at home are not changing remain open to debate, and the debates continue to swing from arguments about women's nature to arguments about the culture in which women live.

In her compelling narrative of girls' and boys' development Nancy Chodorow[16] described how girls, raised by mothers, developed a sense of self that was linked to others, whereas boys, raised by a different-sexed parent, developed a more separate sense of self. Hence girls emerged as women who were more likely to 'mother' than were men: they were more responsive to other's needs, more preoccupied by issues of attachment and caring. The change in the domestic order would have to be effected over generations: as fathers, impelled by ideology rather than psychology, took an equal part in parenting, boys and girls would become adults with different, more flexible gender identity. Yet to get to this point, fathers had to share parenting, to be as involved with daughters and sons as mothers were. And this, though occurring in a few families, was not becoming a general trend, even among parents who believed that it should.

This stubbornness required its own explanation. One account, which gained enormous currency in the early 1980s, was that women could not sustain their willpower. Though they wanted to become economically independent on one level, at another level they wanted to remain Cinderellas,[17] leaning on the princely male to provide for them. Women's domestic roles were not changing because women were afraid to change them, and they were afraid to, because they felt inadequate and dependent in a male-dominated society.

Hence women were advised to blame themselves for the status quo. They were afraid of success, afraid of the competition, afraid to make their kill. So conditioned were they to be nice that they imagined gross punishment heaped upon them if they proved themselves to be outstanding, or grabbed the prize in a competition.[18] But sociologists and economists challenged this psychological location of woman's fall. Women's careers progressed at a snail's pace because at every step they dragged with them the same heavy domestic weight they always had. As Colette Dowling berated herself for playing with her children, for staying home to sew curtains and make jam, Sylvia Ann Hewlett[19] defended her behaviour and derided her theory by pointing out that it was probably very difficult to do anything else. Who else would have looked after the three children, entertained them, fed them, and chauffeured them? Who else would have made the new country house, in which Dowling caught herself reenacting feminine roles, into an idyllic home?

Women 'decided' to remain at home, economically and emotionally dependent, because it was so very difficult to do anything else. The processes of having children – pregnancy and childbirth – create gaps in working life which are sometimes not accommodated by employers at all, or, when they are tolerated, nonetheless stall promotion. Some researchers found that a hiatus in working life – usually caused by domestic obligations; in particular, by the birth of children and children's need for care – is the factor most detrimental to women's advancement.[20]

The single most important factor was again identified. What women need, what would solve their problems, is, Hewlett persuasively argued, a set of social policies that make work feasible for mothers: child care facilities and maternity leaves and allowance for absence in the event of a child's illness. Women will be able to compete with men at work when women's lives outside work are like men's.

One-shot Theories – Convincing, and Inadequate

Each 'single most important factor' that has been identified can also be shown to be a part of the picture, neither being necessary to impede women's progress nor sufficient in and of itself to do so. Institutional child care does not pick up the entire maternal tab. In the Scandinavian countries whose social policies Hewlett lauded, women's careers are indeed far more advanced, but not equal to men's. Job segregation is still common, and when there is job segregation – jobs for men and jobs for women – there is always job inequality: inequality of pay, of promotion, of prestige. When employers design jobs with women in mind, these jobs are virtually always less well-paid than jobs designed for the 'principal breadwinner', thought to be male, and have far fewer routes to promotion. Furthermore, women remain primarily responsible for domestic labour in the home, and this changes the conditions under which they offer their services to employers. The 'second shift' becomes a feature in their lives on the basis of which they calculate their energy and time commitments.

Whereas men with young children work longer hours – over four times as much paid overtime as childless married men of the same age[21] – women with young children find it very difficult to obtain suitable work, and hence employers design jobs for them. As their husbands work longer hours for good overtime rates of pay, women have less help in the home. As their domestic obligations increase, they seek jobs which can accommodate them. These jobs offer rates of pay far below what their partners earn, and so it becomes 'irrational' for men to take time out of work in order to give more time to the home. Men who face the primary responsibility for their families have far less access to 'good jobs', and face constraints similar to those faced by women.[22] As soon as men are forced to take on 'maternal' functions, their work opportunities are jeopardized.

In Soviet countries, too, which supported women's employment through fairly widespread child care institutions, job segregation has ensured quite marked wage differentials between men and women. Moreover, the government's decision to put little money into the services and manufacturing that would make domestic life less burdensome means that women, who continue to do unpaid 'women's work' in the home, subsidized with their unpaid labour the economic policies of the Soviet government: they work harder to maintain the home because the government allocates less funds to services which would ease the burden of home maintenance. State-supported child care has allowed them to work (though in 1970 less than half of children under school-age, 7, were catered for by public child care facilities).[23] The cultural ethos forced them to work, and the shortage of men in the Soviet population immediately after the Second World War made their work essential;[24] but they were shunted into jobs specifically designed for them as women. Throughout the former Soviet bloc (CEE) countries working women are in the poorer-paid and less-prestigious occupations. They are also under-represented in the managerial and higher-level positions. Women dominate employment in the service sector, particularly in education, health and social care sectors (where they represent over 70 per cent of all employees in many CEE countries). Women also constitute the majority of workers in the trade, culture and arts, communications, and finance sectors. This occupational concentration reflects a link between the 'feminization' of certain sectors and the related decline in status and hence the average wages of those sectors. So though the stereotyping of certain occupations according to gender may be different in CEE countries and in the West, the effect is the same.

The gap between men's and women's wages in the CEE is not so very different from Western wage differentials.[25] As in the Soviet Union, social structures altered radically, but there was no concomitant equality. Though the liberation of women was originally high on the agenda of the Bolshevik revolution, in practice ideals of equality narrowed considerably. The falling birthrate fostered a backlash against the erosion of traditional notions of femininity.[26] The traditional division of labour in the home was never changed, in spite of Lenin's outcry against housework. With a government that failed to meet the service needs of its people, in an inflexible and inefficient economy, women became so burdened by the daily tasks of their domestic lives that they did not and do not have 'the time, the energy, or the psychological reserves to look beyond them'.[27]

Though greater structural changes might have helped women in these countries to progress further, it is striking that despite the impressive structural changes which did take place, traditional attitudes towards the relations between men and women changed relatively little.[28] The strength of traditional mentalities in part explained the failure of these regimes to adopt policies which could have created structures more facilitating for women. The argument that inequalities stem from traditional structures is incomplete.

If child care facilities do not offer the final solution, if there is still simply too much women's work in the home, however well provided-for are the children during working hours, then perhaps the problem is that men do not help enough, that the working woman remains a wife, taking on a second shift at home after her working day ends. Some accounts of why women are not making greater strides towards equality at work involve subtle and ingenious descriptions of how the pressures of the second shift affect women's happiness, self-confidence, and career determination. Though there might have been a revolution in the workplace, domestic life remains much the same. The revolution is stalled because only half of life is changing. As much as they want to move forward at work, women are blocked by lazy, stubborn husbands. Wanting to protect both their husbands and themselves against their frustration and anger, they actually disguise from themselves the extent to which they retain traditional wifely roles.

Sociologist Arlie Hochschild[29] looks at how women manage the domestic burdens they still incur by what she calls the second shift, or an excess of domestic work brought about by the stalled revolution in the home. As their ideals of domestic collaboration crumble in face of their husbands' persistent lack of participation, they seek to protect themselves from disappointment and frustration by disguising the relative amount of household work and child care tasks performed by each: they see their husbands as contributing far more to the home than they actually do. They suppress their anger – and their job commitments. Hochschild shows how this way of coping with men's stubbornness reinforces rather than undermines the status quo. In accommodating their husband's domestic laziness, women support it. This startling, insightful account of women's work and men's withdrawal in the home, however, does not question the work structure which refuses to take into account people's domestic responsibilities – nor does it acknowledge that work structures have become more, not less rigorous, in the past decade.

Whose Fault?

The second shift is not an isolated remnant of previous family history but a continuing symptom of the divisions between the personal life of the home and the more public, institutional life of work. For Hochschild, the stalled revolution in men's domestic input is a remnant of habit, laziness and prejudice. We have to ask what makes the man a couch potato, a television ogler, an idle zombie, when he comes home. For the amount of television watched at home is often linked to very long and demanding hours at work, after which one simply does not have energy to do anything else. Home becomes a place of soporific passivity when work drains and threatens, frustrates and demeans. Hochschild sees the women's revolution as stalled by men's persistent expectation that a wife will fulfil in the home her wifely roles whatever she may do outside it. Women, she argues, to preserve their marriages, accept that second shift which takes them out of the running for fast-track promotion. Hochschild's analysis, however sharp and amusing, places the blame on those stubborn men who will not change and on the women who allow men to have their way. It does not investigate the structure which makes change for men so difficult.

For if men's victory in the battle between the sexes continues unabated, as measured by indicators of occupational achievement and political dominance, the price of this victory is increasingly judged too high. Not only quantitative indicators such as accident and mortality rates measure the toll taken on men, but the process of acquiring a masculine self-identity has come to be questioned. Those exploring new ways of being masculine reject the sacrifice of intimacy and openness and other costs which old ways so often imposed, where men have been distant or absent parents, have an impaired and superficial relationships with partners and male friends. Damage to the capacity of young boys to feel and connect closely with others is as harmful in different ways as that experienced by their sisters.[30] This upbringing gives rise to mentalities and enacted structures which are oppressive of humanity and nature. But this cycle is deeply resistant to change. In reassessing themselves, in redefining their identity, their expectations and their capacity for action, can women inspire men to undertake such a process themselves in new ways? Can they so engage together in more human interaction? Transformative feminism, which insists on the need to 'craft new alternatives'[31] in light of the recurring constraints of contemporary work structures, highlights men's and women's victimization in recurring structures, and the potential power women have in refusing to follow traditional paths both at work and in the home.

Whose Conspiracy?

The demands employers make on men influence their behaviour in the home. There is growing evidence that many men want to work less, and would be willing to forgo some of their earnings in order to reduce their hours of work.[32] Many men may want to participate more in the home and family life, but find it impractical, given the demands their employers or their firms make on them. Yet many feminist writers remain convinced that women's slow progress towards equality results from a male conspiracy which, having felt the threat of female power, is working harder than ever to retain male supremacy and male power. Suspicion and fear and greed enforce already-prejudiced structures.

This conspiracy is thought to emerge in many forms. Not only do men directly and deliberately, it is thought, lock women out, but they also undermine their will; they drain women's best energies and sap their self-confidence. Naomi Wolf[33] argues that a woman's obsession with appearance holds her back, and that this obsession is foisted upon women by commerce and the conglomerates that control commerce. Women's advance is now in retreat as massive medical, cosmetic, fashion and retail

11

industries manipulate her. Trapped by unrealistic ideals of beauty and daunted by their inability to fulfil them, women remain masochistic and infantilized.

Though Wolf's explanation is less plausible than many for the stalled revolution, she nonetheless exposes an area in which women themselves do not feel they have made significant strides. Though they are trying very hard, individually and collectively, to shatter the glass which engages their preoccupation and fosters self-doubt, they remain enthralled.

The supposition that there is a conspiratorial backlash against women may seem reasonable: it organizes the myriad of reasons into a single principle. The guardians of power are maintaining their stand, and sending into retreat the women who pursue masculine privilege. Women are being punished for the advances they made: women are being warned that success will cost them dear. In constructing a conspiracy from a combination of prejudice, restrictive social policy, popular culture, media images, common assumptions and predictions reinforced by statistics, Susan Faludi[34] gives a definitive shape to a medley of social, economic and intellectual mishaps. Yet the superimposition of a structure without outlining the precise ways in which this structure functions creates a brooding sense of malice alongside images of paralysis. We see, vaguely, men shooting arrows at women from the wings of the theatre. We see society in terms of 'them' and 'us'. We see victim and oppressor, rather than a system of interconnected circuits.

In fact, this vision is both excessively optimistic and excessively pessimistic. Its simplicity gives it optimism: if only women could shoot back and kill, all would be well, is the supposition. Hence the extensive social structures which work against equality are ignored. But at the same time, the vision that all one can do is battle, neglects the most complex ways in which women can influence the conditions under which they live. None of these explanations can be final or ultimate. They work together and reinforce one another. Each woman confronts her own cocktail of problems. For some women some constraints fall away as though they never existed. Others come up against them at every turn. Some constraints can be negotiated individually, and some need political or social control.

We need to understand the ways in which individual events occur in complex, organized situations and partake in wider processes. Individuals – both male and female – are not passive components of social systems but active in collectively structuring the systems of which they are members. Individuals make sense of their experience, engage in power relations, enact outcomes, negotiate the social order, structure their system. In this way we can see both that change is difficult because so many functioning systems resist change, and secondly, that change is possible and within our power.

Systems and Circuits

Explanations of women's stalled advance are usually stacked up like layers on a wedding cake. The bottom layer is packed with solid accounts of market forces. Women lack 'human capital', or the development of skills, either because they have failed to invest in them, or because others have prevented, or persuaded them, from such investment. Hence women are packed into low-paying jobs, competing with other unskilled women for low-paying, low-prestige, low-prospect jobs. Since so many women compete for these jobs, employers have no incentive to improve their terms.

The second layer consists of a mix of male conspiracies. Men want to sustain their privileges and their powers, and so keep women out, with biased hiring policies and, when women overcome these, with harassment. Male power at work is enforced with male imperviousness at home, as men refuse to work towards a domestic lifestyle that would allow a woman to compete in the workplace on terms equal to men.

The top layer is iced with explanations of women's psychology. Caring more for others, more psychologically dependent on relationships, she has less bargaining power within the home. She gives up non-domestic goals in order to preserve the harmony of her marriage, or to be the wife her husband wants her to be. Geared to accommodate others, she is afraid to compete with them at work. Socialized to be dependent, she fails to invest in skills.

Cut through this cake, and one is given a slice from which one can pick and choose. Any of these different explanations as to why, in general, women's career advance is stalled, is sometimes true; yet none of these truths offers a satisfactory explanation of women's condition as a whole. Each of these, however drastic, actually underestimates the obstacles to equality, for it is in how these various explanations link up with one another and interlock that they are given structure and stability – and resistance to change. The difficulty lies not with the particular problem named and the specific solution proposed, but with the type of analysis that sees one thing as a problem, and believes that one thing, or even one set of things, if changed, would change women's position. The difficulty lies in the uneasy way women are presented as both having the potential for power and as being disempowered by the conditions in which they live.

I hope to unravel the social processes which reinforce one another and are deeply embedded in mentalities and economic life. At first the idea of interlocked structures sounds pessimistic. If structures interlock then nothing can change before something else changes first. Every change seems to depend on a change somewhere else. But in fact what it means is that there are many points of possible change, many paths of escape, many possibilities of avoidance or release.

We need a new perspective which allows us to focus on the ways in which women are constrained, and the ways in which they are agents. We need a perspective which allows us to see how women 'collude' with the society that constrains them, without losing sight of the external constraints which fashion their constraints. We need to focus on collusion without losing sight of women's agency. We need to see how the structure in which we act both constrains and empowers us. We need, finally, to seek ways of change.

Explanations about why women do not succeed in their careers in the way that men who have wives do, shift clumsily between the mentality of women and the mentality of men, between the structure within the home and within the workforce. We need a new way of framing both the problems we see and the questions we pose. Single-direction explanations – tracing myriad effects from a single cause – have not provided any satisfactory answer. Tracing a single effect from many causes seems like an intellectual mud-fight: undesirable effects are seen to emerge from any number of undesirable conditions. We need to trace circuits, to show a system which is reproduced daily, which constrains day-to-day actions, and which we participate in through our day-to-day actions: we need to understand how our lives work.

Exceptional Women?

In the first phase of the women's movement the similarities between men and women were emphasized as a means of winning rights for women. The assumption was that women had a right to equal opportunities because they were equal to men in the sense of being the same as men. Now a different angle is suggested. We begin with the assumption that women have a right to equal employment, and ask what conditions must hold for that equality to be gained. We observe that women's lives are different from men's. Do we obliterate these differences, or do we accommodate them? This was the puzzle faced by the women I interviewed for this book.

The women described in this book are women who aimed for a masculine-type career pattern and who also were mothers of children under 18. They were not simply working mothers, but women who saw themselves as ambitious in their work, as ambitious as working men. Their careers were central to their ideas not only of satisfaction but also of self. They had children, but expected that motherhood would not shift or detract from their goals or their ability to attain those goals. They were on the whole very careful to avoid employment in jobs designed for women. They followed careers which are protected from job segregation, and the discrimination of pay and promotion linked into jobs 'designed' especially with women in mind – jobs thought to be low-skilled because employers believe women can do them, jobs designed for women who often require shorter hours to accommodate their domestic shift, jobs offering low pay and poor promotion prospects because a 'captive' labour force is expected to fill them – a labour force looking for jobs near their homes, who need flexibility, who have low expectations of advancement and fairness from an employer because their lives as wives and mothers come first.

To some extent this determination was based on class differences: those who were well-educated, those whose mothers were articulate and understood the potential for change and the danger of stasis, were forewarned of the pitfalls of employment designed for women. Yet many of the women had discovered for themselves the need to mark out a strong career along other lines. Some had the role of breadwinner foisted upon them: the cruel experience of women's financial vulnerability and unpreparedness stimulated ways and means of rising to the challenge. Others looked back at their mothers' lives, or looked around at their friends' plight, and determined to be different.

Whatever the various and unpredictable routes to their ambition, these women were determined to eschew women's work; yet, as women, and especially as wives and mothers, they faced women's constraints. The long hours expected of corporate employees demanded more than a daytime nursery; they required – as most ambitious men have – a traditional wife, looking after the home, the children and the husband. However much these women succeeded, they were all at times confounded by the ways the systems of domestic work and employment functioned against them.

The career structure itself may block women's advance. This structure has evolved in a society in which employees have had wives, and though the number of employees who do, in that traditional sense, have wives, is falling, the demands of the jobs which have been fashioned on the assumption that they do, have not changed: in fact, employers have become increasingly demanding of their employees' time.[35] Promotions of women to top occupational places are rare because women are seen to be unwilling to work the long hours their male competitors work. Given the fact that women, unlike most male corporate managers, do not have wives looking after them and their children and their homes, they cannot afford to work the same hours.

Reframing: Decade-old Problems in a New Context

As an update of my previous study was proposed, and I wondered how to rewrite it, I quickly saw that it needed reframing. I wrote *Why Women Don't Have Wives: Professional success and motherhood* between 1981 and 1984, when I found myself transported to a modern feminist America, from the far more staid setting of Cambridge, England. In Britain, ambition and determination to succeed in a career were recognisable and acceptable occurrences, but they were still exceptional; in Washington, DC, where I lived from 1981 to 1983, they were mandatory. Yet as these women pursued their careers, they remained obsessed by child care problems, by fatigue, by fairness to family versus commitment to work. They were developing the language of checks and balances, of guilt and resistance, of self-assertion and self-doubt which was even then immediately recognizable as belonging to achievement-oriented women with families of their own.

My new sample of women for this book was mapped on my old. The first sample was small to begin with: though I contacted 75 women (60 in the United States and 15 in Britain), only 20 were interviewed at length (three two-to-three-hour sessions in the course of three months) and of those it was possible to contact, after ten years, 17 (nine in the US and eight in Britain). In looking back at my original sample of women I interviewed in depth, I thought, at the beginning of this project, that many were exceptional rather than representative. I had sought out 'names', women notable for their achievements. It was the highly successful, the vastly talented, the most ambitious whose strategies and tactics I wanted to reveal. What I found of course was that these were just other human beings with the full assembly of reasons to be both happy and unhappy. In this subsequent book I sought to extend the frame of the ordinary, and reduced the emphasis on stardom. Even my repeat sample of women previously interviewed aided this effort, since several of them, either through choice or as a result of economic changes, no longer had the professional glitter they had ten years before.

As I turned to investigate more commonplace lives, my choice was vast. I tried to find women who represented various recognizable categories: the career woman who had been educated to ambition, the late starter who had discovered ambition in midlife, the woman whose unexpected financial need had stimulated the discovery of marketable skills, the woman whose God-given talent guided her career. But among the 15 women I subsequently contacted (in addition to the 17 from the original sample), and whom I interviewed for a three-day period, and whose work life I tagged in order to see what it involved and how they engaged in it, I discovered that in these 'typical' categories, women succeeded by finding an atypical route. It was by being innovative rather than representative that women fashioned their success.

At the time I conducted my first interviews, between 1980 and 1984, there was a sense that women were moving rapidly towards equality. The awareness that the ease of such progress had been vastly overestimated was just emerging. There had been two simple miscalculations in this optimism. Few of the women planning to be working mothers understood just how time-consuming child care and domestic work were. The emptiness they saw in the housewife Betty Friedan described[36] was mistaken by them for an emptiness of time. For Betty Friedan was complaining about the satisfaction and breadth of roles available to women, rather than about the absence of things to do. Yet these exacting women spotted the unnecessary input in their mothers' care, and guessed wildly, along with Germaine Greer, that children grew up without being 'raised',[37] without that constant care and attention they were soon to discover their own offspring needed. And, like all young women, whatever their ambitions, their imaginations minimized the hard work of women's traditional work. They did not realize that even half-time parenting involved long, hard hours.

Secondly, just as women were joining the workforce in ever greater numbers, and aiming for ever higher rungs in the occupational ladder, something was changing in the workforce they were joining. When, as young adults, they had begun to conceive their futures, they still looked askance at their parents' dull working life. They believed that in the new, efficient age they would work fewer hours, and have more time for leisure and for family. The working world they were to participate in, however, involved increased hours, increased pace, increased competition. So the greater demands they did not expect on the home front joined up with greater demands made upon them in work.

In an economy which was stagnating, among dreams of equal action and equal power, it seemed that when partners shared work which brought in a joint income, then domestic duties would also be shared. But domestic duties are far more onerous than very young adults appreciate, and a shared second shift does not complete the task. The mothering and domestic functions left over from the parents' second shift have to be paid for. Women's work itself became a form of consumption. Women's work was necessary both to the family's economy and to feminine ideology, but it was also expensive, involving paid child care and paid household help. It was high, too, in anxiety costs as children were perceived to need excellent care.

Many women drop out from, or cut back on work after they have children: working itself can become a huge expense as child-minders are hired and fired, as one pays for the services which that now elusive wife once performed. Yet often their work proceeded because it had become economically necessary: the one-salary-maintained households so common in the 1950s were becoming more and more rare. Job security was being phased out, too, and two jobs in one household spread risk more thinly: with two people in jobs a family was less likely to be without an earning adult. Sometimes the household expenses had already adapted to two incomes: as thinly spread as she was, a woman might believe they could no longer afford to live on one income. Between 1973 and 1983 the real income of the average 30-year-old man fell by 23 per cent, yet the prosperity of many families was maintained. 'Working mothers are

preserving family living standards', a congressional study proclaimed in 1986.[38] The 'yuppie' lifestyle became its own badge
of success, and was perceived by some as a necessity.

The ethos of working hard and working long was being
established. The overworked American emerged just as the
working woman set her target for success. The good life was
costly, but people apparently were willing to pay. The ethos of
hard work latched on to the age of high living.

For a very brief time the 'solution' to all this was to become
superwoman – doing everything, she did not have to give up
anything. Though the image was derided nearly as soon as it was
labelled, it has in various forms been practised by women who
simply do not know what else to do. To expect women to do
everything at home just as they had always done, but to work,
and compete as workers, alongside men, was to put the burden
on them. Nothing had to change at home when superwoman
was in charge. It was a clear sell-out.

But this sell-out had a good pitch. Many women bought it in
some form or other even as they saw the sham. The question
remained why; and the question impinged on other questions
about why women were not succeeding in their occupations to
the extent that men were, or that the training they had would
indicate. There were various reasons proposed: each one seemed
definitive. Each one was true, but not definitive.

The domestic structure is reinforced each day as women do
jobs they feel compelled to do. The occupational structure is
enforced as women accept jobs with poor pay and poor prospects. They could change these systems by taking better jobs
without giving up the wifely or maternal or feminine roles they
valued. This, at least, was each woman's agenda.

The book I set out to write was meant to address women who
followed career patterns that were once more typical of men.
What I then discovered, however, was that their life patterns
were very different from men's. Each woman I spoke to, in very
different ways, confronted obstacles to equal employment and
equal opportunity in employment. It is in this sense of being

bound that conspiracy theories gain plausibility: men become a single force acting against women; society undermines women; there is a backlash against women's advance. Yet there was no single factor working against women, nor even any single set of factors. There were many variations within the system of work and home. There were many different circuits of response, effect, decision, choice, dilemma, but each different circuit could be seen as part of the same system. The successful women found loopholes, or loosened the joints at which different structures intersected.

The obstacles to equal opportunity are generally underrated. The social practices underlying prevailing structures of disadvantage which affect women are deeply embedded in social and economic life and strongly reinforced in the household, in the labour market, in the organization of economic life, in the regulations of the political authorities. This does not make stagnation inevitable; but it explains why headway is so slow, and why progress on any one front is insufficient.

Beneficial Structures: Compounded Issues

Women cannot afford to disregard the task of understanding themselves and the structures which constrain them and the impulses which confine them. New critical views of women's lives are, as Adrienne Rich wrote in *Of Woman Born*, 'more than a chapter in cultural history [they are acts] of survival'. As we work towards understanding how women act within their historical and social structure, how they reinforce it and how they might change it, we should focus, too, on how the structure is not purely oppressive: many constraints arise from women's desire to preserve what they have and what they value. For many women, offering their domestic and emotional services to others is not oppression but a rewarding fact of life. Thus the responsibility to change the system becomes a series of questions and negotiations rather than a set of battle plans.

We need a vision which gets away from many concepts which feminism is, or should be, outgrowing – concepts such as 'conditioning' wherein education or childhood training or others' stock responses are seen as 'programming' a woman in some way. Like the animal 'conditioned' to a response, a woman is seen as programmed to act, rather than choosing to act. Her choice is then seen as escape from the program; but this leaves out both the choice of her previous behaviour, and the benefits such previous behaviour might have had to her – thus polarizing different types of women as one type sees the other as conditioned and unfree. We also need to minimize conspiracy theories, as less central than questions of action, choice and influence. We need more flexible interpretations as to why women confront certain choices, and how their choices affect their futures. We need greater sensitivity to individual circumstances within a general framework; for women's very different stories involve varying patterns and common structures.

But the idea of a conspiracy against women, or a backlash against their progress, in many ways *underestimates* the obstacles to equality in the workplace. It presents obstacles to women's equality as requiring some special effort, some distinctive intention – whereas in fact many of the obstacles to women's equality are structural and, as we maintain and reinforce and accept these structures in our daily lives, we block progress. Things are not advancing as quickly as we thought not (simply?) because there are mean males tripping women up, but because the social system in which they seek equality is rigidly maintained, and since it is we who maintain it in our day-to-day lives, we must learn how – in our daily lives – to dismantle what constrains us and maintain what we value. Some of these structures function under the influence of addiction to certain types of gains and practices and uses. Others arise from constant human need.

The extent to which things must change if we are to achieve equality is disheartening. Yet we should take heart, since the need for change is becoming more and more widely acknowledged. 'The prevailing social order is so damaging that the rationale for current patterns of production and consumption – as they affect women and as they affect nature – must be thought through again',[39] writes industrial sociologist Elizabeth Garnsey. As we look at the life patterns and choices of the women who have been prepared to fight for equality, while they preserve what they value in their domestic roles, we see a creative force aimed at balance and reform. To make good choices women often have to change the stark terms of the structures in which they act. They often develop ways of thinking, ways of seeing, ways of valuing and ways of managing which should, eventually, find their way into the mainstream of decision-making. The selfishness and greed, the single vision and the single track, which once were thought to underpin progress, now threaten to undermine it. Our future is now recognized to depend upon new orientations towards care, nature and nurturance. The choices we all make now snag on a wider range of consequences and costs that, over the last few decades, were admitted to. The 'different voices' of the women described here show alternative routes for the future.

1
What Do Women Want?

The question which Freud asked two generations ago: 'What do women want?' expresses a prejudice rather than a puzzle. Freud was puzzled because he could not see that women were dissatisfied by social, sexual, financial and family constraints. He did not see that this dissatisfaction was often expressed indirectly, in symptoms of mental illness, because women lived in a society which as yet had no language for expressing the variety of their needs or discovering among themselves common dissatisfaction. As the voice of what women should be and should do and should feel was so loud, the individual variance from these feminine standards was experienced as a quirk, an isolated deficiency. It was through a common voice, a recognition of common dissatisfaction, that women's unhappiness became a movement.

Well – Freud saw this and yet did not see it. He saw that there was a psychological crippling in women, a condition he believed to result from denied sexual desire. He guessed that they were mournful or bitter about their biological destiny, which he failed to recognize as a social construction. So, too, he recognized the short shrift women had as adults, though he blamed them, rather than the society he analyzes so critically in other ways. He wondered why it was that a man of 30 seemed so full of promise, with the best of his life in front of him, still open to growth, still eager for experience and challenge, whereas a woman of the same age seemed psychologically inflexible, old in her rigidity, with no further paths to development before her.

In reading Freud on women one experiences a strange division: on the one hand he is portraying what was then a common human reality, and a common tragedy, stemming from the fact that at the age of 30 there often were, for a woman, no further paths to development. Many still suppose that there is nothing further to be said of a woman after the plot of love and marriage brings her story to a close. What is strange is that Freud is not expressing sympathy but petulance. In another version of his 'What do women want?' query he expresses irritation at the fact that girls are so bright and precocious, so curious and eager, but that they turn into women who have frittered this promise away. He ignores the link between that evaporated potential and the premature ageing. He see the effects on the woman of her blocked future, without sighting its causes. He fails to consider that she might grow rigid in response to the impoverished future she perceives as available to her as a woman in Freud's society.

Sensitive to sexual constraints on both men and women, Freud was apparently blind to restraints on a vast area of women's needs. In reply to a question 'What do people need in life?' Ernest Jones reports him as saying: we need to love and to work. What he failed to see was how this answer applied to women as people, too, and how his wise reply reflected on the plight of women. Women, like all adults, need to love and to work. But women still do not find this easy.

Women and Work

The most important social change in the past 25 years involves the status of women – particularly of women at work. Nearly half of the entire workforce in the United States is female, and nearly half of women with children are back at work within a year of a child's birth. In the last decade of the nineteenth century 19 per cent of all women were in the labour force. In 1977, 32 per cent of all mothers with small children younger than a year were in the labour force; in 1988, 52 per cent were. Recently, the percentage of women at work has exceeded 60 per cent. More women are entering the professions than ever before. More women are aiming at high political office than ever before. The numbers of women college graduates are converging with men as are the numbers of women in graduate education; and the choice of subjects women study are no longer distinct and separate. Women are also engaging in heavy manual labour, both skilled and unskilled.

What is important about these vast changes in women, education and work is not simply a leap in the numbers of women employed; for what changed in this generation, after so many generations of simply being on verge of change, is women's expectations. Women gained a wider vision of their future, and a greater sense of their control over it, and a greater sense of their responsibility for it.

Women's outlook is changing, yet the number of changes so many of us witness and experience somehow do not amount to as much change as we expect from them. Frequently women enter a career only to remain in 'women's jobs', jobs segregated from mainstream promotions and benefits. Or, they enter professions which are thought to promise much, only to find that either promotion eludes them or their desire for advance clashes with a need for balance in their lives. Having geared themselves up to gain the goods which once were men's only, they discover within themselves a different scale of values.

One problem is that structures in the home and in the family have only changed in parts. The working mothers of today are more demanding of the fathers, and fathers do seem to play a slightly increased role in child care and have an increasing input in parental responsibility. But in the home as in work the changes are minimal, or appear minimal where they seem to matter most. If women are less successful at work, or if they find success at work tough and trying in ways men do not, then they tend to invest more in the home; but if they are forced to invest more in the home, then they have reason to give less to their jobs and careers. And if women, as mothers, give less to their jobs and more to their home and children and partners, then it certainly makes sense to their partners to spend more time at work, to earn more money, to establish security in an increasingly insecure employment environment.

As economist Claudia Goldin noted, this generation of women is not unique in its sense that change for the better, a progress towards equality, is at hand: 'Each generation of Americans', she writes, 'at least since the mid-nineteenth century, has claimed to be on the verge of an unprecedented and momentous change in the economic position of women.'[1] The fact that women continually feel on the brink, but never there, has convinced many feminists that the cause lies with male power and male malice. The breakthrough, therefore, is thought to depend upon wresting from men what they do not want to give: control, power and privilege.

Others believe that progress is not made because women do not really want it, or because they are somehow not psychologically equipped to get what they want. But each view fails to take into account how these are interlocked, how decisions for women are made particularly difficult by the series of clashes between norms and needs, both at home and at work. Any point seems a reasonable starting point, because we are looking at a circuit.

Women's Work: A Very Brief History

Women are not new to the work force. They have always worked in one way or another. Before the industrial revolution women worked alongside their husbands in the home. When only very poor women worked in factories after marriage, unmarried women still worked before marriage, or as casual workers after marriage.

For most of this century the inequality of women at work has remained constant. In fact, occupations were nearly as segregated by sex – into women's work and men's work, with women's work being lower paid, with far fewer opportunities for promotion – in 1970 as they were in 1900.[2] Inequality of pay – with women being paid less for their work than men for theirs, was fairly constant between the mid-1950s and the early 1970s. Throughout the 1970s there was a considerable closing of what is called the 'wage gap', but this gap is very hard to define. It is meant to chart the difference between men's and women's pay for the same work. Different pay scales for the same work are not technically illegal, but it can be very difficult to determine what work is the same when it is not absolutely identical. There have been attempts in Europe to legislate for equal pay for work of equal value so that jobs which are largely female – such as nursing – remain attractive to women while being financially fair to them. These policies, however, are slow to take effect.

Indeed, if we consider the increase in women's education and work experience within this thirty-year span, one can see the economic discrimination has actually increased during this time – though the wag gap remained the same. Far more women have education and training equal to men than they did in 1950, but this is not reflected in women's careers and pay. And economic discrimination, at its most basic level, is a difference in earnings between two groups of workers which cannot be accounted for by differences in their work experience, their education, their tenure with a firm. So economic discrimination at work may increase even as the gap between men's wages and women's wages narrows.[3]

Inequality at work is based on a number of things. It has been based on ideas of what women were capable of, what kind of supervision they needed, and what predictions were made about their future work. The policy of refusing to hire married women, or insisting that a female employee resign when she married may have been based on the assumption of what she owed her husband, as well as a prediction of what she would soon decide to do anyway. These marriage bars (policies against hiring married women or of firing single women when they married), once nearly universal, were highly prejudicial to women's progress at work, but though they may not have been founded on prejudices of workers and employers against women, they were fuelled by these prejudices. Marriage bars were based on the belief that women should be at home with their children and that they should depend on their husbands to support them. These policies, which were enforced for the most part between 1900 and 1939, were expanded during the Great Depression as a means of ensuring that the scarce jobs would be filled by men. The majority of marriage bars were lifted in the 1950s when there were far fewer single women to do women's work – for women married particularly early in the 1950s.

When employers believe that most women will work only for a short period then, even though they know this is not universally true, they decide to channel all women into dead-end jobs involving little job training and skill acquisition. This is called 'statistical prejudice'. So common assumptions about what women will do have vastly wide-ranging influence on all women's work opportunities. Marriage bars were not, however, made on black women and women immigrants. Housework (performed largely by African-American women) and crop picking (done by immigrant – usually Hispanic – women) could, apparently, be done by women whether married or not. In such jobs – without security of tenure or promotional prospects – women were neither feared nor controlled. These women were 'protected' from protective legislation because their employers did not see them as setting an example, and their services were needed by employers as labourers, rather than as wives.

Marriage bars were successful because they could be rationalized and justified in the current climate of opinion. Married women were seen as neglecting their families if they worked, endangering their well-being. Married schoolteachers were fired because they might become pregnant – and that was judged to be objectionable in the classroom.[4] Yet in the late 1940s fewer women were available for work, and those who might have been available were marrying earlier and having children earlier. So, as there was a squeeze on the number of single female workers available, the marriage bars were lifted. Older female workers in the mid-1950s were suddenly praised for their maturity, reliability, neat appearance and less chatty nature.[5]

As women returned to the labour force in the 1950s, many of

its features were unchanged. Jobs were still segregated by sex, and women earned about 60 per cent of what men earned. Yet some things did improve – older women were more likely to be hired, and many firms saw the advantages of part-time work, though retail establishments were more likely to tolerate part-time workers than were manufacturing companies: Scott Paper Company, for instance, claimed that the situation had to be 'more desperate' for them to consider 'bringing in married women on a part-time schedule'[6] – which has always been and continues to be important in attracting women, who remain primarily responsible for running the family.

Women have gradually participated more in employed work as they have made advances in education, as clerical and sales jobs have increased and as the workday has grown shorter. The decrease in fertility, and the greater ability to predict and plan pregnancies have also made a difference. So too have advances in household production.

Before 1930 nearly 80 per cent of all women who worked before they were married dropped out of the workforce when they married. This protected men's jobs in conditions of declining employment. As Claudia Goldin studied the records of hundred of firms, she found that though these policies were discarded after the 1950s their effects are long-lived. If no women were accountants, then it would take a special woman even to try to train to be an accountant (and she might well be dissuaded by others). The marriage bars of previous generations created a world of male employment, which may reproduce itself. Deviation – seeking non-feminized work – may have some perks, may be exciting, but it carries costs. If women's jobs were dead-end (when women were denied access to promotional ladders) then there was little incentive to stay on at the job longer. And if women did not stay on the job long, if they saw their jobs as short-term, then even when they were allowed access to promotional ladders they would not be eligible for the climb. And so the effect of prejudice lives long after its demise – and that is what we are still living with today, and why we need new ways of understanding the odds against us.

Constraints are often placed on women on the basis of what is taken to be common sense. Expectations of what others will do forms, and justifies, policies. Employers once justified putting women in jobs with no promotional ladder because they believed that women were not ambitious: women wanted to marry; in marrying they became wives; in becoming wives they became housewives. Because they wanted to marry and become wives they were not ambitious in their work. This lack of ambition made them casual workers, inefficient and, in the long term, unreliable. Hence, employers felt, it was fair and reasonable to restrict women to 'subsidiary, uninteresting, and monotonous occupations'.[7]

Protest: The First Phase

Why did it take women so long to complain? Perhaps social norms seemed stiffer then. Perhaps the punishments for protest, for challenge, for deviance, were greater. Perhaps they too saw some necessary connection between marriage and housewifery. Being unmarried was dangerous. It exposed one to poverty and loneliness and stigma. If to be married meant that one had to give up work, then that was a worthwhile sacrifice – especially since the jobs available to them were so restricted. Women's acceptance of the marriage bars was based on their expectations of marriage, and these common expectations of marriage allowed employers to allocate unattractive jobs to them, which made it easier for women to accept relinquishing those jobs.

Women's conditions had to improve *before* they complained. Women had to change their perceptions of their abilities and their expectations of their careers, and their sense of what is fair. They had to summon the strength to fight custom and prejudice of which their silence hitherto had been a product. They had to develop new self-images, and new ideas of support. They had, also, to face disappointments – not to soften them or disguise them but to experience them and to gain energy from anger and frustration. The discontent Betty Freidan described may not have been new (it had been heard before in the 1920s) but it newly mobilized 'college-educated women whose expectations greatly exceeded their realizations'.[8] This was the generation of women who saw themselves as having equal access to employment, and who believed in their power to erase persistent spots of prejudice and constraint. As the psychologist Gilbert Brim has recently noted, it is when protest groups are successful that they begin to demand more.[9] In seeing themselves as having power, they raised their expectations, and their demands.

As in all forward-looking and forward-moving positions, backlashes are inevitable. The people who are comfortable with how things are resist change; and those people, comfortable in the status quo, are often more powerful than the dissatisfied, who seek change. And sometimes what looks like a well-constructed backlash is really something which others, in their frustration, construct as an explanation for the bewildering slowness of progress. For as each aspect of women's lives changes, which should, we think, make the big change, we find that certain crucial things remain all too much the same. While women's role in the economy increased drastically, many gender distinctions remained constant. While both partners' ideas of which domestic roles are appropriate to whom are transformed, the actual role-taking persists.

Industrial Change, or Repetition?

Work structures reproduce themselves. Either they repeatedly, and continuously, and persistently take into account women's domestic roles, and in so doing reinforce those roles, or they ignore the work and time of family life, and restrict the work opportunities of anyone who might have to tend to the young, the old or the ill. Studies of industrial change and women's employment, which looked at employment practices in newly-industrialized countries – such as Malaysia, Mauritius, Singapore and China – have found that 'light' industry (textiles, clothing, pharmaceutical and electronics) has provided a form of 'female-led industrialization' where women are preferred as workers for most factory jobs because they are hard-working, easy to control, willing to accept tediousness and monotony.[10]

When women have low expectations of employment and

make few demands of employers, they become both highly desirable employees and trap themselves in low-paying jobs, with little protection. Employers looking for women with such qualifications (docile workers who are accustomed to monotony) often prefer very young women, without family obligations, and with a high turnover rate, who often leave when they marry – a process employers call 'natural shedding'. Such a label expresses an employer's attitude and expectation: women will leave when they marry because the job is not suitable to a married woman. This expectation maintains the type of job available to women. Given the assumption that they will leave when married, the employer sets up jobs which will attract women who want to work for a while rather than women who want employment to be a career. This means that there are fewer career-track jobs available to women. This means the employer has no reason to create a better type of job.

Marriage bars to employment sound like relics from the past, but current jobs are often designed with either unmarried, or childless women in mind. In newly-industrialized employment, which was once seen as a ticket to women's progress in developing or newly-developed countries, virtual marriage bars remain – not as defined policies of employers, but as practical impediments. Conditions of employment in these modern conditions are generally incompatible with family responsibilities. Few women in developing countries have industrial jobs after the age of 25 – at least in the modern section of employment. Those who do feel pressed into such work by dire necessity – usually because they have no male wage-earner in their household – and explain that when they work they 'entrust their children to God' – in other words, leave them uncared for, and unprotected by any human source. Midlife women in developing countries usually work in informal industries, doing piece-work, or in cottage industries, rather than in factories: informally they have less rigid working conditions, but the conditions are often more difficult, employment is unstable – and constantly threatened by new developments in modern industry whose working conditions they are unable to meet.[11]

Once, it was hoped that these newly-industrialized countries would provide the basis of industrial equality: they would be the base wherein women would be welcomed into jobs at the beginning, where they might remain, and rise. But this is not the trend. The fact that these factories welcome women workers seems in itself to contribute to the persistence of low wages and short-term employment, with little training in skills that could be transferred to other jobs.

Overtime and Overwork: Inefficiency and New Bias

Overtime presents a major problem for women in employment in almost all countries, whether developing or developed. Employers find overtime an advantage: it allows them to make use of current employees when there is a sudden need to increase productivity. Overtime becomes a substitute for the shift work, or the part-time work that would really suit women. It is far more efficient to 'overuse' current employees because then employers do not have to train new people, or provide more insurance and pension benefits. Should the demand for production slow down, they do not have to lay off workers, but simply cut down the amount of overtime work available. Men with young families take greatest 'advantage' of any overtime work available; women with young children find extra hours most onerous. Hence overtime for them is a handicap.

The costs of overtime are rarely counted by employers. The increasing inefficiency of fatigue, burn-out, poor health – even drug abuse – is ignored because work time is assumed to be productive time – however strong evidence is to the contrary. The new ethos of overwork, too, is remarkably inefficient, yet it is sustained by the prejudice that increased hours of work must somehow increase productivity. These extended hours employers demand of their workers, and punch in themselves so as to oversee their workers, are in part a response to the proliferation of activity at work – through rapid communications, through the ability to respond to changes on the other side of the globe, through the wish to communicate with all countries, in all time-zones. Yet firms seldom question whether this sense of urgency is actually productive.

'The control over time is absolutely critical, in terms of what one wants to do with one's life', says Lotte Bailyn at MIT's Sloan School of Management.[12] Time is a scarce resource, especially for people who lead and sustain personal as well as working lives, yet employers are now asking more time from their employees. It is a badge, a proof, a token of commitment. Many feel its demands, and its costs, yet few realize what a useless token it is. There is something tough, nearly macho about these 60-hour work weeks, the willingness to prolong a meeting, to finalize a document at midnight, or just to sit at one's desk, with one's light on and the computer humming, for a little longer than anyone else.

The link between time and productivity is outmoded, based on a simple model of the production line. The longer the production line is switched on, the longer those workers assemble objects, the more things are produced. For most people at work today, work and productivity are very different from this assembly-line model. The expectation that one will stay on to the bitter end, often leads to time-wastage, time-whiling, time-spinning. There are myths of seriousness and commitment, of what is sometime called 'presenteeism', and sometimes called 'face time', where being seen at work seems to count for something over and above simply being there, where putting in time has an unquestioned mystique, even though being present involves extra work for others – for secretaries and colleagues. Time becomes 'a proxy indicator for performance, based', Bailyn says, 'on some crazy assumption that the more time, the better'. These costs are not counted. Nor are the costs of overwork, which is a strange version of overtime. As the normal hours of work increase, overtime becomes normal, and part of an employer's expectations. Hence it becomes easier to obtain extra work without overtime pay. The incentives are in the prestige of being seen as a hard worker – especially in large firms where it is difficult to measure each individual's output, or in jobs which do not have strictly measurable output. Hence time makes the workplace even more alienating for women, and though this limits men's lives too, it is difficult to refrain from suggesting that the tough new hours are a challenge to women's participation.

Haunting Images

This brief account of women's employment with the pitfalls built into the structure of both 'female' and 'male' employment, is relevant to the dedicated career women described in this book because even though these women have avoided such pitfalls, they are aware of them. They manage their work, and their domestic lives, within this context of dangerous slides into 'female' jobs and the challenges of good jobs. The tension their ambition breeds, the doubts that beset them, the barriers they are determined to overcome, the persistent fear that they will give up too much, and that having given up ground it will not be regained – this is the context in which they act and plan. Every determined woman is haunted by her more traditional roles. Whereas a man (however career-oriented his partner) lives and thinks and acts on the assumption that he does have a wife, a woman is haunted by the prospect that however independent and determined she is, she will become a wife.

The women described in this book were determined to follow what were once considered masculine-type career patterns. Nor were these pie-in-the-sky dreams, which crumbled in the face of women's reality. Instead, they were genuine directives, real working goals, which were either modified or hardened in the face of their experience as women in this world. This selective approach to women's emotional and occupational lives may initially seem inadequate to the task of answering very general questions about women, their work, their motherhood and their futures. Yet this is the best window to such realities: the complex social structure is made up only of individual lives, and our interest in that complex structure is in the way individual lives are affected by it.

New Beginnings

When I began this project I searched for women who had already become successful. After the fact, I wanted to know how they had scrambled up the vocational ladder, how they had found the openings and marched up the rungs, how they had managed their lives. Stories of women's success remain both interesting and inspiring, but I now believe that they should not be told in isolation from women's employment as a whole. When exceptions are studied in isolation from a wider number of cases, a certain ease may sneak into the narrative. If we look only at those who have made it, then we may come to the conclusion that making it is a natural conclusion, one which more women would come to if they only stuck at it, tried hard enough. This was not the conclusion of my first version of *Why Women Don't Have Wives* but this implication sometimes hovered at the edges of the stories. There were many paths to success, I argued, and each successful woman created a different one.

Two thing were implied here. First, few women followed ready-made paths to a career success. Even those who began their careers with male ideals and male images of success, eventually took time out to change both their personal and their professional lives. Second, the going is tough, because there is no set pattern. This lack of set patterns exists not only because women as a whole are new to vocational success (though there have always been exceptions) but also because many aspects of their experience impede usual career patterns, which have been established by men who have wives.

In the previous book I asked how we can make progress in a working world created for men, but with a mother's responsibility. The question has changed. A woman's life is far more complex than many of us thought. We all recognized that it was unfair. What we did not appreciate was just how difficult it would be to redress wrongs; for it is not only a matter of sharing out the working pie, but reshaping the pie while we learn new ways of cutting it.

This new book at times had to be written in a dialogue with the previous one. Whereas I first perceived this task as a challenge to women and women's ingenuity, I now see the process as more complex, and more widely rooted than I did ten years ago. The task women confronted was far more radical than anyone originally had supposed. It was not quite recognized then how inhospitable the workplace was to women – not simply in terms of attitudes and policies but also in its persistent structures. It is not so much that there has been a backlash against women's progress, but the voices of conservatism which were evident then remain as strong today as they were then, and the structures both of work life and domestic life have not changed enough to make integration easy.

Moreover, though I was aware of a 'cutting down' effect during intense phases of motherhood, I had not yet noted (or it had not yet become evident) that women at any phase of their lives are apt to change course suddenly, because they do not have one-track minds, because they have high standards for a balanced life, because they are unwilling to incur certain costs whatever the gains. Though such meticulous care for one's individual well-being is found in men too, it is far more widespread among women. Not only do women have trouble gaining access to promotional ladders, they have a habit of climbing down, or to the side when they are high up. Yet what sometimes seems like a lack of career commitment may be a response to progressive conflict and progressive stress. It may, too, be a rejection of work patterns which do not suit them, because women are sometimes more aware than men that people need both to work and to love – and they may, too, have higher standards and a deeper sense of what it means to love.

Women, Love and Dependence

Women have often been seen as centring their life on love and on the family. Byron's Don Juan[13] says, 'Man's love is of Man's life a thing apart, 'Tis Woman's whole existence', and at one time this seemed true. This quote is often taken as an apt description of the different importance love has for men and for women – even though this remark was made by a character who centred his existence on making women love him.

There has been a conceptual revolution in the idea of what it is to be female. This revolution involves changes in views of how women are focused on others, and hence how far the need to love, and the needs linked to love, shape their identity. In 1972 a study was set up to explore how psychological professionals saw women and men and women's and men's maturity.[14] The study yielded devastating, unintentionally witty, results.

A list of personality traits was sent to three different groups of professional psychological workers, with three different sets of instructions. One group was asked to indicate which traits on the list would be found in a 'mature, healthy, socially competent male'. A second group was asked to indicate which personality traits would be found in a 'mature, healthy, socially competent woman'. A third group was asked to consider what traits would describe the 'mature, healthy, socially competent adult'.

The first group, all members of the psychological establishment, consisting of both men and women, indicated that the mature, healthy socially competent male would be dominant, aggressive, in control of his feelings, rational rather than emotional. The second group, who had been asked to tick traits which would describe the mature, healthy, socially competent female, also consisted of men and women. They were unanimous in their descriptions of the mature, healthy, socially competent female as dependent, submissive, home-oriented, susceptible to influence, quick to express emotion and prone to endorse the emotional rather than logical side of an argument – subjective rather than objective. She was also less competitive, more easily hurt, and more conceited about her appearance than healthy mature men.

So, it seemed that the men and women who were professionally involved in helping people adjust, helping people overcome any conflicts which prevented them from being mature, psychologically healthy and socially competent, revealed a gender bais – or quite simply a sexist prejudice. The prejudice is against both men and women, since healthy, socially competent men seem 'forbidden', in this vision of normality, from being emotional and dependent, as every human being has a right to be. The study, however, has become notorious in its bias against women for the following reason.

The final group of psychological professionals, consisting of both men and women, was asked to tick the traits that would most accurately describe the mature, healthy, socially competent adult. This group agreed that the mature adult was independent, aggressive, logical rather than emotional in argument and firmly in control of his feelings. In other words, the group describing the mature healthy socially competent *adult* indi-cated the same traits that a different group had used to describe the mature, healthy, socially competent *male*. The male and the adult were identical, but the mature female was something else altogether – and not a mature adult.

Ten years later, different researchers set up another study to see whether they would get the same results.[15] They did not. It was difficult for them to explain why. Perhaps the original study had been set up with some built-in bias – or perhaps the preju-dice revealed by that study had become part of a wider con-sciousness-raising, so that people were more aware of prejudice, and more cautious about revealing it. Or perhaps ideas about men and women really had changed in ten years, and mature men and women were no longer conceived so rigidly, and so distinctly.

There have been enormous changes in the way women see themselves, and what they expect of themselves. But often women, too, made the mistake of equating a mature, healthy, socially competent adult with a mature, healthy, socially compe-tent male. Feminists were much quicker to spot the demeaning aspects of the stereotypical feminine than they were to question the value of being like the typical mature man. The ideal of some feminists who were writing at the same time the first study was published did, after all, try to inspire women to be like men, to think like men, to get what they wanted in the ways they saw men as pursuing their goals. Their sense of what it was to be liberated was to be more like men, to have what men had, and to do what men did. Even in 1981, Colette Dowling wrote about her quest to stamp out all the home-oriented dependency and emerge as a woman who never relied upon anyone, who would always pursue her career and her career interests, who stamped out weakness and need. This shallow, distorted ideal became vastly popular because it showed a quick, clear path to adult-hood: women would change from being socially competent females to something quite different – to socially competent adults, who were just like mature men. The idea that women were different from men, and adults in their own right, with their 'subjectivity' based in reality and a validity in their 'vacillation' and a strength in their 'dependency', was a long time in coming.

Expansion and Affiliation

It is not easy to change one's identity, especially when social norms reinforce it – especially, too, when much of one's own experience reinforces the previous self-concept that, intellectually, one is trying to discard. As more women committed themselves to identity work – or to employment or careers that provided them with a sense of who they were and where they were going apart from the traditional woman's world – psychotherapists noticed a new range of conflicts which emerged in these women. The American psychoanalyst Alexandra Symonds found that many women were seeking her help because she was a female analyst and, they believed, only a woman could understand their problems. These problems emerged in apparently liberated women who pursued careers previously considered male – such as law, medicine, business, television management, photography and psychotherapy. They were women who felt strongly that women's lives should change, and they were determined to change their own. They embraced the new maturity – the maturity of aggression and drive and control. But their new life, their goals, their promise of opportunity, had not brought them happiness.

To explain the conflicts she was observing, Symonds identified a split between two sets of needs which she called dependency needs and expansive needs. Dependency needs are what women have been traditionally encouraged to develop. They involve needs not so much to be supported by others – as the name Symonds gives them suggests – but the need to be attached and involved with them. They have been more aptly named, by others, affiliative needs, since they are needs for attachment and involvement, needs satisfied by companionship, communication, nurture, care and love. Expansive needs are needs to meet challenges and solve problems, to develop and test one's skills, to feel oneself as someone able to act in and control and interact with one's environment. Traditionally, women have been denied these needs, or encouraged to see them as being fulfilled within the sphere of human relationships and domesticity.

All people have difficulty combining these two types of needs. Common practices and habits and images in our society make the division between these two types of needs especially difficult to bridge. Home and work are separate. Separate identities are developed to accommodate the ethos of these different spheres: business is business, not personal; attachment makes one vulnerable, but life (outside the home) is tough and toughness obliterates need. At home one is oriented towards others and others' well-being; in the workplace one looks out for oneself.

Many people, men and women alike, are more comfortable in one sphere than another. Many people, men and women alike, try to bring the best of one sphere into the other. And all people make compromises, accept trade-offs, as they juggle these needs in a society that does not provide friendly patterns to combine them. Psychology is rich with studies of such conflicts and their failed solutions. In the film *Citizen Kane*, the young Kane was given money and power as his innocent childhood pleasures and affiliations (represented by his sled 'Rosebud') were taken from him, never to be retrieved. Power and wealth offered success, and success isolated him. Though the film may have offered consolation to many men who were unable to have such wealth, and may have stabilized their dissatisfaction, it also told a story that has been often told and often verified: success does not bring happiness, and success often demands the sacrifice of happiness.

Women do not have copyright on compromises and trade-offs, but they do experience recognizable problems with compromises between dependency and expansive needs. Recent generations of women have experienced their own special forms of conflict as they rise to the challenge that new admission of their expansive needs has brought, while remaining socialized, and psychologized, to dependency needs. Women, it seems, also have more difficulty in compartmentalizing their behaviour and their personae. They have more trouble than do men at switching off their concerns about their families when they are at work,[16] and they are more troubled by impersonality and competitiveness at work than, it seems, are men.[17]

Three-faced Gorgon

In her practice Symonds discovered a range of means of managing, or failing to manage the conflicts between these two sets of needs, and their accompanying divisions in self-identity. At one extreme Symonds found women whose dependency needs were so deeply denied and repressed that they were not accommodated to any extent. These women avoided affection and intimacy and become controlling and exploitative people. They mimicked the man who embraces the macho image. They appeared to be stunted by lack of emotion, by denigration of attachment. The point of every encounter with another person for these women, Symonds found, was to 'prove' oneself. Like the man always intent to prove himself a man, these women were intent on proving themselves competent, independent, tough.

At the other extreme of women suffering from contemporary conflicts between dependency and expansiveness, were career women who have deep, intense, and indeed insatiable needs to be taken care of, underlying a thin facade of self-sufficiency. Their development appears paradoxical, for they expend a tremendous amount of energy on their education and careers, but they feel that without a man, and without children, they have no true status. These women believe that self-identity can only be found in challenging and rewarding work, but they feel they are worthless if they do not provide the traditional female supports, or fill the traditional female roles.

Between the extremes of women who totally deny dependency needs and those who feel they are nothing without a man, is the largest group of career women. These women have achieved success in their working lives and some satisfaction in their personal lives, but they none the less feel dissatisfied, and believe that their dissatisfaction comes from not succeeding enough either at home or at work, and so they try doubly hard at each. Many studies of women and men in the professions, for example, show that women tend to have more children than their male peers, and that they have more children because they want to prove their femininity but at the same time they want to pursue the careers that are important to them.[18] If women are more successful at work than their husbands, then they are prone to develop other compensating strategies to prove that they are still set in female roles. For example, they may do more domestic work than a partner, thereby assuring him that career success does not shift the traditional balance of power in the marriage.[19] These women hope to prove they are not cheating anyone at home or being left out of anything at work. They give a great deal to everyone because they want to feel that they do their best, because they want to prove that no one will suffer from their 'double' life.

This middle group of women of course falls prey to the superwoman syndrome. This is fuelled in large part by guilt, as women feel they must give themselves to work as men typically do, and to their families as women typically do. The superwoman syndrome allows men to be unchanged at home, and it allows women to accept male careers unchanged. It allows women to have everything, because they earn it by doing everything.

The description of Symonds' patients is both easily recognizable, and a little old-fashioned. It harkens back to an earlier image of what the new woman was, and what she expected herself to be. So determined was she to be equal to men, that she determined to become just like men. But recently when Suzanne Gordon exposed the women who are 'prisoners of men's dreams' in her book of that title, the puzzle was that she supposed women had become equal to men. For one of the most noticeable things about women and work is that women often decide to give up those expansive tracks, whatever their previous investments. They are trained, they are educated, but somehow in the end seem unprepared, or unwilling, to keep up the climb. Either the rigid division of labour in domestic life[20] or the masculine cultures of the workplace[21] or the lack of direction, the muted drive for power,[22] catapults them away from the goals they once were so determined to achieve.

Yet as I described the spectrum of Symonds' conflicted women to the women I interviewed, they immediately recognized themselves in one of these categories. This did not mean that they exhibited the symptoms of Symonds' women, but that the conflicts described were real to them.

The conflicts that Alexandra Symonds identified fifteen years ago are still recognizable today, and they are recognizable as having special reference to, special preference for contemporary women. The conflicts that were described have been redescribed again and again since then, and they do identify two different extremes, and a middle ground. The fact that the two extremes and the middle ground are all unsatisfactory also rings true for many women. But what this schematic account ignores, and what we must now appreciate, is that individual women have taken individual responsibility for refashioning both their home habits and their work habits to make each viable. Hence these conflicts can be constructive. Over the years, conflict in women's lives has given rise to a new female thinking, a new sensitivity to the as-yet-undiscovered balance of their needs.

Yet we must not slice the language of inner conflicts from the social realities in which women work and love. To see women's problems simply in terms of inner conflict is to ignore the ways in which the stacks are loaded against them. On the other hand, to see their conflicts merely in terms of social structures is to forget, too, that they often willingly reinforce those structures because certain aspects of those structures meet their needs.

These polarized explanations spring up and then crash down because, when the complexity of women's aims and women's lives is minimized, when the interconnections are ignored, it seems to make sense to emphasize one persistent flaw, one prejudice, one failing over all others. When we know change is necessary, when we are trying to change our lives, when our best efforts get stuck, we seek explanations, but they tend to be overspecific. We often feel some constraints, and fail to spot others. The progress of women is linked, as is each woman, to the home, to the family, to her education, to her past socialization, to her present responses, and to her assessment of future risks and securities. The highly complex nature of her needs, alongside the commonplace rigidity of career success, the tight interlocking of career decisions and personal outcomes, contributes to the slow and sometimes backsliding progress.

The interconnections between different aspects of women's lives – their sense of their own needs, the economic conditions in which they live, the structure of the jobs available to them, the domestic habits they inherit and maintain – make any account of their choices, dilemmas, compromises and gains difficult. Yet by tracing both the plans women make and the paths they followed we can make some headway in mapping internal and external aims and constraints. We can see how the ways in which they experience both love and work often pressure them into special female compromises which provide both satisfactions and conflicts.

Choice and Consequences

The difficulty in observing what women want, and the difficulty women may have in obtaining what they want, result from the fact that the packages in which choices and consequences come do not fit neatly into their lives. They are aware, more often than men, in different ways from men and in ways typical to women, that they have to compromise. For women, marriage often involves living where one's husband's work is. Even the career of Zoë Baird, with its strong trajectory, is grounded in a husband's relocation, in crippling difficulties with childcare, and in the hostile response to a working mother's desperate solution. This grounding may involve living where a woman's best job is not, or it may involve leaving a good job, or being unavailable to move to a good job. Being married often involves children and having children involves a commitment in time and energy and emotion. For men, typically, being married involves having a wife who will move with him when his career requires a move. It involves having someone to care for his children, and someone to ease the burden of ordinary, domestic life and personal care. These are not necessary consequences of being a woman. Nor are they necessary consequences of either marriage or motherhood. But they are ready-made patterns, which are difficult to break clear from, and very difficult to feel safe from.

Moral philosophers and, recently, educational psychologists, have paid attention to the doubt and anxiety involved in making compromising decisions, but on the whole sociologists and economists have taken a more simplified view. It has been said, and repeated many times since it was first said, that economics is all about why people make choices, whereas sociology is all about why people, as socially determined beings, don't have any choices to make.[23] The economist supposes that our aims are simple, and the sociologist supposes that our thoughts are pre-cut cultural patterns. But we see ourselves, and experience ourselves, as at least nominally free agents, and though we often feel constrained by the circumstances in which we make decisions, or would prefer our circumstances to be different, we nonetheless do choose, and women of recent generations are working harder and harder to gain control and responsibility for their choices. But difficult choices remain difficult.

For one thing, we can never predict all the consequences of a single decision. In economic theory it is generally assumed that people have sufficient information about alternatives to make reasonably intelligent choices. In some areas it is easy to obtain such information either before one acts or through experience, and mistakes are not very costly. For example, one will steer clear of a restaurant which is known to serve poor food. If one chooses a restaurant and it serves poor food, then one need not go there again.

This model of choice is very limited. It does not cover the important decisions of our lives which are important because they involve other people, and burnt bridges, and foresworn paths, and unknown turnings. The special, and different power we do have in making consumer choices is in fact what makes shopping so enjoyable to many people: they enjoy the special, unusual sense that they are in charge as they complete or reject a purchase. The recreational aspect of shopping involves stepping out of the real-life arena in which one does not have such a simple method of control. People tend to avoid shops where salespeople practise the hard sell, because they then feel that they are not in control. The store that promotes itself through service grants the customer far wider control than stores usually do: any item can be returned at any time after purchase for whatever reason. Hence the customer retains the control she has before the purchase, whereas the anxiety many people have about making a purchase is that once their decision to buy is made, they lose all power. The shopper's sense of power lost is suggested by the fact that in 80 per cent of unsatisfactory purchases people do not bother to complain or to try to return or replace the unsatisfactory item.[24]

Though there is nothing comparable to this in human life – in what we think of as moral life, in which commitments and obligations follow from our interactions with other people – there have been some attempts to present our lives as a series of 'passages' during which we try out and seek various paths to self-fulfilment. The once-fashionable notion that one's duty to one's self was the highest duty, has now shifted to the position that one's duty to oneself is one duty among many, and has to be balanced accordingly. Though it never quite fitted in with actual experience of attachment, especially attachment to a partner and children, it did register the growing awareness, which continues today, that life patterns are not firm and fixed, that personalities and personal needs and individual skills change throughout adulthood, and that we should respond to this flexible potential. Yet if one marries and has a child and either decision turns out badly, the situation can be changed, but not easily and not without distress. It is not the kind of mistake that can be 'corrected' or 'rectified' along the lines of the economist's decision and choice.

We do not live our lives like travellers wandering from place to place hunting and gathering experiences and leaving the land unchanged behind us – and by 'we' I mean especially women. The travel novel is a distinctly male genre: the backpack in Bruce Chatwin's *In Patagonia* or *Songlines* is always ready. The experiences are sharp and poignant, but the self remains intact, gathering up a piquant interest in its collection of lost friends and precarious situations. In comparison, the voice of the female backpacker in Ruth Prawer Jhabvala's *Heat and Dust*, takes up the thread of common female experience. Adventure becomes entwined with sexuality and fertility. The demands and expectations of others confine the female 'traveller' to a very different set of experiences. Interactions change her course, and each move forward remains entangled by past relationships and their implications. Decisions about love, marriage, child-birth, fidelity, isolation, often come in tightly-wrapped packages. One small decision may lead to a situation in which one feels forced, in which one no longer sees options for choice.

Not only do one's own reactions and actions and feelings have irreducible complexities, but they also have consequences for the lives of others. The restaurant which does not please its consumers will go out of business. This may be economically logical and legitimate. But unloved spouses and children are not so easily written off. If they are written off by one person, then others have to pick up the pieces. Abandoned children suffer, they may go into state care, they may fail to thrive, they may form an underclass and become delinquent.The costs of 'free choice' in the human world are high.[25]

Choices are difficult for many reasons. Some alternatives are never considered because current benefits tend to loom large in people's thinking relative to future costs of which they may be only dimly aware. Even when the future costs are known, individuals can conveniently ignore the social, as opposed to the private consequences of their behaviour and will usually act accordingly. Sometimes people follow patterns because they take those patterns for granted. They fail to realize the extent to which they can choose. They may be imitating the behaviour of a previous generation which is often codified in a set of social norms. These may once have served as a reasonably inexpensive surrogate for the accumulation of individual wisdom but they may be inappropriate in a more modern context.[26]

Women, in making choices about work and marriage, about work and motherhood, about motherhood and child care, face all these unknowns, along with the probability that inherited assumptions and policies and expectations will haunt their de-cisions, while there are as yet no easy ways of paring off the inherited superstition from the not-yet-fully explored reality. Once, it seemed simple – to assume equality between men and women and work up from that assumption was the ideal. Though this starting point is sometimes referred to when progress seems slow and sticky it is hard to return to it once we become parents. Motherhood changes us, plays havoc with clear lines of identity and determination. It is not that we suddenly become different people, or that all energy is channelled into our children, or that we no longer need to strive for mastery or creativity in other areas: 'I still want to compose', shouted Elisabeth Lutyens as she was giving birth to her first child. The prewar period in which she became a mother, and saw herself identified as a mother, demanded a deliberate, shocking rejection of the proposal that her creativeness would be, finally and fully, satisfied by child-birth. Instead, what women find as they become mothers is not that they lose the determination and ambition they had before, but that their lives become subject to more contradictions as the idea of equal opportunity for self-fulfilment clashes with the need to create conditions in which others can thrive.

These areas in which choice fails, or in which poor choices are made, have become hot spots of scrutiny. There are many reasons why progress is slow. Sometimes young women, looking to their future, depend more on a mother's pattern than a peer's – hence the old patterns are repeated even when conditions may be favourable to change. Also, women may for many reasons find it difficult to predict future conditions and future needs – their futures are far less straightforward, far less planned than the career patterns of men. But while young women in the 1960s were very bad indeed at forecasting their future economic needs or the future opportunities that work might offer, young women in the 1970s were much better at forecasting their economic futures. As the divorce rate continued to climb and had a much higher profile, as women's education increased, and as the women's movement increased women's awareness of both their power and their vulnerability, young women were much better-equipped to predict where they were heading. Since young women in the 1960s did not anticipate the large increase in female employment in the 1970s and 1980s, many severely under-invested in skills needed for continued employment. But in the 1970s young women began to invest more wisely in skills.[27]

Women now understand more fully the costs of failing to invest in work skills, or in having children at one time of life rather than another. This understanding of how independence and self-determination are often linked to a job and career progress can very easily clash with questions about what our children need, and what consequences follow from not being constant, perfect mothers, or being working mothers, or being home mothers who may be unhappy. It becomes especially difficult to make decisions when we believe these issues are at stake, and when our perception of these issues is skewed by ideas of motherhood and childhood, of self-fulfilment and commitment, which contain as much that is false as is true. Abandoning children is surely bad: but what does abandonment mean? Are mothers abandoning children when they work full-time? Are they selfish when they aim for self-fulfilment? Does the responsibility for raising children rise only with the family? And in the family does it reside mainly with the mother? If she thinks not, then how does she negotiate this change? When change is difficult, how does she resist the enormous moral pressure that traditional notions of motherhood exert? How does she discover what she needs and what her children need? If she is able to discover this, can she meet both? If not, what steps does she take to change her life so as to accommodate both herself and her family? And as she takes steps, either practical steps in her own life, or 'cognitive manoeuvres' whereby she tries to change her needs and her outlook, what changes does the workplace allow, and what changes are effective within her family?

2
Why Do Women Mother?

'Motherhood', I wrote in my earlier study of women and work, 'has always been a poor relation among feminist topics'. In the heady days of the 1970s, when radical change seemed imminent, motherhood seemed like a worn-out institution that, given a modicum of enlightened good-will, could be refashioned and updated. Motherhood was frequently perceived as a primary impediment to woman's self-realization. It sapped her energy, sexuality and power.[1] Parenting was a task that could be shared out equally between parents, if only women overcame those subversive dependencies which made them want to stay at home rather than go out and seek their fortunes in the workplace.[2] Though some researchers had already developed theories about the powerful habits of motherhood, these had not yet spread to more general questions about women and work.[3] The difficulties surrounding women and work were sometimes sensitively managed, though usually in heroic tales of women who did attain balance. More commonly, the problems were glossed over in one of two ways. First, there was the image of the forward-looking superwoman who did it all because she was so smart, so energetic, so well-directed and self-controlled. For her it was easy, seemed to be the message; and hence those who were having difficulty, it was thereby suggested, lacked the right stuff. Secondly, there was the new conservative image of the women who realized work was not worth it, that for women career goals were empty in contrast to the fulfilment of motherhood. In novels, in television advertisements, in films, the high-powered woman was tamed by her child's needs. Often she found a new partner, for her new traditional self. Often, too, she found a new career, but this time something home-spun, home-run, offering a new package deal.[4]

This was not quite a backlash; it was simply the voicing of a conservatism that had never disappeared. More importantly, however, these images also provided answers to continuing problems. It is so difficult to follow male career patterns while mothering that a retreat into traditional roles is sometimes a tempting solution. These films and novels often tried to deal honestly with the reality of the problems women faced. Some of them also (such as the film *Baby Boom* and Maeve Haran's novel *Having It All*) acknowledged that for women to combine the good aspects of traditional motherhood with a career, then the careers had to be transformed as much as did traditional parenting. But so controversial has this topic become that traditional solutions are 'exposed' as enemy infiltrators. The dictum that once had a great deal of truth – 'The personal is political' – now tends to wear its truth like a noose. Sometimes the personal is a genuine discovery about an individual solution for problems which are embedded in the particular situation in which one works and lives. Each woman should still be allowed to decide and to act without making a general political assertion. And yet, the individual decisions we do make, as social beings living in our society which, like any society, is made up of individuals acting individually, either sustain or undermine the practices which either constrain or enable women.

The women of today constantly tread that tricky line between living as an individual and being a living representative of a type. Women frequently spoke about the awareness of different perspectives: they saw themselves from both inside and from without, and these angles did not match up. The stereotypical interest in 'reflection' and a model-like appearance has been replaced with a concern for one's capacity to be a role-model.

Motherhood is no longer the neglected child of feminism. It is no longer an afterthought, or aside, to the common issues of feminism, but it remains its sorest point.[5] Women who are not mothers feel that women who are mothers see them as hard, limited and selfish. Women who are dedicated to their careers believe that women whose primary work is their children are missing out and opting out. Women who have jobs often oppose them to the careers which they see their families to be, and feel defensive when their priorities are perceived in any other light. Women who do not work in paid employment and prefer being fully available to their families feel that they are marginalized by working women. They feel they have to counter the charge of not doing anything, or not making anything of their lives. They answer that they care more about their families' emotional well-being than the gross family income. They are sacrificing, not opting out.

The arguments hinge on a poorly constructed but passionate base. They involve anxieties and suppositions about what children need and what mothers ought to be. They involve the knowledge that motherhood may threaten and confound one's plans. Many women find that the odds against their ambitions which once which seemed manageable are experienced as overwhelming. But the needs which gave rise to those career goals are not so easily obliterated, and hence the conflict recurs. The most false note sounded by the clichés is that there is an easy way to resolve this conflict, if only one is clever enough to find it.

Researchers look into these questions, but scientific information seldom answers these passionate queries. The 'typical' mother/child bond has changed far less in past decades than the 'typical' family. The mother/child relationship seems so basic to development and to the family and to society that any change arouses fears, and as fears are aroused they feed on a variety of problems. As education seems less good than it once was, as discipline seems less strong than it once was, as the two-parent family that is imagined as right and representative becomes less common than it once was, the most visible changes are blamed; and the most visible change in society during the past few decades is the change in women's idea of what is involved in being a woman, and the change in their working patterns.

But ideas about children and mothers and even the family remain entrenched in spite of these changes. Even young women of today remain of the opinion that child care should primarily be a task of the family. Any state or employment facilities are seen as distinctly secondary, supportive to a mother's role. Women want to achieve both aims in their lives, and they often realize, or come to realize that they will have to lower expectations regarding their career prospects as a result. The male-breadwinner marriage continues to be seen as an appropriate framework to this end. There is no obvious nor attractive alternative to marriage as the main location for the socialization of one's children.[6] Alternatives are found, and found to work, but they are endorsed as being just like a 'regular family' which, however fictitious, sets the standard.

The Experience of Hope

Motherhood is often perceived by young, determined women, as more pliable, more mutable than it turns out to be. From the outside it seems like a tired formula ready for change; but the experience is far more compelling, rewarding and exasperating. As Ann Oakley wrote in *Housewife*: 'it is first-time motherhood which forces women to confront the feminine dilemma. Before that . . . you can pretend you're equal. Once there's a baby to care for, you can't.'[7]

The institution of motherhood – the social form that mothering usually takes – has evolved within the housewife's role, and this role has been seen by some feminists as the focus of women's oppression. This is a role allocated exclusively to women. The crux of this work is that it is unpaid in a society which largely sees money as the sign of value. Being a 'valueless' occupation, it is nonetheless demanding and confining. It is hard work, but, since it is associated with economic dependence, it has the status of non-work. Yet the housewife's work is productive in that she produces workers for industry. Its productivity is to produce neat, presentable, disciplined, happy workers and potential workers. Ann Oakley explains that the housewife produces 'her husband with his clean clothes, well-filled stomach and mind freed from the need to provide daily care for his children; the children fed, clothed, loved and chastized ready for their own adult gender-specific role as workers or worker-producers'.[8] And just as the housewife is seen as important as producer, she is seen to be enormously important as a consumer who keeps the consumer productive culture alive. Her free time, her empty time, her service time are, economist John Galbraith noted, 'critical to the expansion of consumption in the modern economy'.[9] Hence, the unpaid role of housewife was both without value in contemporary currency of value (it was unpaid), and it was enforced as essential to the maintenance of the family, wherein socialization of future generations took place, and to the expansion of the economy, for the housewife learned what consumer goods she and her family and her home required. And as the housewife saw much of her role as monotonous and lonely and fragmented, it was also supposed to be the central role of a woman's life, one that took precedence over others.[10] It was also, in the early years of the women's liberation movement, seen as the key to women's subordination.

Was this role just a crude fact of domestic labour? Would its contradictions one day be transcended by technology? In Woody Allen's film of 1972, *Sleeper*, he wakes to a future 200 years from his present in which all menial domestic tasks, which usually structure the housewife's day, are to be taken over by a domestic robot. This expectation was endorsed in the futuristic cartoon series *The Jetsons*, though in that household where domestic tasks are performed by a domestic robot, the roles of father and mother, daughter and son, remain rigidly stereotyped, with the wife still 'at home', spending through compulsive shopping the earnings of the husband whose daily working life is terrorized by his boss's whims. In fact, these images of unchanging roles alongside domestic technology are far more accurate than the supposition that the washing machine, not the vote would be of prime importance in the liberation of women, which ignores what has been discovered about the social impact of technology: 'housewifery expands to fill the time available'.[11]

Technology could not liberate the housewife – but could it replace her? Perhaps her job, with its menial, monotonous and fragmented roles, could be better performed by a non-person. In the two films about the Stepford wives, the perfect suburban housewives with perfect suburban homes are not sufficiently controlled by their husbands through domestic roles. Their individuality, their potential for complaint and change, their need for love and responsiveness, for truth and care, remain a threat of which, through male consciousness-raising, each husband becomes aware. To fulfil this role best one must either be robotized (this is the account in the first film) or lobotomized (this is the account of the women's passivity in the sequel). The emptiness of this task accounted for the hollow centre in the housewife's routine which Betty Friedan identified as the problem that had no name, and which a generation of women immediately understood with that 'click' of recognition as someone did name it. The life to which education, custom, and social norms assigned them was not fulfilling. In assigning them to domestic roles they were losing out – financially and psychologically. Women were not properly 'adjusting' to gender roles, because the gender roles they were assigned were for a somewhat less than mature human adult. These films pulled off the satisfying trick of presenting a horrifying fantasy, which some men might have, while satisfying angry women with a vision of man's urge to dehumanize them in the home.

The futuristic vision of domestic chores being done by robots might have signalled some promise. Perhaps the housewife's roles which filled her time without offering satisfaction were like menial tasks in employment which might someday be taken over by technology. Material progress would free woman from her oppression, just as it had freed some men from oppressive conditions of employment. But the duties of housewife have a strange, sticking link to notions of femininity. For one thing, they are not transferable to a person of a different sex. In Britain, in 1970, Albert Mills tried to convince the Department of Health and Social Security that he was a 'housewife': he stayed at home and kept house while his wife went out to work and brought home the money. Vera Mills wanted to claim for Albert Mills the 'dependent wife's benefit' for her husband under the National Insurance Act of 1965; but the Millses were unsuccessful.[12] Such a claim seemed reasonable because surely the rationale behind this benefit was that in a domestic partnership while one individual went 'out' to earn money in paid employment, the other remains responsible for home maintenance, and for this reason the individual in paid employment is allowed to claim a benefit for the economically dependent partner.

But this line of reasoning, this assumption that it was the role rather than the sex that mattered, was not supported by the DHSS (Department of Health and Social Security) or the law court. The DHSS lawyer successfully argued that when the Act referred to 'wife' it was used with the meaning given to it in English law, which is the female part of a monogamous male and female pair.

The role of wife lies on this strange boundary between biological type and social role. For the woman it implies social roles, but it is also intricately linked to the fact of being female which on the whole she cannot change. It is also intricately linked to the family, to the dynamics between the male and female partner, and the dynamics between mother and father and children. This set of dynamics and the intrigue and power and complexity which underline it, tempt researchers to see it as the real problem behind that stalled revolution, behind that stubborn slowness of women's progress. What has not yet been achieved, in spite of all that has been written, is a map which shows how the structures of work and the home interlock with women's own outlook and desires.

The family, as experience and institution, is a point of passionate interest, of love and ambivalence, of enormous personal investment. Consequently it is packed with potential for rewards and disappointment. 'Of all the words in the language 'family' is for me the most powerful', Ann Oakley writes: 'it excites in me a far greater range and depth of emotional reactions than any other word. It signals both the most loving and the most hating of relationships, both the highest degree of liberation and the basest level of oppression. . . . When I was a child I used to cry myself to sleep at night worrying about how I would exist without my parents – when I had to go away from them or when, unthinkable thought, they died. The next morning I would get up and scream at them about some minor matter and write my mother searing notes of loathing.'[13]

The high emotional impact of the family and its life-long influence have been recognized since the beginning of psychology. The tendency for adults to repeat the familial dynamics they experienced as children has also been observed, more recently. In fact, the repetitive patterns of the family have accounted for that tricky question as to why women continue to be mothers. Setting aside the biological facts of reproduction, which clearly account for some but clearly do not account for all aspects of traditional mothering (and housewifery), Nancy Chodorow described how the usual pattern of being raised primarily by a female parent gave rise to sons who grew up not to be primary mothering parents, and daughters who did. The social fact that mothers become the primary caretaker of children forms the personalities of both their sons and their daughters whose first attachment is to the mother. As the boy grows aware of himself as male and masculine, he breaks that first tie of identification with his mother as he sees himself as different and separate from her, whereas the daughter, seeing herself as female and feminine, remains attached to the mother. Hence, 'the basic feminine sense of self is connected to the world, the basic masculine sense of self is separate'.[14]

The psychology of motherhood as both girls and boys, women and men, normally exhibit it, is reproduced by the social conditions in which they normally experience it. And yet this recurrence of patterns we would like to change, but have such difficulty changing, is reflected and enforced not only by the personal relationships within the family, but also by the economic conditions of their society.

Economics of the Family

These passionate psychological dynamics affect our economic reality – or the individual's relation to money and to work and to productivity. It is hard to credit it now, but as recently as 20 years ago economists paid virtually no attention to what went on within the family. An economic theory of marriage, however, was developed by Gary Becker,[15] winner of the Nobel Prize in economics in 1992. In his account of marriage the underlying assumption is that the division of labour in marriage involves rationality and choice. This is a common assumption. It is how many economists account for the way markets work. People, they believe, make choices based on a fair knowledge of the consequences. They control the market, it is thought, through their choices. Their choices reflect their pursuit of what they see as good or desirable.

In Becker's view people marry because they want to have children – their own children. Though this is not the only reason for marriage, or a necessary reason, it is, Becker believes, the 'primary motivation'. In addition, the economist sees marriage as an efficient arrangement. The frequent contact and sharing of resources which people who love one another find desirable can occur more efficiently if the individuals share the same household on a relatively permanent basis. This is a version of the adage 'Two can live as cheaply as one'. Though this saying is strictly false, two people can live more cheaply under one roof than under two; it is easier and cheaper to prepare a meal which provides enough for two consumers, than it is to provide two different meals for two people in different places at different times. Even if twice the same food does not cost less than half of different food items, economies of scale arise with cooking time and cleaning time and use of cooking materials. Moreover, when two people love one another and enjoy one another's company, then the sharing of 'resources' (accommodation, work, and time) is an enjoyable offshoot of companionship.

A third motivation, in Becker's view, stems from the efficiency associated with the specialization of male and female time within marriage. It is here above all – in this specialized male and female use of time – that we can see a circuit of cause and effect, and as the effect is anticipated it becomes itself a cause.

The Reproduction of Dependency

At the same time Becker was depicting this rosy, rational view of marriage, many other writers were beginning to expose the human costs of this smoothly functioning unit. What more and more people were pointing out was that women had been co-erced into a series of choices which limited their lives far more than they had hitherto recognized. The rationale of the tradi-tional division of labour was to men's advantage, and the con-sequences for women of this traditional division of labour were disastrous: they became less than fully human. They lost self-respect, they lost power, they lost control over their lives.

But Becker's theory of marriage is not simply wrong. It is strangely enlightening. For as it explains how and why the traditional division of labour in a household works, we can see how it links up to women's stalled position at work, and how it reproduces itself – not as a result of male malice (only, or primarily), or of habitual male laziness in the home (only, or primarily), or of male bias at work (only, or primarily), but as a result of a circuit of causes and effects, of anticipations and ensuing realizations, of interlocking structures wherein one does not budge because the other does not budge because the other does not budge. It is this that makes change slow and difficult – but as we come to understand this further, we can see how the rate of change can increase.

The traditional division of labour within the home is efficient and rational (in the economist's sense of rationality wherein an individual's choice is based on good value for money) because in paid employment, women get a raw deal. The economist's theory supporting the rationality of the housewife's role has nothing to do with biological mothering or female socialization. It is meant to justify the housewife's role on the basis of employ-ment practices, but what it in fact does is expose the unfairness of employment practice which makes it much more difficult to justify a different division of labour in the home, giving rise to 'reasonable' decisions by both men and women which then sustain the unfairness in the workplace which in turn makes decisions to sustain the traditional division of labour 'rational'.

If women's market productivity and wages are lower than men's, then marriage permits a substitution for the wife's less expensive time for the husband's more expensive time in household activities and a corresponding substitution of the husband's time for the wife's time in the labour market. 'Each marriage', Becker writes, 'can be considered a two person firm with either member being the "entrepreneur" who "hires" the other at . . . [a] salary and receives the residual "profits".' In other words, because women earn less than do men in paid employment, it is more efficient for men to spend more time in paid employment (where their time earns more than a woman's time would) and women to spend more time in domestic work, for though this is unpaid work, they are losing far less in pay than would a man because they would earn less than a man if they were in paid employment. As a couple makes this calculation it sustains the traditional division of labour without challenging work conditions outside the home.

Becker's theory of marriage suggests that marriage is not exploitative, but even-handed. Nor is he cold-blooded in his calculations of economic efficiency, for he calculates that one perk of the team effort is that in this team which is bonded by love (what he calls 'full caring') each individual will take pleasure in the 'consumption' or well-being of the other. The gains of marriage are therefore doubled, as each enjoys what he or she does, and each enjoys the 'profits' of what the other does. The roles are divided, but as each partner takes one rather than another role, each also enjoys, through sharing and caring, the role one does not take but the other does.

But if women choose this division of labour, then any individual woman might choose to do something different. If marriage is actually sustained by individual choice, then an individual might choose to allocate her time differently. Yet this division of labour becomes a system which is difficult to change. Women become housewives because it is more efficient for them to do home-oriented work while men work outside the home and earn money. It is more efficient for them to stay at home while their husbands earn money in the workforce because women are not offered good, well-paid jobs in the workforce. The expectation that women who marry, or who believe they will marry, will fail to invest in labour force skills because they believe they will not need them or use them in adult life leads employers to provide few good jobs for them. Employers who believe that women will decide not to invest in their work skills will offer them few opportunities for promotion and less training, on the assumption that there will be high wastage. Hence, when women do want to change they will find structures in place that make change difficult. They will also have to confront the choice of spending less time in home-oriented activities whereby they will either seek their husband's help, at an inefficient wage rate, or they will employ someone else – usually a woman – to do the work they have been expected to do, but who may be a little lower down on the wage scale than they, though this still becomes costly, because they have to pay in wages for the work that in the traditional division of labour was free.

The image that Becker drew of the traditional family is of a team whose labour is divided, but who have equality: either can be seen as hiring the other to do the job that he/she chooses not to do. Men 'hire' women to bear and rear children and to do housework because they are incapable of bearing children, because the 'mothering' roles which are linked to biological motherhood fall more naturally to the woman, because while the woman is at home mothering she might as well do other home-oriented (wifely) activities. The woman 'hires' the husband to go out to earn the wages necessary for maintaining the home.

What is neglected in this even-handed description of marriage is power and dependence, how this allocation of time leads to an asymmetry of resources. Men, when they are traditional breadwinners, have more immediate access to the family income: it is theirs first and foremost, thereby giving them a privileged position in this 'hiring' scheme. When a woman does want to change this arrangement, she finds constraints in the workforce and impediments at home: for when she goes out to work who will look after her children? Where will she find a wife?

Can Fathers 'Mother'?: Role-Reversal

Though the question, 'Why can't a woman be more like a man?' has been frequently heard, the question about whether a man could be more like a woman, was until recently a rarity. It was not until women became aware of how their mothering roles constrained them, and how other options should be available to them, that they began to reconsider, too, the role the father should play in the wear and tear of his genetic investment. Margaret Mead believed that it would be easy enough for men to assume a mothering role. In a television documentary she pointed to the ease with which men become 'hooked' as an infant grabs a finger with that instinctive response which, to others, seems to carry such emotional weight. But no one ever questioned the fact that men get 'hooked' on their children. The question is whether they are as easily drawn into the daily chores, the attentive planning, the concern, the anxiety, the practical nitty-gritty – whether they find the institution of motherhood as welcoming and as confining and as encompassing as do women.

As a child I remember reading in a 1950s school storybook about a man who slighted women's work and claimed that his wife had an easy time while he went out to do hard work all day. His wife, enraged by this slight on her tasks, challenged him to change jobs – just for one day. The man laughingly accepted, believing that he would be having a 'day off' while his wife struggled with the labour on the farm. In fact, the wife managed brilliantly, for she already knew about farm work, having helped in most of the farm chores already. She ended her day re-freshed, still brimming with energy. The husband however, had no idea how to proceed with women's work. The kitchen was full of mysterious and unpredictable gadgets. The baby was malevolently distracting and fractious. There was too much going on, too many different demands on his concentration to complete even one job. By the time his day ended he was tired, bewildered and humiliated.

Role-reversal is still sometimes seen in this comic and superficial light. In the 1982 film *Mr Mom* a husband is made redundant, while his wife finds a lucrative job; he takes over the housewife role. He comes up against his own ignorance of domestic appliances, which he tries to use creatively and sensibly, but only creates messes and disasters. He tries, for example, to dry a child's hair with a hoover. Though this plays with the idea that a woman works harder, and is better-organized than a man, this film, like the 1950s school reader, enforces the idea that women's sphere is separate, and that men fail if they try to take it on. The idea that women know best about these things actually protects men from having to deal with them.

Anger and humour are often closely linked, and as Nora Ephron cracks jokes about the retinal blindness that hits men as they open the refrigerator, unable to see the butter they are looking for until a woman points it out and hands it to them, as she mocks the man who sets the table and sits back to let praise wash over him for a week, she both derides men for their inability to see what is in front of them until a woman serves it, or to see how extensive domestic jobs are, and gives up on them. The fact that men do not take an equal share in parenting and domestic tasks, the fact that progress towards equality in this area is particularly slow and sluggish, does arouse anger, and makes men the legitimate butt of feminist wit. But this should not be the end of the story. Men may not be naturally good at certain things, but this ineptitude does not let them off the hook.

Does Mother Know Best?

The question about whether women are simply genetically better at mothering has to be addressed. Mothering – as we know it today – is not instinctive to women. The type of behaviour we think of as caring and nurturing is simply not unlearned, instinctive behaviour. But nurturing behaviour in women is a strong and persistent tendency. Perhaps women tend to remain the primary parent today because they have been so in the past.

Through natural selection women pass on genes which make them good mothers, which attune them to the needs of others, key them into others' feelings and needs, prod them to feel linked to others and feel safe only when they are caring for others.

This bioevolutionary argument has been presented sensitively by Alice Rossi, who is careful not to conclude too much from it. She found that sex differences persisted, especially in regard to parenting practices and attitudes. The sexual division of labour occurred in the earliest societies because it aided survival. There were many reasons why women should stay close to their infants. There was no alternative to breastfeeding. Pregnancy hindered movement, and so much of the time they would not have been good hunters. Therefore the men hunted, and were separated from the women, and the skills of strength and characteristics like aggression were favoured among them; whereas the skills and characteristics appropriate to child-rearing and domesticity were favoured among the women. The division of labour has become biologically built into human sex.[16]

But this conclusion is less of an affront than it may at first seem. Rossi is not arguing that our choices are now more limited because of our genetic make-up. The fact that mothering skills have evolved in women does not mean that women should mother and men should not. It is simply an hypothesis about what most women will find easier or be naturally better at than most men. The genetic argument says nothing about any individual, because there may be greater differences in skill and characteristics between two women than between any individual woman and any individual man. All Rossi's argument does is to suggest why certain things may come more easily to women than to men. She is careful to point out that she is not arguing that women should devote themselves to mothering, and to nothing else. She is suggesting, however, that if we want to change the traditional division of labour, we have patiently to teach men the skills they require to do these jobs. We cannot assume that they will learn as easily, as 'naturally' as women seem to.

Kramer vs Kramer was a sophisticated attempt to study role-reversal from this angle. Men could learn, but it was not easy. The father learned about terror for the child's well-being, about the difficulties of balancing his work-time against family-time. He slid from anger to guilt to empathy as he battled with his son's despair at the mother's abandonment and the need to discipline the child. But like most cases of role-reversal I witnessed, this was forced upon the father. Role-reversal is taken up by default, rather than by a decision, by an ideal of equality. Men who are forced into the primary parenting role do not have an easy job. A study of 'motherless families'[17] shows how men suffer the constraints and drawbacks women often confront as they offer their services to employers under the conditions that their family responsibilities allow. This is not a position, not a set of restrictions, that one can easily choose. It is one that men may rise to, if necessary; and this is very different from a chosen, deliberate change in the division of labour. Ann Oakley described how her husband took care of her and the house when she suffered a post-natal depression. But she also realised that this was 'help' offered, that the husband was tending things until she was able to, that this sensitive contribution to domestic organization was not a change in the division of labour, but a temporary provision in response to someone else's need.

I learned of several instances of role-reversal, but these were always shortlived. Divorcing fathers were left with children, but swiftly acquired girlfriends or new partners who helped them. The distress of such fathers on their children's behalf was genuine, but they were far more tolerant of the upheaval in their work and domestic lives, living with this breathless unease, because they saw it as temporary. They were as persistent as the most career-oriented women in finding good childminders. They were ruthless in requesting others' help – and they were often granted help on the ground that others saw them as overburdened. The fact that Bill Stein was dealing with a toddler and doing the laundry roused the pity of the College President's wife. She rapidly offered her assistance. The entire college community was activated to help this poor bereft single father of two young children, while his many female counterparts went unnoticed.

However responsible fathers felt, they were adept at getting others' support. The havoc they experienced as primary parent was a crisis which they frequently overcame. When they did not, they were constrained just as women are.

Contradictions and Resistance

At the same time as Gary Becker was outlining his enormously influential theory of marriage, feminists were investigating human capital from a very different angle. Instead of asking who will pay what for what they can produce, and how people spend time according to what it will earn, they suggested a new query. They asked whether the market value of women's time was fair. They asked whether the traditional division of labour was good for women. Rather than wondering whether traditional roles made sense of the family as an economic unit, they asked whether they satisfied women as individuals. They saw that women often had access to men's earnings as a result of their domestic work, but that this monetary gain was insecure. Women's access to men's earnings was indirect, based on individual assessment, perhaps, of what the housewife needed or had a right to. Though some men were fair, others were not, and in face of unfairness a housewife had no redress. Even in a fair household the housewife had no direct control. In consequence men gained power, authority and control. In consequence, women lost self-esteem, self-determination and social power.

There is something very strange about Becker's theory. It was inaccurate when it was written, and it is totally defunct now; yet it is a formula which many women feel as a threat, or as the point towards which marriages tend to gravitate. It does not represent the ordinary marriage, and yet its form requires deliberate resistance. The system Becker described in which the domestic-based woman and the male breadwinner live well on their shared profits began to recede more than a generation ago, but even in the last century it was not universal – nor as common as many of us have believed. The story of wages and earnings in economic history has been confined to men's wages and earnings. Women's earnings have had no place in past economic history.[18] As a result, women's earning are deemed to be insignificant. Their invisibility seems to be on two levels. Women's financial contributions to the family, and their financial role in the family, are absent from history books. They have been deemed unimportant, irrelevant, too small to make a difference.

Many of the structures in the home and at work that women confront are sustained and maintained on the assumption that the traditional formula for marriage is accurate. It is this which makes it especially difficult for that formula to be changed significantly. It is this that threatens women's employment. As governments believe that public spending on child care facilities would undermine the family, they are arguing for a family that no longer exists but, as they do so, they make it much more difficult for change to be positive. Mothers do go out to work. Fathers very often are not breadwinners. Mothers are often left both to look after their children and be breadwinners. Hence they need child care facilities. Or, women work to contribute to the family income, which often cannot be sustained by one wage. But even then women's earnings are often seen as marginal. Since they are seen as marginal they can be kept low.

A Failed Compromise

Mothering and mothering tasks and the costs these incur on careers are seen as central to women's employment, which in turn is seen as central to women's equality. Motherhood and the domestic tasks which are linked to it have been seen as accounting for the stalled progress in women's employment – either because social policies do not allow women equal opportunity at work[19] or because the inequality in the home spills over into the workplace.[20] Since women now do expect to work, while they also expect to have children, and while they expect to play an important role in the care and raising of their children, part-time work seems like providing a wonderful solution.

Women more often try to combine work and motherhood than to give up one or the other. They try to combine many traditional aspects of mothering with their work, and one means of doing this is to work fewer hours so that they can spend more time with their families. The idea of part-time work is generally highly appealing to women, and several studies have found that the possibility of flexible working hours and flexible working conditions plays a central role in their decision whether to return to work after having children.[21] Several surveys which chart individual wishes regarding working hours have shown that part-time work fits in with women's preferences for working hours, especially among married women with children still needing care.[22] These surveys have also found that almost half the women in full-time employment would prefer to work part-time if this were offered to them by the companies or institutions they work for. The demand for part-time jobs with pension and health benefits far exceeds the actual supply of such jobs. In fact, the rise in protective legislation (maternity rights, eligibility for sickness pay and other non-wage benefits) often acts as an incentive for employers to avoid hiring women on a full-time basis and instead to make use of them as part-time workers, or as informal workers who are not eligible for such benefits.

The inadequate supply of worthwhile part-time jobs leads to a substantial proportion of mothers with young children living reluctantly as housewives rather than working. Many women who do not work would like to work but cannot find jobs with hours which suit what they see as their domestic obligations: 42 per cent of women who were housewives said that the reason for not working was that they had not been able to find part-time employment in their occupation. Part-time work has many of the perks of the superwoman image, yet without making superhuman demands. Like the superwoman syndrome, it allows a mother to work, while leaving essential domestic roles unchanged. It allows the mother to be employed without giving up a mother's primary responsibility for her children. It permits her to contribute to the family income without actually shattering the male breadwinner/housewife marriage, for though her earnings can play an important role in the financial comfort of her family, they are 'secondary' and unnecessary to its survival. However, the image of a woman's earnings as 'pin money' is inaccurate. Women tend to spend proportionately more of their income on their family needs than they either save or spend on themselves. The low wages a part-time working married mother is often paid may alleviate a family's financial strain while it leaves the issue of her financial dependence unchanged.

Just as the superwoman image of 'having it all' sustains many of the typical, even cliché images (of the woman as wonderful cook, entertainer, proud involved mother, attractive alluring lover, supportive wife), the more modest part-time option often leads to gross inequality at work, and sustains the unequal structures both at home and at work. The women I interviewed in the early 1980s were well aware that a good part-time job was very nearly a contradiction in terms. For many companies reject part-time work completely. Other firms allow it, but not in skilled jobs. And part-time management positions are virtually unheard of.

Women who plan masculine-type career patterns for themselves in early adulthood often change their goals as they experience the rigidity of conventional job schedules. They resist the single vision and the single track. They seek a balance in their lives, rather than a Holy Grail of success. As a result they work hard to find more flexible forms of employment, and one obvious form of flexibility is part-time employment. Some of the most determined and successful women have made good careers within part-time work, but it often remains second-class work, without insurance benefits, or pension contributions, or paths to promotion, or paths to full-time employment in which these benefits might be gained. Employers often refuse to take on part-time workers in any area other than menial employment. They find them 'unsuitable' as skilled workers. And yet part-time work remains enormously attractive to women.

Many women were persistent and inventive as they discovered or created part-time work. Mary Hoffman, the children's writer, worked the hours her three young children would permit to her, until these hours increased and her stature increased so that full-time investment was reasonable. Judith Guest, author of *Ordinary People*, began writing only when her children began school. A fashion designer worked piecemeal, from home, until she had more time ('given' her as her children grew) to invest more time in her work. A half-time museum curator organized worldwide exhibitions when her children entered college. The part-time work was a learning process, a way of keeping in touch, a way of remaining in practice, so that when the circumstances allowed, they could go full steam ahead. Women transformed part-time work as a trap into part-time work as a bridge which could accommodate their various needs and achieve a balance. These women were capable of making use of practices which are not automatically friendly to them. But there are strong odds against their success.

The odds against them arise not from simple malice, or man's deliberate urge to keep hold of the jobs and promotions and salaries and control which he now has. Rather, it has to do with tacit expectations and assumptions and norms, with habits and patterns of interaction which form interlocking cycles that are very difficult to break.

The first cycle is domestic, and involves the structure of marriage and the feelings of those within the marriage. Since it is a cycle, there is no starting point, but we can begin with the fact that these women want to be mothers. They see the family as primarily responsible for the care of the children. They find that within the family structure the mother is primarily responsible for the children. Hence the mother is far more likely to cut down on employment outside the home than is the father. Hence the father devotes more time to paid employment so that he can earn more money. Hence the mother devotes more time to child care and domestic tasks because the father is not available in this capacity.

The second cycle involves employers' and women employees' expectations about the terms on which they engage in transactions with one another. Employers expect that women will be mothers, with less time to give to their work. This makes the employer less eager to invest in training and the costs of job security for a woman employee. Hence the jobs whose flexibility often appeals to women are in many ways less attractive than more rigid employment. Women are nonetheless likely to apply for and accept such jobs because they see their primary responsibility as the care of their families. Hence part-time work and flexible hours are essential to their employment. They do not believe they can offer their services to an employer under any other conditions. Their desire for job flexibility will incur disadvantages which they have to accept because they need flexibility. Because the flexible jobs are not attractive, employers expect a high turnover. Hence the employer has no reason to make the job attractive or to put it on a promotional track. Hence the employer sees it as a job designed for someone who accepts lesser working conditions and opportunities – the employer sees it as a woman-designed job.

These two different cycles interlock as the woman at home decides to cut down or resign from her job because she is not earning as much or likely to advance as far in her job as is her husband. Thus her role as child-carer and domestic organiser is confirmed, as is her husband's role as breadwinner. Enforcing these cycles are not male meanies determined to suppress her, but a variety of accepted expectations, choices and structures.

The challenge to women is to break this complex cycle – rather than to change one thing – either within the home or within the workplace. Progress is slow and difficult because changing one thing in interlocking patterns will not be enough. The individual challenge is to find the point in the cycle at which the woman has the most power and will incur the least cost.

Sometimes this is found when need conflicts with habit. A divorced or widowed or separated woman who may be accustomed to the housewife role, or a 'secondary' income, is pushed by need to find a better, more equal place in the work structure. Sometimes this is found when individual ideas conflict with the status quo. The educated women of the 1970s challenged the notion that they would not plan careers. Sometimes the points of interlocking become weak as expectations clash with experience. Many housewives of the 1960s discovered that they were deeply unhappy, confined and isolated in the traditional housewife's role. In such circumstances women are inspired (both through hope and anger) to break the structures which confine them.

Yet points of conflict frequently appear where none was suspected. Couples who seem to share ideals of gender equality discover themselves enacting traditional roles. The marriage itself may be threatened by the sense of betrayal. At work, some firms try to welcome women as employees, but exhibit such strong masculine cultures that women feel uncomfortable, and cannot thrive. In such cases women may feel too bewildered and confused and ambivalent to put forward an effective battle. This experience is disheartening because it has been more muted than other constraints on women, because the constraints are harder to define, and because it becomes very difficult to apportion blame. Is the woman herself unable to adapt? she may ask; or are male structures making adaptation impossible? Would not their task be so much easier if only the family were not forced to take virtually sole responsibility for the child, which would be the case if only the wife were less likely to find herself primarily responsible for the family's well-being, which she might be if only her partner did not have to work so many hours to be breadwinner whereby he tends to see his job as done when he comes home?

Controlled Change

The housewife/breadwinner marriage model is now in a fragile position. As our economy changes and our view about what women want changes, we also want to change the shape of marriage. The expectation that the housewife/breadwinner marriage is still valid makes it difficult to change, and incurs enormous costs for women when it does change so that they become the breadwinner. The division of labour which one expects, and which employers expect, enforces the old forms even as many people agree that they should be changed, even as many people experience them as changed.

As we look to other countries which do seem to have changed more thoroughly, more deeply and more effectively, it is tempting to cite one thing as cause of their success and of other countries' consequent stagnation. Surely it is the institution of motherhood – the fact that child care falls to the mother – without support from government policies, and without enough paternal participation – that stalls progress.

Yet because of the interlocking of perceptions, expectations, individual practices and social policies, this simple diagnosis, intuitively appealing, does not really work. It is motherhood which creates the greatest difficulty in breaking the cycle of structures, but the problem of women fitting into today's typical work schedule is not simply a matter of needing others to do their mothering for them – it is that they want to do the mothering for their own children.

One Single Change?

It is easy to see why many believe that nothing will change unless social policies are implemented which help change the division of labour in the family. It is easy to see why some have argued persuasively that child care is the crucial factor in the continuing wage gap – or difference between earnings by men and by women. Responsibility for the children should be shared between parents and society, so that men and women would be equally disadvantaged by their children – with the assumption that if child care time becomes an equal responsibility, the norm for both men and women, then neither men nor women will be disadvantaged by it.

If women are forced to take time as mothers – first in being pregnant, then in giving birth, and then, often, in caring for children and raising them and being available to them – then it does seem reasonable that widespread, affordable, good-quality child care facilities would allow women to work in conditions equal to men – and then, perhaps, the remaining inequalities would be eased out. Most people who argue this look to the Scandinavian countries for support. Here indeed the gap between what women earn and what men earn is less than in Britain and less than in the United States. Yet in Nordic countries, in which preschool children (under 7 years old) are entitled to day care in an institution or family while their parents are either working or studying, part-time work is often preferred, and only 1 per cent of women who did work part-time reported insufficient child care as a reason for wanting to work part-time in 1987 in Finland and in Sweden.[23] Despite the wealth of public day care facilities for both preschool children and school-age children, and despite the fact that these facilities, many of them run by local governments, are virtually costless to the parent, women still want part-time work, and they want it for family reasons.[24]

The argument that women with small children are prevented

from working full-time because there are inadequate facilities to care for their young children assumes that women with young children want full-time employment. But this does not seem to be the case. Most women with young children want to remain in some kind of employment on a permanent basis, but they also want to have time with their children and to look after their children themselves. And hence part-time work becomes enormously attractive. Part-time work is 'gendered' – it is almost exclusively sought by and given to women. The differences in women's work patterns have a deep cultural base which results in a set of practices and policies and patterns.

Moreover, in the countries of Central and Eastern Europe, which have, in the recent past, had good state-supported child care, and which do have the world's highest rate of women at work, nonetheless have persistent wage gaps. These will probably increase as jobs become scarce – as the state deserts its policy of insuring every citizen's right to a job, and ends its accompanying support of institutions which make work for women possible. For women in what was once East Germany often feel they are living in what is now a foreign land. Not only do they, along with their husbands, confront entirely new issues of tax schedules and housing benefits, but they also find that familiar landmarks have been devalued.[25] Child care has become an impediment to work, and as the conditions of employment change to become competitive with the West, new restrictions are made upon them at home. Their 'liberation' diminishes their freedom.

But the socialist ideology of gender equality was never enough to offer equality, never enough to put equality into practice. Jobs were always segregated. There were jobs for women and jobs for men, and the jobs for women became 'feminized', which means that they lost status and pay. It seems strange to someone from the West to see which jobs were feminized. Heavy manual labour in Soviet Russia was seen to be suitable for women, and was less well-paid than lighter labour, which was labelled 'skilled'. The strides women made in medicine, because the working hours were less and because women did have good access to the professions, became labelled more as a caring profession than the image of technical and intellectual expertise that clings to it in the West. The extensive maternity leaves and child care leaves, the rights to return to employment after leave, the provision of crèches and kindergartens all make work easier for women – but they are not enough to make work equal for women. Now, as state support for both jobs and child care is coming to an end, women in what was once the Soviet bloc face new gender inequalities to add to the old.

Fertility

Feminism and contraception are issues that have invariably been entwined. The early crusaders for women's rights, like Mary Wollstonecraft, felt highly ambivalent towards sexuality since, without effective birth control, sexual activity did threaten women's well-being. Fertility may in theory have been a blessing, but it also led to poverty – of time, energy and health, as well as money. For Mary Wollstonecraft's daughter Mary Shelley, the division in male-dominated culture of a woman honoured as begetter of children and resented for her power, was imaginatively realized in her novel *Frankenstein, or the Modern Prometheus* wherein male intelligence ousts the woman's role in fertility, yet in usurping this feminine role the results are crude, cruel and dangerous: men, in their envy of a woman's fertility, control her through it. And a woman can easily be controlled by her children: Margery Spring Rice, one hundred years later, described the 'working class wives' whose every minute is dominated by child care and household tasks, who define leisure as the ability to sit down and mend the family clothes in peace, whose only measure of health is their ability to continue as housekeeper and child carer.[26]

As women became more reliably able and more widely able to control their fertility – to determine when and how many children they would have – the new woman on a large scale really had a chance to emerge. The increased education of the young women growing up in the 1950s and 1960s raised their expectations, which were not crushed by excessive child-bearing but which nonetheless, puzzlingly, failed to materialize. Their education was often seen by their families and by them as a kind of increase in marriageable value: a college education would make them a suitable mate for a more desirable man, someone himself with a college education and the earning power and prestige that would bring him. College also was itself a peripatetic marriage market where young women would meet eligible men. But these motives did not abolish the education they received, and though in many cases it took many years, the disappointment, the sense that they had not got from life what they had expected, what they perceived themselves as promised, made the time ripe for change.

The ability to control when one has children is of enormous importance to women's lives and their ability to plan their lives and to negotiate changes through situations. The best-laid plans of women give way to another child; and though there are persistent guesses that women become pregnant deliberately to avoid the challenge of certain attempts and certain successes,[27] the issues surrounding fertility are so complex that the notion of control – though possibly a legitimate ideal to use in shaping policies – is never an achieved fact. And the women who believe strongly that sexuality and fertility are inextricably, morally linked, are themselves people who face problems of balance between affiliation and expansion, though the terms under which these are balanced are different.

The cares which arise from having too many children – all those mouths to feed, all those clothes to wash, all those noses to wipe – are to some, residual concerns: they are, according to Elizabeth Anscombe, 'wisdom of the Flesh – and that is death'. For Elizabeth, this is a religious and moral belief, which sees marriage and sexuality to be offered to people for the purpose of procreating children. Professor of Philosophy, Anscombe shocked her empiricist colleagues by strongly supporting the Pope's encyclical on birth control. Children are not chosen – nor are they unwanted: they are given. They are a natural outcome of the sexual aspect of married life. This is a not a belief about women's role in life, a prescription of how she ought to spend her time or what she ought to be thinking about. Children engender responsibility, but such responsibilities can be managed.

The 'trick' to any success for women involves changing or escaping set patterns, which so interlock and constrain women in various ways. For Elizabeth, who has enough of the eccentric academic about her to appear both sharp and vague, seems to escape certain patterns simply by refusing to see them. All souls are equal before God; she is as important as her children. Her 'bug' for philosophy need not compete with her children – it is a fact of her life, as they are, and arrangements are made which must accommodate these facts – they are not terms to be negotiated.

But strategies and outlooks, though they affect what we do and what we can achieve, are not rigid. Because she sees children as 'given' and not as something one chooses to have or not to have, her outlook is different. This does not make everything easy. Yet whatever complaints she has are distanced by the concept of 'grumbling' which she described to Valerie Grove: yes, I will grumble about this one, she reflected when she learned she was pregnant with her fifth child.[28]

In interviewing people about such important and unshapely issues, researchers quickly learn that different interviews from the same person yield very different information. At the first interview one may well hear only the bad things – or only the good things. A second interview might well frame a thoroughly different picture. In the end, one feels that all one has is a handful of scripts. But these are not worthless. These are genuine efforts at interpreting and reinterpreting our lives.

New Visions

The women interviewed for this book all understood how in various ways they faced special obstacles as women. They were all mothers, too, and faced this special feminizing influence both in their feelings and in the structure of their daily lives. The great social change their generation has witnessed and is participating in, is not so much change in the number of women who work – or even the number of adult (married) mothers who work, but changes in ideas about a woman's right to claim equality at work, to view her career as a moderately ambitious man typically views his, to avoid the pitfalls of sex segregation at work, and to accommodate her family in ways which accommodate her working needs.

What the polarized approaches neglect is the real way in which women in the past 15 years have experienced negotiation in their lives, how they are neither dupes of men nor duplicitous women – though it is easy enough to make them out to be either because in negotiation, in compromise, words can be taken out of their mouths and actions taken out of context to prove a given point. The context in which they make decisions and choices, however, reveals that complexity of circuits while showing their power to change the shape. It is only by seeing these small acts and everyday victories (and everyday compromises and defeats) that we can understand precisely what has happened during these decades of change.

Enormous changes in women's lives, in women's working lives, in their outlook, their anticipation, as young adults, and their goals throughout adulthood, make it plain that there has been some progress towards equality. The interlocked structures which impede progress have had some flexibility, but we want them to have more. If we want to change these interlocked structures we should do two things: push at the points of weakness, seek out inconsistencies of outlook and practice, find out where there is the greatest ambivalence, and push on that. To follow through arguments of change we need to realize that arguments for equality will not always get us very far. We have to understand why the status quo is unsatisfactory for everyone. Men are increasingly coming to realize that the demands on them are unsatisfactory. They pay for them with ill-health, with tension-related habits and characteristics, with feeling tied down and bored, and if they are unsuccessful as breadwinner, with a sense that they are worthless and have nothing to contribute to their families. The structure of the family demeans their emotional contribution, and their overriding value to the family as husband and father. The disappearing father may be a result of the father who believes himself useless as he is unable to fulfil the role of breadwinner, or 'used' as his earning power becomes his only value. The aim of change is equality, but equality does not mean that while women will gain more, men will then have less. Greater equality is a vision which should lead to greater good for all, with less division and less hostility and greater cooperation.

Women constantly ask questions about the costs of their work, constantly assess the value of the work they do and its effects on them and the people around them. They work to understand the conditions in which they make decisions. Women cannot disregard the task of understanding themselves, and of revisioning the roles which play such an important part in their lives, both as constraining and enabling experiences and structures.[29] An important aspect of research into women's lives, and sharing accounts of their choices, decisions and reflections, is to move beyond 'taken for granted' views of reality, in order to see their limitations and how they tend to confine action to forms which sustain the current social arrangements. The task of each woman's life, wrote Adrienne Rich, is revision: 'Revision – the act of looking back, of seeing with fresh eyes, of entering an old text from a critical direction – is for women more than a chapter in cultural history: it is an act of survival. Until we understand the assumptions in which we are drenched we cannot know ourselves.'[30] Motherhood, both as experience and institution, both as a personal and a political relationship, is usually considered by means of a series of questions of what children need and what mothers ought to be. Instead of pretending we have answers to these questions, which would really be another way of attempting to find the 'right' place for women in our society, we have to understand the network of constraints, and decide where in our individual ways we can best attack them.

3
What Do the Children Need?

Mothers may be adult humans, with a range of adult human needs, who suffer the mixed blessings of human complexity and are justified in their pursuit of happiness, but what about children? Do they not need full-time care, especially when they are young? Do they not need love and admiration of the kind a mother is very likely to give? Surely the infant's and child's demands for a mother's constant presence signal a real need? There may be social and domestic 'institutions' – widespread habits, expectations and assumptions – which reinforce mother-hood, but if it is an invention meant to control women, it is surely a child's construction rather than a man's. It is not a male, but a child's conspiracy that stresses the importance of the mother being at home, staying at home, remaining at all times available to the child, with her attention fully focused on the child. Whatever more subtle ploys her partner may or may not use to keep her at home, whatever encouragements he may offer, whatever support society may fail to provide, the child's grasping hands and fierce anxiety home in on the mother's searing empathy to 'keep her in her place'. It is the child's, not the man's power, that makes the strongest bid. Thus, in one of the first novels of new maternal conservatism, the would-be liberated career mother in Freda Bright's novel *Futures* returns home, anxious to check up on the new child minder. Caro finds the woman to whom she has entrusted her baby watching *General Hospital*, oblivious to Sasha's screams of terror. The mother embraces her: 'Baby . . . lambchop . . . Sasha darling . . . I'm sorry . . . I'm sorry . . . it's all my fault.'[1] Whatever the sentimentality or subversiveness in this novel's theme, there is no working mother who has not felt the absolute pull of a child's need, or the hypnotic panic in which such scenarios are envisaged.

The Mother Knot: Tied and Tried

Questions about what children need from a parent are passionate and passionately biased. They touch our deepest fears, for children are experienced as our greatest vulnerability. Harm to them seems like our greatest danger. Recently women have come to experience this magnetic orientation towards their children as both a potential fulfilment and a potential threat. It is a relationship that clearly is packed with consequences beyond what one can control or predict. It is a relationship in which one is virtually trapped, without the power of choice one can exercise in friendship, love and marriage. When a child is born to us we have a set of expectations about what is needed, and what will be the outcome of meeting or failing to meet these needs, but such expectations can fall far short of the actual requirements. This sense of responsibility, of it being 'all my fault', registers the typical allocation of responsibility in the family which is greatly reinforced by social allocation of responsibility wherein it is supposed that the family is fully responsible for the well-being of the children born into it.

Women I spoke to during pregnancy, or while they were anticipating having children, spoke in two distinct voices. When she was six months pregnant Sue was still working as a fashion editor. She barely looked pregnant, yet spoke about her baby constantly:

> I keep thinking what it'll be like. A child in my arms – my child. Don't gloat like this – this isn't sentiment – it's terror. Will I drop her? Will I forget her – leave her somewhere? How will it all stick in my mind – this change? Some people [in the birth group she was attending] talk about being afraid they'll be baby bashers, but I wouldn't do that – or, that's not what I worry about. It's the mental heaviness, like you always have to keep your baby in your brain, you know, and maybe my brain won't.

Eight weeks later I interviewed Sue at her home. She was on maternity leave, and seemed very calm. 'I've hired someone to look after the baby from eight to one. She already knows her way around the house – where I shop, all that sort of routine. She'll visit from time to time, before I go back, and I'll be half-time for the first few months, maybe taking a lot of work home with me.'

These different sessions highlighted the very different voices women commonly used. On the one hand they spoke about scheduling and organization, of time allocated to physical recovery, to child care, to work. This was the voice of control, expressing the belief that difficulties could be managed and challenges met. On the other hand they expressed a host of anxieties: that the child would have special needs, requiring more than normal medical attention and care. They worried, too, that maternal love, which enlivens most women's hearts and gives them the power of maternal care, would elude them, and in eluding them would transform them into monster-mothers, in whom vindictiveness would grow from inadequacy. Here they spoke about things over which they had no control, or expressed fears about losing control: if they were no longer able to direct their energies towards what they wanted to do and who they wanted to become, motherhood would usurp their energy and their identity.

The Subjective and Objective Image of Motherhood

For some women, the image of their own mother is daunting in its constraints and repressions. The 'self' identified as 'mother' in Nancy Friday's *My Mother, My Self,* is one who forbids sex, who denies the daughter's sexuality and along with it her independent adulthood, who casts a net of fear around the daughter's explorations that confine her forever. But while some women focus on the unhappiness their mothers aroused in them, or the constraints their mothers tried to impose upon them, others try to discover how their mothers themselves dealt with those constraints. They look upon their traditional mothers as unhappy but distant. They are enigmas, seemingly happy yet clearly in despair. Ann Oakley writes, 'my mother spilt out the moods inside her with that well-recognized feminine incapacity to keep the floodgates closed, and with that common feminine response to a constraining and frustrating all-domestic environment'.[2] Alice Walker constructs a new female world by searching for (and exploring) her 'mother's gardens':[3] the mother's subjective experience forms landmarks in the daughter's own womanhood. Though many women in this sample acknowledged that their (traditional) mothers had contributed to their development, and were glad to have had them at home,[4] they were sensitive to what their mothers might have been. They tried, as adults, to imagine new possibilities for her. They were eager to describe her abilities and her suffering. Many women saw their mothers as having been unhappy in their traditional roles. They feared that in becoming mothers themselves they would be forced to follow the same patterns. This made them edgy and determined. Whatever brittleness or coldness the new woman has stems more from self-doubt than from certainty. The image of their mother's unhappiness became a motive: they would not follow in the footsteps of unfulfillment.

Advantage: Uncertainty

The experience and practice of motherhood does not diminish that uncertainty about a child's hold over one's time and energy and soul, nor does it increase the volume of that voice of control. Child care, among working women with young children, remains a highly charged issue. Women discuss it, boast about good arrangements, are in despair when minders or nannies or a child care centre has to be changed, and often glaze the drawbacks of their arrangements with bland optimism: non-English speaking caretakers encourage nonverbal communication; inadequate stimulation is seen as encouraging the child to amuse himself; the constant colds and infections suffered by a child in group care are seen as building up his immune system.

Whatever false encouragement women give to themselves is out-matched by the wealth of arguments against their right to entrust their children to others' care. Freda Bright's novel, blatantly conservative in its message about women, love and children, gains its effectiveness by touching that ever-tender doubt: will my child be all right in another's care? And Bright depicts the nightmare with which every working mother is familiar. It plays on the worry that she does not know what happens to her children in her absence, and that no one can be trusted to care as she does. The conservative force of that book in which the solution is a return to rigid gender roles – romantic husbands and suburban wives devoted to the children – is no longer either plausible or possible. Family lives, family finances, have changed. New fictional conservatism is more flexible. In the film *Baby Boom* the infant wields power over the mother figure, but still the story offers the woman a choice and a balance. She can return to the big business in the big city, or she can create her own successful work in a more friendly environment. In Maeve Haran's novel *Having It All*, the 'conservative' issue again is balance and sanity, rather than a return to a stereotypical past.

Forward, and Back Again

Women's ambition continues to snag on questions about what their children need – and in particular, how much their children need of them. The image of the new woman devoted primarily to her career is as slick as it is sleek. However committed women are to their careers, their sense of their children's, and their family's, needs are seldom brushed aside. Even when women intend to stick close to their career goals, they find themselves drawn into traditional patterns of response and action. However strongly they believe family obligations should be shared, they find that the best path and shortest cut to meeting their family's needs is through their direct action and care.

Among the career women I interviewed, both in 1982 and again in 1992, was a strong awareness of the importance of family and relationships and children's well-being – along with pressures to succeed, along with a desire to succeed. The rising hours of work demanded for success in today's career have put an additional, unanticipated strain on mothers, who are all too aware of the potential costs on their children.

For a little while, in the 1980s, the significance of the cutback on time parents had available to spend with their children was minimized. Perhaps parents were spending less time with their children, but, it was suggested, the time they spent with them had more *quality*. The distinction was drawn between a parent who was ever present, but distracted, bored, and burnt out, on the one hand, and a parent who spent the day at work, away from the child, but who returned home fresh for the child, keen to engage with her. During these shorter than traditional periods of engagement the parent could pack in a lot of parental input.

The notion of quality time, once a life-saving, or conscious-salving notion, has now become a joke. Working parents are tired at the end of a working day. It is hard to save up special freshness for one's children. Children have their own rhythms of daily life, their own times of needing and connecting. These arise coincidentally in the ordinary course of an ordinary day. Under the pressure of their multiple jobs, parents may try to redefine children's needs. A six-month-old baby is described as 'independent',[5] as a mother battles with her sense that all is not well in leaving him at a child care facility. The description of her infant son eases the stress between her two competing sets of obligations.

Such hopeful definitions may become self-fulfilling: child psychologists have expressed concern at the phenomenon of the 'the independent child' who becomes independent because she does not expect help and responsiveness and comfort from adults.[6] Her independence, it is thought, arises from the lack of closeness to people on whom she might depend. But as women did discover that their children were shortchanged by them, they changed their lifestyles either by paring down their actual jobs to the bare minimum, or cut down their obligations, or changed their jobs. This pattern of decision-making in response to their need to meet their children's needs is the primary reason that, in general, women have not progressed up the career ladder with the speed that had been anticipated fifteen years ago. Their outlook on a career clashes with their experience of motherhood. As they feel the discrepancy between their imagined goals and their complex reality, the inconsistencies of attitudes and practices towards women elsewhere aggravate their doubts further. The isolation many mothers speak of is not only the isolation an adult may feel at home caring for a child, but the isolation involved in having no markers on a desired and expected path. How, a mother may ask herself, does she deal with the (now) socially accepted career goals and that tug towards her children's needs, which is also socially enforced, both by social norms and expectations of what a mother should be and do, by the slowness of men to share the parental tasks equally, and by the paucity of social institutions to aid 'their' child care tasks? In this way, questions about what the children need become the mother's problem.

Expert Development

Mothers and fathers are hostage to theories about child development and children's needs. Usually, when the father feels concern that children are not getting enough parental time, the practical changes arising from this concern are carried out by the mother. Many women described how husbands had been supportive of their decisions to cut back in their work, describing 'joint decisions' which involve a woman's return to full time mothering. 'We went over it – over and over again. And every time we realized that the best thing for the family was for me to stop working. I'd keep swinging back to the idea – well *she* can do it, and *she* can and *she* can. And I was always asking: "Why can't I?" But Jim said, "Look, we have to do what's right for us. This is our baby, and our family." He's helped me with this, helped see this as positive, not just giving up. And it's only for a while.'

In her study of how couples manage the conflicting roles which often conflict with their ideals of equality between men and women at home and at work, Arlie Hochschild reports how men may console or support women who have decided to stay at home to look after their children. ('It was worth it, wasn't it?' a husband reminds his wife as their son seems easier to handle after she resigned from her job.)[7] This return to more traditional mothering styles may seem like a manipulation by the man, but it is experienced by the woman as responsiveness to her children's and family's needs, and to that persistent need of the woman to act as mother to the child.

The overwhelmingly strong image of motherhood and the importance to women of seeing themselves as a good mother make two questions indistinguishable: what do the children need, and what do parents perceive their children as needing? Because children perceive their own needs as endless and, especially when very young, express their 'views' with vehemence, parents in doubt about how much giving is reasonable turn to experts for answers, and child-care experts have seldom given women's needs priority.

The history of motherhood since the Second World War has been strongly influenced by theories about child development – and as these theories spread, they flourished in the economic and social climate of the 1950s. The urge for stability which spread after the war, the common ability for one breadwinner to earn enough to support a family, relative job security, all combined to create an image of mothering – which is now seen as the traditional image of motherhood. Economic and social forces gave this image plausibility, and psychologists made it seem inevitable and necessary.

The groundwork for questions about what children need from parents was laid immediately after the war by studies of war orphans which later, in the 1950s and 1960s, became popularized by psychologists and child development experts. John Bowlby reported to the World Health Organization about observations of infants in institutions which cared for orphans, and in hospitals, which at that time did not permit parents to have much contact with child patients. When infants – ranging from six to twelve months – were separated from their mothers, they displayed anxiety, crying, withdrawal, lassitude, dejection, insomnia, loss of appetite, weight-loss and extreme slowness in growth development. In somewhat older children the effects of separation from a mother were clearly marked by dramatic stages of anxiety, mourning and an awful resolution, wherein a kind of peace reigns as the child no longer expects to find the mother. The 'peace' is a sickening depletion of expectation.

On first being separated from the mother the child is restless and tearful. He appears to search for the mother, as though he cannot really believe that she is absent. This stage of protest is followed by despair of recovering her. The child remains preoccupied with her and watchful for her. Later, however, the child gives up the hope of finding her, even seems to give up interest in finding her. He becomes in this third stage emotionally detached – not only from his mother, but from all people. During this stage even if the mother does return she is treated with indifference. The image is of an attachment which has been stretched during the anxious and protesting phase of separation, which then finally snaps. Something is lost and gone. The lack of interest in the mother becomes a failure to retain any attachment, any interest. With this emotional disconnection, potential development, both intellectual and emotional, is stifled.

We have to be careful with our children. We care, terribly, about them. Their demands often confuse us, and because we are so concerned, we turn to experts to tell us what they need to be happy and what they need to thrive. They represent our greatest investment in the future, and so we are often prepared to give anything towards their development. We are often ready to set aside our own needs at an expert's recommendation, even if there is only a small chance of the dire predictions being realized. Our children have only one childhood.

Maternal Deprivation versus Temporary Absence

The descriptions of these children who suffered from a condition called 'anaclitic depression', or depression resulting from the absence of anything to 'lean on', was heart-rending, but, for many, oddly consoling. It revealed how that urgent maternal responsiveness was a suitable response to a child's need. It showed, too, the power of the mother, who seemed essential not merely for the child's happiness and comfort but also for her very survival. Children do not live by bread alone. They fail to thrive, fail to grow, can even die, if they are not held and cuddled. They need that special physical attention that parents seem to want to give them. For infant's love is not, as was once thought, cupboard love, or attachment linked to the source of food. Physical contact, instead, is a stronger force of attachment than food.[8] But did any of these studies which poignantly re-affirmed the importance to the infant of physical love and care ever have any bearing on the question of whether the mother harmed her infant by working outside the home?

The idea that any of these studies had anything at all to do with working mothers was a glaring misuse of such studies. Temporary absence from a child is very different from the cases of maternal deprivation that Bowlby recorded. Nor was there any indication that the important attachment had to be to the mother, that a father for example, could not do the same work; or even that very good care by a non-parent could not soften the pain of separation and help a child thrive during a parent's absence. The questions that were *not* asked, as these studies of infants and young children in institutions were linked to children left in non-parental care during working hours, reveal the underlying prejudice. But parents care compellingly for their children; they know that their children have only one childhood and do not want to take risks with them. The images of these children were so vivid and horrifying, that they helped persuade a generation of women who were kept at home by a variety of other factors that their continuous presence in the home was a necessity to their children's well-being.

The extension of Bowlby's work on maternal deprivation to ordinary homes with ordinary working mothers has now been discredited, and Bowlby himself in more recent work, admits that an infant may be more secure, and more skilled at forming attachments if she has more than one 'attachment figure' – or more than one person whom she recognizes as caring for her and upon whom she can depend. But though studies of maternal deprivation are irrelevant to the temporary maternal absence of a working mother, there remains a bias in child development which romanticizes the position of the mother, and in romanticizing it suggests that the traditional position of the mother at home looking after the children full-time is the position that is optimal for the children.

What child development psychologists describe is the use of the intense relationship with the mother. They continue to discover new, remarkable ways in which the infant engages with the mother, elicits responses from her, then takes rest breaks from this intense, exciting conversation, or shows distress when the mother fails to respond.[9] The active engagement between mother and child has been described as a love affair; and this relationship is seen to flourish in the presence of a third person who admires and cares for the parent who is so besotted by the infant. 'So what a surprise', exclaims a psychologist who described this scenario: 'We have reinvented the wheel', and reestablished the psychological roots and rationale of the traditional family.

None of the investigations into the importance of attachment actually has any bearing on questions about whether it harms children for their mothers to work during the day. Some psychologists, however, have suggested that it does. They insist that children require someone who has an irrational appreciation of everything they do and achieve. But of course even children who have parents who work have parents who take an irrational, exorbitant pride in them and their normal developmental progress. Yet the debate continues. The British parent adviser Penelope Leach has issued a virtual diatribe against working mothers.[10] She does not refer to theories of child development, but to her own sense of what children can and cannot tolerate. Though 'tiny gaps' she believes, in the mother's continuous company can be withstood by a child, even these are wounds which need time and attention to heal.

Leach recalls looking after another's child herself and being unable to interpret the whimpering and fretting: was the child hungry, or tired, or lonely, or bored – or what? The assumption seems to be that mother knows best. But this theory, so flattering and appealing to the mother, is also restricting. Like many arguments about mothers and work there is a recursive circularity: the fact that a mother tends to know her child better than others becomes a reason for suggesting that the mother is derelict in her maternal duty if she puts someone else in the position of learning how to interpret her child. But the mother knows her child well because she is in the position of getting to know her child. The mother may be the first to understand and interpret the infant's responses, but she is not the only one able to do this. It is her position *vis-à-vis* the infant that makes her learn this. Like anyone else, she learns what she has to.

Some women guard their special knowledge and their special position. It is a privilege, and they do not want to pass it on to someone else. Hence Lynn Maris explained why she was resigning as assistant manager from a large store chain to which she had to commute from New Jersey to New York: 'I look at my children and think – how can I be so lucky? It is luck, to have normal children, but there's something else – it's temporary. Not only because they grow up and go their own way, but because your control is so limited, and anything can happen. How can I trust anyone else with them? I know there are good, responsible people who look after other people's children. And I know other women who spend less time with their children love theirs as much as I do, but it's at this gut level, that it's my responsibility, and my privilege, and I can't see why I should give it up.'

Other women are frustrated by this 'privilege'. The child's special need for them gives them a special, unyielding responsibility. As Alice began once again teaching when her second son was twelve months old, she said: 'He grabs my leg when I get up from a chair. He doesn't even want me to close the bathroom door. I want to work. I have to work, and this clinginess makes me want to scream.' Many women feel ambivalent: this importance and this skill are both privileges and binds. They wish they could spread the responsibility around, yet they feel threatened by diluting this role. They want peace, they want time, they want more energy for themselves, and yet they want to be constantly involved and constantly available.

Children often learn to need the mother only. The traditional division of labour teaches the infant to depend, most, on the mother. But this is not a necessary, immutable need. Children, it seems, function very well cared for by a number of people. Though too many caretakers confuse the child, at a very young age she is able to distinguish between people and recognize them and has no trouble with as many as five or six people. In fact recent research shows that a child feels more secure if more people look after him.[11] Babies who are bathed regularly by their fathers show less distress upon being separated from the mother. Children are more flexible than has been supposed. The child's power over the mother is, like mothering, learned.

Full-Time Mothering: Uses versus Needs

There is a sharp split between two types of approaches to the question about whether maternal employment adversely affects children. The first looks at mothers and children interacting. These studies reveal how much is going on in these ordinary interchanges, and how crucial such exchanges are for sound, normal development. But to show how deep these ordinary occurrences are, to explore their intricacies, and trace their importance, does not provide a schedule of necessary time. It does not show how much of this kind of interaction the child needs or for how long. It does not rule out the possibility that interaction with people other than the mother is adequate.

The other way to approach the question is simply to look at children of mothers who work, and to see whether any differences in emotional or intellectual development can be observed. This is not easy, because researchers have to be careful to sift out the effects of divorce, of single parenting, of separation, of paternal unemployment, and poverty from the effects of maternal employment. Children may survive all these things, and even thrive after having experienced them, but they are different issues. They pose different problems, different puzzles; they involve different strategies, and the researcher does not know which behaviour is an answer to which problem.

So each new study has to refine itself, be more specific, sharper than the preceding one as it hopes to draw the perfectly simple line between a mother's work and a child's development. This is no easy task. Three months after one apparently definitive study was released, which 'proved' that children suffered no ill-effects if their mothers worked, a new American study funded by the Department of Education contradicted the previous findings by the National Institute of Education. In white, two-parent homes, school students whose mothers worked full-time during their school years scored up to nine percentile points lower on tests than students whose mothers never worked. The magnitude of the effect was directly related to how much the mother worked. Part-time working mothers' children scored better than full-time, and the amount of time the mother worked was directly related to the child's score. Recently other startling and puzzling results have emerged. It has been found that in African-American families the performance of children, academically and intellectually (on IQ tests) was higher in families where mothers worked full-time. Indeed, African-American families and African-American women tend to show very different results from white middle-class families.

Children of black working mothers do better than children of non-working black mothers. This may be accounted for simply because the working mother who lifts her family above the lower 20 per cent income level of their community has an overriding advantage. Any children of any race or ethnic group who are in the lower 20 per cent income level of their community have higher scores on mental maturity tests than do their peers, if their mothers work. The morale of working when one's income is essential to the family's well-being is very high. Full-time employment raises the self-esteem of the mother, raises her hopes, increases her security, her sense of control, her vision, her sense that she is setting a good example to her children. But even in black middle-class families, where the income was well above the lower 20 per cent level of the community, working mothers expressed far less ambivalence towards the stressful complications of their work. It seemed that this might be a result of their different attitudes towards their achievements: work was not a luxury, but an achievement, which set a good example to their children and their community. The black professional women in this study had a pride in their achievements, and an awareness of how that pride could serve their children well.

Why shouldn't similar results be found in white middle-class families? The income level is usually raised by the mother's employment – though not always, because when the mother is in paid employment child care and domestic management involve costs that may rise to the level of her income. Many women spend more on child care and domestic management than they actually earn, but work for them is part of their quality of life, and its costs are judged to be worthwhile. The white woman who works full-time should receive as high a boost to her self-image as does a black woman. Should she not be able to provide as a strong an example to her children as does a black mother in full-time employment? Well, yes, all these seem to hold for the daughters of white middle-class mothers – but not the sons. In white middle-class families, it seems, the daughters benefit from the mother's full-time employment, but the sons do not.

How can these differences be accounted for? Why should daughters benefit, and sons not? Is it that girls benefit so much from the model of independence and outside interests that working mothers offer, that the poor effects of any diminution of control or attention are overridden? Or do girls have too much control and attention in the traditional state of affairs, with the mother looking after them, at home with them whenever they are at home, gearing her time and interests to theirs? Do they get more attention and control than is good for them? Do boys, on the whole, get just about the right amount of control in traditionally mothered families, and so lose out when they get less adult control and attention?

These are questions which have been posed by researchers

trying to make sense of the studies so far. But the samples researchers are dealing with have changed. When researchers first started challenging the psychologists' guesses about what would happen to children of working mothers by studying actual children of working mothers, they had trouble finding enough 'clean' subjects – children of full-time working mothers who were not divorced, who did not have unemployed fathers, who did not live in poverty. Now, it may be difficult to find 'clean' or pure subjects – that is, children of mothers who do not work at all, who do not have sufficient outside interests that are tantamount to working, who do not see themselves as only temporarily following the traditional role of mother.

Maternal employment is the norm. Most families now rely on a woman's paid employment. When something becomes the norm it does not seem so dangerous, and does not invite such scrutiny. When a practice becomes necessary, the consequences are accepted. In the end, the theories about child development and maternal employment were brushed aside when they no longer made economic sense. When female labour was needed in Britain during the Second World War, the state provided nurseries, and it was assumed that the children would be all right. It was when men returned from war, and women were required to forgo employment for the men who had fought for their country, that the state nurseries closed and theories emerged which suggested fearful consequences of child care, which was often lumped quite simply with maternal deprivation. East Germany, or the former GDR, was heavily dependent on female labour. As this necessity is eased and it is no longer held that it is every citizen's right to gainful employment in the new unified Germany, East German women have come up against the opinion in the West that young children are harmed by being cared for in state nurseries.

The question of whether nurseries and child care centres are 'needed' has always faced a contradiction. From one point of view, they are needed if the mothers who care for children want them and would use them. They are needed, too, if employers need women who are mothers who need alternative care for their children. But either of these 'needs' can be countered by 'experts' who believe that child care facilities should not be provided because they are not good for the children. So while nearly two-thirds of mothers of children under 5 would like to share their child care tasks,[12] the Ministry of Health in Britain, and successive governments in the United States, have resisted the mothers' needs, finding them 'alarming', and seeing the children's needs in opposition to the mothers'.

The power of theories about what children need does not rest simply on psychological considerations. Economic conditions can rapidly shift the balance of considerations. The theories which were so prevalent in the 1950s have lost their economic backup, and so have lost credibility and even relevance, as the economic position of the family changed. The phenomenon known as stagflation, wherein unemployment is high and there is inflation, which has occurred in the past 20 years and shows no sign of diminishing, reinforces the trend already set: that women will work and women will continue to work when they are mothers. The question simply remains as to how stressful this will be.

Abandoning Women

The theories about children's needs for maternal care are a little different now. Psychological supposition has given way to common sense – which emphasizes that children need their parents, that they need more of their parents' time than they often get. Questions focus on how much time working parents give their children, rather than whether a parent should give all her time instead of working. The tension is seen not so much as between a job and parenting responsibilities, but in terms of fast-track parents who have no time for their children.[13] The scare theories now are less likely to describe the range of emotional and behavioural problems among children of 'working mothers' than among children of 'absentee working parents'.[14] There is after all strong evidence that the presence of the father in the home has a much closer link to non-delinquency than does the presence of the mother. In *What Shall We Do with the Children?* Judith Hann quotes a study which found that 98 per cent of a cross-section of juvenile offenders were without a father (or father-substitute), but only 17 per cent were without a mother. She found that while researchers studied links between maternal employment and delinquency, they had not bothered to report the numbers of delinquents who experienced a father's absence. The stunning effect of the 1991 film *Boyz 'n the Hood* rested on its identification of the deadly epidemic faced by young urban black males who have been abandoned by their fathers. Sons need fathers if they are to mature into adults who can function in this demanding and often unfriendly society. Parental neglect was laid at the father's, not the mother's, door.

Images of Abandonment

Yet abandoning means very different things when it describes a mother and when it describes a father. The father who leaves the family home, and lives apart, is not seen to abandon his children as long as he sees them from time to time and contributes to their financial support. But a woman who does this is seen – and sees herself – to be abandoning her children.

This different standard has nothing to do with the actual measured effects on children. This discrepancy registers a shared sense of what motherhood is: its commitment, its significance, its responsibilities. This prejudice reveals the ground beneath those difficult decisions women have made to leave their children; both the women and the decisions have virtually gone underground. Each brave decision to write a book about this subject, by mothers who have left their children, seems to founder. Sylvia Paskin wrote an article on her experiences, and was flooded with so many replies that she decided to write a book about it. Once one women spoke up a hundred others were anxious to tell her she was not alone, so relieved were they to discover through her that they were not alone. Women described how they had kept secret from everyone who knew them the fact that they had children, whom they had left in the care of others.

Yet the 'crimes' these women had committed did not involve abandoning children on snow-covered mountains, or selling them to slave traders, or even thrusting them into the care of the state. For the most part, they had left children with fathers or grandmothers. Their crime was not cruelty or neglect, but the malfunction of the maternal bond. They described pacing the darkened house, alone with a sleepless baby whose cries spoke of huge needs, but in some foreign language, addressed to an alien being.

A television documentary was aired in England, making use of the wealth of responses. Women who had left their children spoke about their experiences as mother, as renegade, as shame, as stigma, and finally, as these feelings were shared, as hope for acceptance. The book that was planned on this subject, however, was set aside, as requiring more exposure, and inviting more opprobrium than the author could tolerate. Rosemary Jackson took up the task from her similar experiences.[15] In an early draft of the current book she describes sitting in Germaine Greer's lectures at Sussex University – already a young mother, listening to the call to liberation, too late, hearing how it was woman's duty to stand up for herself and her rights, aware both of the truth of what Greer said, and the enormous difficulty of putting it into practice. In this vignette of the solitary mother in a classroom full of childless feminists, we can feel the young woman's call to individual development crashing against the sense of being bound to her children, and realizing that in this setting, the maternal tie had no voice. It was unravelled like a confetti of sentimentality and male convenience and male control.

Few feminists in the 1970s admitted how difficult maternal entanglements were, how deeply they worked their way into one's soul, whether for good or ill. The inevitable discoveries by this articulate generation of women came a little later, but the voices of passionate ambivalence were always resolved. Jane Lazarre, in *The Mother Knot*, described her thwarted goals for finishing her thesis as her baby woos and rules her. She described her despair and frustration and boredom as she counts lonely hours of her child-care-filled day. She described the fun and exuberance of community effort as she and other parents worked to set up a crèche. She wrote this book a little too early, perhaps, to confront the question of her husband's peripheral support. He remains the strong masculine presence, strong in his separation but ineffectual in releasing her from the mother knot, however sincerely he sympathizes with her. However much he shares a love for their son, he is quite clean of the miasma of maternal feelings.

Perhaps she protected him from them, as Sylvia Plath did Ted Hughes – or as she aimed to do: 'I find my first concern is that Ted has peace and quiet', she wrote to her mother, 'I am happy then and don't mind that my own taking up of writing comes a few weeks later.' She understood that 'it is impossible for him to work in this little place with me cleaning and caring for the baby'.[16] After all, she herself felt, 'it is so frustrating to feel that with time to study and work lovingly at my books I could do something considerable, while now I have my back to the wall and not even time to *read* a book.'[17]

For Plath, as the marriage disintegrated, as she was left to cope alone with her children, the despair and isolation, the obliteration of her sense of identity in her new isolated situation and forced fragile independence, the conclusion of her dilemma was resolved in suicide: in death there are no more contradictions. For Lazarre, as for most women who write about their own maternal feelings, the intense ambivalence was resolved into an intense pride. There comes a time for most women when, at least temporarily, there is a reprieve in the demands made upon them, when schedules work, and unpredictability no longer rules. At such times the widely appreciated benefits of parenting make the costs seem worthwhile, and the feeling – however shortlived – is : 'Look, we have come through'.

But the women who do not reach that point are silenced. Many women now admit – as they perhaps would not have done in the 1950s – that residing inside them is someone who identifies with a mother who chooses to leave her children. But even among women who are willing to talk about almost anything, this admission is muted. When Jane Rogers gave a reading of her novel *The Ice is Singing* she explained that she had written this story about a woman who leaves her children, when her own children were very young – but hastened to add that she had not left her children – no, nor wanted to, but that she simply understood how someone could come to such an impasse. I am not doubting the legitimacy of Rogers' protest, but that she thought it appropriate to make it in the context of this vivid (fictionalized) account of a mother who does, temporarily, leave her children underlines how dangerous this discourse appears to many of us – even now, even among women who know themselves well enough to know better. In the conclusion of Rogers' novel the woman who has left her children decides to return – not because they could not survive without her, but because without fulfilling her role as mother she would have lost her voice, her self, her ability to think and reflect as a sane and viable being. The woman who leaves her children has no other identity left to forge.

In Rosemary Jackson's as yet incomplete text, she follows this theme in literature. Women who leave their children in fiction are punished, never finding the goals they seek – unless, of course, the story's reward is to the father, as in *Kramer versus Kramer.* The discrepancy between the novel and the film is intriguing. In the novel Mr Kramer becomes a much better person as a result of having his son thrust upon him. He becomes deeper, more caring, more connected. But not only that – he advances further in his career as he plumbs his human depth, with a wonderful Czech nanny on the side.

The popular film, from Avery Corman's novel, reveals different consequences for the man and the woman. Whereas the novel may be more realistic in its depiction of what chances a woman has to make it on her own within a year, the film highlights the realistic drawbacks to a man of finding himself primary parent, as well as breadwinner. As in the 'motherless families' described by George and Wilding's book of that title, a father in sole charge of his child suffers the same tensions, setbacks, frustration, humiliation and anxiety that Mr Kramer learns about as facts of parental life – limiting, not merely ennobling, facts for the afterwork drinks and the promotional camaraderie, the obsessive dedication, the overriding urge to make it, lose the simple forms they once might have had. Or, it may be that employers and clients guess that this is bound to happen, so perceive it as happening, because he is in sole charge of a child. So we sympathize with him in the witness box, pleading to keep his son, but having to admit that his salary is lower than his wife's: his public shame at being below par in salary is sweet and forgiveable, since we know how he came by this reduced status.

In the film, the structure of 'motherhood' is constructed around the parent and child, however grudging and doubtful both father and son are, initially, as this new relationship is forced upon them. The mother, having freed herself from that structure, sails to a generous salary and professional position, but cannot return to that domestic structure which the court awards her as her right, but which she, in her self-seeking goals, has foresworn.

Perhaps there is an unhappy suggestion in this 1979 film that women in pursuit of their careers must foreswear motherhood, and become the child-abandoning monsters who haunt every woman who makes such a decision. The supposition is that women destroy something of their womanhood when they do leave their children, that in behaving as so many men in fact behave, they are doing something which demeans them especially, because they are mothers. The novel, however, is far stronger in its condemnation of Joanna Kramer. She does not win in the work world, either, and her action is seen as senseless and cruel, a crude bid for a self-fulfilment she will not attain. In the book there was little of that ragged tension portrayed by Meryl Streep at the beginning of the film, when her raw nerves catch on this dilemma: 'I lose my temper a hundred times a day. I'm no longer any good for him, or myself.'

Popular Culture: Thermometer or Thermostat

It is difficult to know how to describe popular culture, and the medley of images and attitudes it expresses. Does it register common beliefs, or does it magnify fears and doubt? Does it portray what people actually think, or think about – or does it try to control their thoughts and regulate their thought patterns? Does it record, or dictate? And if it records, then does it express what most of us feel? Is it systematic, or more like a treasure chest (or trash can) packed with various things each can choose or put back at will? Are we consumers who make choices about popular culture, or are we passively imprinted by it?

Attitudes towards popular culture have themselves had enormous influence on current attitudes. As Susan Faludi describes films and news reports of psychological and sociological studies as prejudicial to women, she proposes an embattled attitude towards popular culture. 'It' is trying to get women; 'it' is trying to control women; 'they' – or those behind the production or the printing – are trying to keep women 'in their place'. Yet if, with Camille Paglia, we see culture as a register of beliefs, then we look to the media to discover what ideas are 'in the air'. Since popular culture is such a mish-mash, and since even the most simple, crude story invites a wealth of ingenious interpretations, it is more plausible to suppose that we are dealing with a set of images which can be used very differently, rather than a design which stamps our thought. *Fatal Attraction* was seen as a warning against Aids when it first came out: the nuclear family was endangered, a man could no longer afford to be irresponsible, even to fill a lonely weekend in the customary macho way. It was 'read' as a warning that casual male privilege was on the way out. It was seen to herald a new ethos in sexual responsibility and fidelity. Yet a few years later it was seen as something else: a fable to expose the evils of the unmarried woman, a portrait of the psychospinster, desperate as her biological clock ticks emptily away, ready to destroy whoever and whatever is in her path in pursuit of a child and its father. The invisible subtext was no longer an illness, but the debunked Harvard–Yale study about the rapidly diminishing chances of women marrying as they grow older.

Interpretations of popular culture change as popular culture changes. We can see the validity of both these readings in the film; what becomes inaccurate is the suggestion of an intentional message, a conspiratorial message by the creators of the film – because even if the scriptwriter and producer and actors sat in conference and decided what it was they wanted to promote, and against whom, even if they were deliberate propagandists, they would not have created propaganda because the audience, the film critics, the feminists, the writers on popular culture would have caught them out. They are too exposed to sophisticated and self-determined views to create propaganda. If the writers and producers had in fact wanted to present a psychospinster, to warn women that they should marry in good time, or to warn others against the predatory nature of the unmarried woman, then they aimed at a task beyond the scope of their abilities. All they can be accused of doing is presenting an image which might be taken by some people in this way. But because issues about marriage, about child care, our children's well-being, our right to work, and our right to be ambitious, involve so many conflicts and downright contradictions in our daily lives, popular presentations are experienced as threatening.

Childhood Investments

The 'proof' of our concern for our children might be offered in terms of what we pay for them. The abiding sense that our investment in children is an investment in their good, and their future, seems basic and unchanging – yet this vision, and the stress it involves, are, historically, relatively young. Once children were an investment of a very different kind. Children contributed to the household labour. They worked farms. They helped in the house. The stronger they grew the more they contributed. They attended school as their farm or household duties permitted (the school year is still based upon the farming year). Children were also seen as an investment in future care, as insurance policies against being ill or infirm or old and incapable of looking after oneself. In some societies today, in rural Africa and India and to some extent Japan, which still teach youth to honour the old and have no public social security systems, this continues, but, for the most part in contemporary Western society, children consume one's earnings, one's time and one's energy. They involve major expenditures, and the pay-offs to the parents are strictly non-material.

The full cost of having and raising children and seeing them through to educated healthy adulthood is routinely calculated and reported in newspapers and magazines. These calculations make good reading, with their shock value. Recent estimates of the cost of raising children range from $171 000 to $265 000.[18] The humour in children's inexhaustible financial demands has been celebrated in family television comedy. Frequent references to the cost of keeping, educating and caring for children have occurred in *The Cosby Show*, and one recent episode was devoted solely to this issue. As Dr and Mrs Huxtable return from a weekend in Vermont, where they are beginning to celebrate the onset of a post-parenting marriage, they return to a houseful of children and their demands. Ruby wants two hundred dollars for an ice-skating course that comes with 'a really neat scarf'. Olivia, their step-granddaughter, breaks the washing machine and ruins all the clothes in it. Theo is accosted carrying a lamp from his parents' bedroom to take to his apartment, and before departing also appropriates the garden hose. Dr Huxtable cannot lend Theo the car to transport these items to his apartment because Vanessa has borrowed it to drive to the library, and returns it after having crashed into a parked car. Yet the Huxtables are caught in this expensive child net because the children are funny and cute – because, ultimately, we are helpless in face of our children's 'needs', even when those desperate, primitive needs of the infant turn into the perceived 'needs' of the somewhat careless, consumer-oriented children we, with the help of our society, raise. But these expensive children cost more than money: they cost time.

Prosperity does not make these costs easier to bear – it increases them. Our prosperous culture, and our ability and willingness to invest so heavily in our children, increase our sense of what they need. We see children as needing far more than children were thought to need fifty years ago. They need stimulation, they need good schooling, they need entertainment, they need constant care, they need perfect health and perfectly formed teeth. The increased demands and expectations we have of our life is transferred to the expectations we have for our children. And within this high expectancy, we live in a world high in danger. Failure is possible, and this high-expecting world is intolerant of failure. The inability to succeed makes children vulnerable to social influences we perceive as common, as ever-present, and yet as not part of the world we want for them. The costs of neglect, or mistaken decisions about our children can be disastrous. Our society is not environmentally friendly to children. We know that delinquency and drug abuse are common infections, and that it is the home, home influence and home control which make the crucial difference (because that unfriendly environment is not likely to change). Flaws and irregularities too are highly punishable in our society. The handicap of a retarded child is far worse in contemporary society than it would have been in past rural societies, wherein difference could be more easily absorbed. High functioning and keen-edged competition are part of normal adult life. We have to hone our children to survive.

In families, time becomes a commodity, and children use time. In contemporary families, time is an emotional issue. 'Quality time', 'work time', 'child care time', 'time for oneself', 'time to think' – these are issues within the contemporary family, charged with ideas of sharing, and hedged round by the increasing demands that work makes on time. As more families depend upon two incomes, as more workers feel forced to work harder because their jobs are insecure, new allocations of time have to be negotiated – a three-way process, involving one's self and one's own capacity, one's children, and one's partner. As these negotiations pick up issues of fairness and equality, of respect and recognition of the value of one's time, they feel very hot as they are handled. They are new. There are no common patterns forged. Each household must create its individual stamp; and this is difficult.

Though the amount of leisure families now have is decreasing, leisure itself changes the meaning of time. In poorer societies alternative uses of time may not be so attractive, nor as readily available. Prosperity makes further demands on time: television, cinema, books, magazines, shopping, exercise and outings are seen as part of a good-quality life, and these are also things which bite into child rearing or child care time.[19]

The desire to have children is, presumably, a biological urge, enforced by our social world, and justified by all manner of means. It seems to survive all our knowledge about children's expense. It seems to survive the belief that children will not support us in later life. It even survives confrontation with the possibility that love will not be reciprocated. It survives one's sense that children increase one's vulnerability rather than one's strength.

But this biological urge can be controlled. Childbirth, once an inevitable outcome of sex or marriage, can now be controlled. It too becomes a matter of time and timing, of when to have children, of having them when the costs seem tolerable. A common solution to the costs of having children calculated as costs of time devoted to children rather than to a career, is having them in later adulthood, at 30 or 40 rather than 20, so that an initial investment in work could secure a career. Yet a different attempt to solve this problem, mostly by slightly older women, was to have children early, care for them, and then invest time in a career, when children no longer require one's time. Both these different timing strategies are sometimes successful, and both of these strategies run up against work structures.

These delays meet two needs: women needed to feel launched themselves, but they also needed to feel financially well-off in order to have children. This urge, very common in contemporary women, meant that in giving up work time to have children and care for them, a woman would be giving up more than her work – she would be giving up, perhaps, the ground she had worked so hard to gain in her career, and giving up the income upon which her family may have learned to depend. The clash between these two investments in her children and her work, increases the stress of making choices about time, and feeling pressured through time.

This pressure exposes that myth of having it all. 'Over the long haul you cannot claw your way up the corporate ladder, work sixty hours a week, *and* be a good parent, spouse and citizen', writes Sylvia Ann Hewlett in her plea for greater care for America's children.[20] In one of the many arguments against the individualism that blossomed in America in the 1970s and 1980s, when self-realization became a widespread goal, when life was a series of 'passages' towards fulfilment, Hewlett asks, 'What about the children?'; for 'you clearly cannot dump spouse and kids and move on to greener pastures without risking the coherence and viability of the children you leave behind. Self-absorption is bad news for families and, in the long run, is destructive to individuals because it can leave personal relationships in shambles and the community at war with itself.'[21] The modern demands of work may be destructive to modern society.

Rigidity of Maternal Responsibility

Traditional queries about what children need, and what mothers owe them, have been fired by the assumption that childhood influences are paramount, that early teaching and early bonding set hard the features of human psychology. The main theories about human development used, invariably, to see early childhood as the making of the adult. Both psychiatrists and psychoanalysts believed that intense childhood conflicts were seldom resolved without treatment: people might find new – better or worse – ways of dealing with them, and new defence against them, but they remained eternal dramas, eternally unresolved. Hence a mother lost to the world of employment was not a minor mishap in the life of a child, but a lifelong loss, repeatedly suffered and forever unresolved. So, too sociologists believed that the way children perceived others as perceiving them had a fixed effect on their identity. Classification of a child as good or bad, beautiful or ugly, stupid or smart, stamped, indelibly, her self-image. Thus people in charge of our children were seen as having enormous power. Perhaps even working mothers cold control nutrition (which was also seen as having irreversible effects on brain development and growth patterns) but they could not control the microinfluences of child care, and the person outside the family who took care of the child. The assumption that the mother was all-powerful had two aspects: first, that the child needed the mother at all times; and second, that the mother, who cared so deeply for her child's well-being, had a responsibility to be in full control of the child's care because she could not entrust another with that power.

This 'one-shot vaccination model'[22] of human development has given way to a realization of how people change and grow and heal throughout their lives. As Gilbert Brim notes: 'One outcome [of this change in emphasis from early influences as deterministic over a lifespan, to an appreciation of continued human growth and flexibility] all of us can applaud is the liberation of mothers from the undeserved guilt they carried when everything that turned out bad in a child was blamed on their infant care practices. Too much emphasis was placed on the effects of parental behaviour during a child's first few years of life, and parents unnecessarily have had to carry the heavy burden of the cultural belief that the child is fragile and that what happens in adulthood is the parent's fault. Children are stronger and more resilient than most parents believe; and injuries, whether physical or emotional, in the early years of life are often remedied by the experience of later years.'[23]

The generation of women who have taken both their sets of need to heart, and who have faced up to their right to work, have to struggle against the single-disaster assumption, which was the assumption of psychologists when they were growing up. Hence many of these women still look to their parents – especially their mothers – blaming them for inherited identities and fears and failings. As these women learn that they can take more 'risks' with child care, they may also ease up on the burden of guilt they often cast back on their parents.

But parents of today also face other fears for their children. There are dangers in being left unattended at any age. Many children dislike being alone at home after school, and those who do not mind it may be making poor use of that isolation. As the number of hours children are left alone increases, the social and personal costs of this are tabulated from various angles. The greater number of hours children are without adult supervision, it was found, the greater was the risk that they would use some kind of drug.[24] Children left on their own, even when they are capable of managing, may also lose out. Children whose homework is supervised tend to do better in school, and are far more likely to attend college. Yet many parents insist that as children look after themselves and help look after the home while the parents are at work, they mature and develop a sense of responsibility.

Children need control and protection, even when they are old enough to 'manage'. Yet parents too have to manage their lives, and make choices in conditions which they themselves do not choose. As parents face greater demands from their work in an employment environment which assumes its workers have no domestic responsibilities, they continue to live in a society in which they are seen as virtually fully responsible for their children.

Futures

New emphasis on what the children need is sociological, rather than psychological. It focuses not on the minutiae of mother love, but on education, social supports, social validation, general concern and care. It is directed at families and governments, not solely on women's behaviour with their children. But their sense of being ultimately responsible for a child's well-being remains. Though during the first wave of women entering careers, working mothers were found, at least in one study, to spend almost as much time with their children as non-working mothers,[25] the commitments to work have grown, and the time given to family has been cut back. The children of *The Organization Man* – that grey nine-to-fiver described in William Whyte's 1956 book,[26] who gave everything to his job and had nothing left over for his family and his personality – are, as parents, even more job-minded, and less leisure-oriented, and see much less of their children than their fathers saw of them.[27]

During the last few decades there has been a sharp decline in the amount of time parents spend caring for children. Economist Victor Fuchs has calculated that children have lost ten to twelve hours of parental time per week since 1960.[28] Sylvia Ann Hewlett believes that for most men and women participation in family life has declined precipitously. While the proportion of adult life spent living with spouse and children stood at 62 per cent in 1960, it is now 43 per cent.[29]

The trick, Hewlett says, is to spread the burden around: husbands and fathers, employers and government, all have to pull their weight. But what researchers of the time-deficit and its effect on children seldom notice is that the mothers are the first to notice this deficit and to act accordingly – to cut back on the working hours, or to compensate by working more at home. When writers reveal the decline of leisure[30] or the phenomenon of family-time famine,[31] they seem to be presenting the conditions under which many of us live helplessly. They ignore the fact that most women respond to this stress so as to minimize its costs to their children.

Since husbands and fathers, employers and governments are making only very slow progress towards sharing the burden, women still make decisions to cut down, cut back, or reduce investment in their careers because they respond to what the children need. Fathers find that the increased hours expected of them at work make sharing difficult. Though attitudes towards child's needs for mothers have changed, the investments we believe we should make in our children continue to grow – psychologically, intellectually and financially.

Women usually do want to mother their children – that is, they want not only to have children, but also to care for them. The special part motherhood plays in their lives works alongside employment practices and domestic habits (and paucity of) child care facilities, to create a spectre of traditional motherhood following every mother as she climbs upward towards her career goals. There is a persistent slide backwards towards the traditional roles. She is the easy alternative when any other child care plans go awry. She is the first to become distressed by imperfect child care. She is quick to take responsibility and the last, usually, to refuse it. Even women who earned more than their husbands, even women whose husbands respected their careers, found that it was up to them, rather than a partner, to defend a change in their domestic routine, and up to them, rather than a partner, to take up the extra domestic work when there was a blip in his routine. These were often small, momentary issues, but the momentary needs of the child can define a way of life. The care of children cannot be put into cold storage. The magnetic pull of the traditional role is not based on its ultimate truth but on ingrained habits. As the woman explains herself she sees the chinks in her defence; as the man explains himself he welds his armour.

It will take a long time for things to change, and the changes will be moderate, not revolutionary. The capacity to mother, the desire to mother, undoubtedly has both biological and social bases. The hotch-potch of feminine traits, some clichéd, some well-founded – from the greater responsiveness to human faces among female, as opposed to male, infants to the continued predominance in the importance women give to relationships – all seem to make it easier for women to mother – though, as Alice Rossi has pointed out, the ease with which women learn to mother does not mean that they should do it all and men should not: what it may mean is that men learn more slowly, and need more help in learning; and on behalf of a fair and just future, we must pursue this change. As more mothers work, as more mothers learn the importance of work in terms of financial security, self-determination and the pleasure of being able to do a greater range of things, more daughters will grow to see themselves as potential workers and potential mothers, and boys will grow into men who have more flexible views of male and female roles within and outside the family and to develop more of their parental potential.

In the meantime we have to do some very difficult things. We have to track the effect of our work and our lifestyles on our children, yet stand back from those studies and those developmental theorists who suggest that things would be better for our children if mothers stayed at home. This is no longer an option, no longer a viable way ahead. We have to ask a new set of questions based on this knowledge. The question is no longer whether maternal employment harms children, but how can we protect children from any adverse effects parental employment has? How can we – men and women – structure our working lives so that we can give our best to our work and our children? We have to re-evaluate the conditions of our work if they do not allow us to be the people we want to be. In fact, this is emerging as a powerful new perspective.

Attitudes and ideas have to change, as do policies. Since we want to continue as women and workers and mothers without committing some form of emotional suicide, we have to accept that there will be conflicts, and that these conflicts are not shams, or the result of a conspiracy, but the result of complex needs within a society that has not yet attuned itself to new notions of the division of labour, and new standards of care – for who we are and what we want of our future. The children need us to work for this. This is what the children need.

4
Having It All – New Options; New Myths

In 1991 two books were published with the same title. The first, a novel by Maeve Haran, was about a television executive, wife and mother of two young children who, in the opening of the novel has it all. She is a high earner, she has lovely children and a loving marriage. She is promoted, however, and as her pay and her power are stepped up, her life begins to crack. Her husband has an affair, and they separate. The prestige of her job turns into pressure. As each rung of the ladder on which she has been rapidly climbing snaps, she retreats with her children to the country. There she collects energy, peace and sanity and eventually is reunited with her husband who will become her partner in a new, promising but manageable business enterprise.

The second book, also entitled *Having It All*, is by former Savoy Woman of the Year Linda Stoker who is managing director of a business development company which she founded. This is not a fictional account of the good life, but a guide for women returning to work. The guide is both a 'how to' and 'how not to' dissertation. Stoker knows from her own experience that balance is difficult to achieve: as her business thrived, her marriage failed.

Each of these books combines promise with caution, and each has strong elements of the superwoman glitz of the early 1980s when it was assumed that high flights were within every determined woman's grasp. Yet they are not quite as slick as superwoman literature. Nor are they backlash conservatism. What they suggest, a little simply, is that having it all is not having all of everything, but finding out what is most important and learning to lift these things of importance out of their usual leaden trappings. Having it all involves crafting new things from what is already there.

Superwoman: A Child's View

I am the daughter of a superwoman, one of the early kind, an embattled woman who had no back-up, no support from her friends, and little desire to be friends with other women whose interests and aims were so different from hers. She despised, under the guise of pity, women whose minds were filled with domestic things. As she watched televisions ads for new ways of scraping out the dirt on kitchen floor corners she would sigh with superior compassion: 'What some people waste their time worrying about.' As for the child care side of things – well, that was 'her job' too. She stayed at home for four years when her children were born. 'Talk about being bored', she reflected back on that time, and as she spoke I remembered the taste of boredom in our home, as we hung about her and nagged her and coaxed her attention. However bored she may have been, she was never idle. I remember her as always doing something else: painting the ceiling (in high heels and a fine wool dress) while my sister and I played with our friends. I remember her knitting while she read to us (the needles clicked and flashed as she read: she did not even have to watch her hands, but there would be a pause, either while she turned the page, or counted the stitches). She was always busy, and always bored, because what she was busy with was quite different from what she had been trained to do and what she wanted to be doing.

At the same time she despised the housewives who were, without exception, her neighbours, she despised her few female colleagues, women who had chosen careers instead of marriage and children. They were 'masculine'; they were 'limited'. She saw them as Betty Friedan saw the one female doctor in her childhood life, who was fat, had short hair, and wore very sensible shoes. My mother too was a doctor, an eye specialist, who was later to become a professor of physics. She was not only a freak of her generation of women – a mother who worked, but a freak within her profession – a woman among the male-dominated medical and academic establishment. Acutely self-conscious of her position, she felt highly ambivalent towards it. On the one hand she saw herself as 'a second-class citizen', a woman who would not be heard, who would not be respected, a woman who had to prove herself capable each day, at every task, because it was assumed that as a woman she would be incapable. On the other hand she felt that she was part of an elite, a unique woman who was better than other women because she was skilled at work which most women deemed themselves incapable of doing, and because in any meeting she attended, or at any conference, she sustained a high profile simply because she was invariably the only woman among men. She both wanted her work to be accepted on the level of a man's, to be viewed on its merits, and yet she simultaneously saw herself as having special merit because she was a rarity. Unlike today's politically correct feminist who spots prejudice in gallant admiration of one's femininity, my mother was thrilled by it.

Since the 1960s women have become far more sensitive to the range of implications in polite or gallant gestures, such as being offered the one comfortable chair in the room, or having a door hurriedly opened on one's behalf. These gestures are usually intended as no more than polite rituals, yet they carry the implication (which may well not be intended or thought of by the person enacting these social formulae) that one needs help with such things, or as a signal of deference, which then opens up other questions – about whether one shows deference towards an inferior. My mother wore high fashion, bright colours – often Pucci silks, those splendid garish prints of the 1960s which bespoke fun and daring. She flaunted her appearance, and then criticized men for noticing it. She flirted with men and then complained that they treated women (represented by her) differently from the way they behaved with male colleagues. She complained that her colleagues could never forget that she was a woman, and yet she constantly reminded them that she was. She knew that women who disguised their sexuality were likely to be promoted more readily than she, yet simultaneously she thought her sexuality was a trump card. Even as she saw how it worked against her, she valued it and sought to preserve it, and tried hard to outshine all young female incumbents.

Well, a daughter's view is never accurate, and certainly never fair. This cannot be a true picture of my mother, though it is as I saw her. But she had, in the beginning of her career, no supporting ideology, no means of weeding out false from just complaints, or ineffective from effective strategies. She was alone in wondering how to have it all, and people managing in isolation often manage in ways which seem, later, a little clumsy.

'A woman can do everything a man can do and have children as well', my mother used to say, apparently reciting a creed. Her confidence seemed to bulldoze prejudice about what women were and what women could do while it expressed traditional bias. Women, not men, had children, so that the having of children became a thing special to women – especially theirs, in possession and presumably responsibility. Indeed, this pioneer superwoman was out to show that she could be better at everything than a traditional woman (except at cleaning the corners of the kitchen floor) and better than her male colleagues at publishing work and curing patients. She had, I learned from her obituary, been awarded more than seventy grants for her research. And while she was not proposing or completing research projects, she was tending and grooming her children. She made most of my clothes herself. These were so special that people were bound to remark on them, and when they did the fact that my mother made them was a punch line which opened up a flood of admiration: 'Your mother made that? She's made that – and she's an eye surgeon, a professor, and I hear she's a fantastic dancer . . .'.

At the time I was puzzled by the excess of other women's admiration, given that I knew in what low esteem she held them. Perhaps that superwoman image protected them from feeling that her example minimized their efforts. Perhaps if they saw her as super-able then they would not be cowed by the message that they might have done more. But on the whole I think they really were generous, really pleased, and their admiration cost them no pain. They were simply amazed that it did all hang together – her sewing and her surgery. And as such, the reaction of the housewives to the career woman thirty years ago may not be so very different from women today looking at other women today, who seem to have got it all together. Isn't it amazing that some people can do it – that some people have it all?

Who Needs It All?

The trap that the superwoman falls into is the belief that she can have everything because she can do as much as two or three people. The superwoman pattern allows women to take on more roles without changing those roles. She manages both at home and at work without asking anyone either at home or at work to expect less of her. Or, she tries to spot what is inessential in certain roles (like clean corners on the kitchen floor) and to separate those out so that she can fulfil the spirit if not the letter of those roles. Perhaps that was a big beginning.

The image of the superwoman has been criticized and ridiculed from many angles, but it remains to haunt us – maybe not in its most standard versions as the perfect cook, hostess, mother and executive, or the finely-tailored woman with the briefcase in one hand and a baby in the other – but in expectations we have of ourselves and our partners and our work. What often remains difficult for each woman to negotiate too is the change that occurs in her own adult life as she moves through the various phases of adulthood. As a young adult it often does seem that a woman's chances are equal to anyone's – especially if she has had good opportunities in education and training. But the dynamics of the family change things, and having children changes women. The stress of tracking these changes when women's experience and their ideas diverge, sometimes suddenly and sometimes drastically, constitutes the developmental story of contemporary adult women. Looking ahead, and making decisions, then becomes a very lonely affair: 'I can't come to a decision – I can't decide to have children or not to', explained 27-year-old Carrie Bray. 'I reach out to the future, and I just see chaos. There is no simple way.' Her extremely promising career as a chemist would, she knew, be compromised by having children. The pressure to succeed had been bred by her past successes and her past identity as one who succeeds, who can compete with anyone, and win fairly. In confronting the question of whether to have children she felt she was facing a very different kind of challenge.

Each woman has her own story to tell about this course of development, which is filled with tension because each woman has the task of doing it herself – not on her own, but the help, or input, she gets makes things more complicated. She often has her partner's ideas of what a child needs – and this may vary greatly from hers, especially if her partner is not the child's father. She has her parents' ideas, her own history, her own assessment of what she gained from the kind of care she got, and what were the drawbacks of her care. But she also at this stage has a more objective handle on her parents, so that she asks not only what patterns in her parents' lives worked well for her as a child but also what patterns in her parents' lives worked, in her view, well for them. Adult women of today cast a critical and sympathetic look on their parents' – especially their mothers' – lives. They are likely to see both what their mothers suffered in their traditional roles, and how they were constrained. Some women too, whose mothers worked full-time, were highly critical of the inflexible hours their mothers had to work. They saw part-time work as a step up in the world. Some children, now in their twenties, children of women who had rigid working patterns, described their mothers as being tired and under stress, and they did not want to live their lives as parents in the same way. Women today have a wide range of ideas and models to draw on. In this respect they are very unlike the housewives of the 1950s; yet their choices involve doubts and ambivalences, and however they arrange their ideas in their minds, they still have to face the domestic and employment features which they may find more constraining – and in many cases more liberating – than they expected.

Moving Goalposts

Young women who saw themselves as competent and ambitious, as firmly oriented towards a career, invariably faced a crisis during that intense phase of parenting when children are young and very demanding. This crisis did not necessarily involve giving up a career, though it often involved a job change. For some women the crisis was stimulated by an external factor – a chance occurrence, such as being offered a promotion which involved relocation. Glenn Edwards was offered a position as materials manager in Cleveland, though she and her family were settled in Chicago. 'As soon as I heard their offer I had the strangest sensation – I was the go-getter, I said yes to everything, things I knew were mad to do I did because I wanted to show that I was all there for them. My twins were three weeks old and my firm wanted me to go to New York, and I was on my way. I'd say yes and think later how to arrange it – you know, who to call, what had to be changed, who would pick up which child when, whether my help could come earlier. I was used to all that, but this was bigger. This wasn't messing about with my family for a few days, this was a whole uprooting, and I knew my husband liked what he was doing, and my older kids were settled in school, and we had bought a house only six months ago. I kept so cool, so blank, and nodded and said I'd think it over, but I was in a panic. I couldn't think, because deep down I knew I would reject this offer, and that turning down this opportunity would be the end of the upwards path that had been a *big* part of my life for the last six years.'

Sometimes even more problematic, in that the residual emotions are more hostile and grudging, is a partner's relocation which involves leaving a good job. Some women commute – but of the four commuting women in my sample three had given it up within two years: one by finding a job nearer to her husband's place of work, one by resigning from her job, turning to a very part-time involvement with the firm which involved only a few days' travelling each month, and one by separating from her husband. Two women did report that their husbands had turned down promotion/relocation offers because their wife's work simply was not perceived as transferable. This was seen by the women as an enormous gift, special proof of a husband's egalitarian orientation.

Widespread policies of relocating employees have been criticized from many angles. Relocation is grossly inefficient, not only because moving and settling in costs money, but also because the mobile manager has to spend time getting to know how the new branch works and who works well in it; yet there is little sign that this practice will cease. Now employees frequently are faced with the option either to relocate or to be made redundant, hence increasing the pressure to move. The cost of relocation to families falls on women as domestic managers, but the cost on women's working lives has been ignored. Firms often encourage a macho image of loyalty so that the valued employee is seen as prepared to put his home on the line for the firm. Not only is this unfair and unreasonable, it is also inefficient; yet it shows no sign of abating.

Crisis in Confidence

Crisis in the plan to have it all most commonly comes from the stress of doing too much and expecting too much of oneself and in confronting a discrepancy between what one sees as manageable and reasonable and what one experiences as manageable. The priorities of two women were changed drastically and suddenly as their children became ill. For them the pull of new needs in their children and the enormous emotional draining of their children's illness shifted their career plans; but even when everything is going well, life with young children can be stressful and straining, and most women spoke of being torn or pulled in two directions, or divided in what they wanted to do because they both wanted to work and wanted to spend a lot of time with their children. These stresses are part of what we now see as ordinary life, but when they reach a point of making us into someone we do not want to be, or preventing us from being whom we think we should be, they stimulate a crisis.

'I have a very clear self-image', Emily James explained. 'I am independent. I do what I want – more or less. What I mean is that what I want affects what I do. It's an important part of the calculation. I'm not set up to please other people or worry about what other people think. That independence is an import-ant part of me and my self-confidence. I make firm decisions. I think of them as good decisions. But after I had my second child I realized that self-image was no longer valid.'

Emily James is in many ways the new professional woman, a graduate of the Harvard Business School in the late 1970s, who planned to have both a family and a career and who believed that determination and training would provide the answers. She has been adept at learning the myriad of rules which allow one to function in the business world, and in many ways her voice and body language provide firm counter-examples to the man-nerisms which are thought to cause some women trouble. Smiles are thought to suggest an accommodating nature which under-mines a woman's authority. Emily James, though very pleasant, does not engage in a great deal of smiling. Her voice is low, never with the high pitch of excitement which many women themselves dislike because they think it signals to men a lack of control. As do many women in managerial positions, she seems deliberately to minimize feminine self-presentation. Absent, too, from Emily's speech, are any tag questions which are common in women's speech, and which are thought to signal uncer-tainty, and invite agreement or corroboration rather than ex-press authority.

Women who plan to have it all know that they have to keep guard over their plans. Whereas twenty years ago Erikson[1] claimed plausibly (though perhaps not accurately) that wo-men's identity did not take shape as early on in their develop-ment as did men's identity: since women saw themselves as partners, a helpmate of a man, keen to aid him in his goals, they maintained a flexibility that would accommodate the man they did marry. For women who hold career plans dear, a partner must accommodate their goals. He (or she) must be tolerant of a woman's career, and must honour her ambitions, and must

accept the domestic sharing and forgo the lack of wifely servicing which can be expected to result from these plans. From my
sample it would seem that such men are not rare birds: men
whose wives were determined to keep on career track were
proud of them. This emerged in how they spoke about them,
and how they presented themselves as willing to negotiate shared
domestic arrangements and the consequences of this on their
careers.

Many women who either stood fast by their early ambitions
or who were quick to develop ambition along with the usual
work experience of young unmarried women, spoke about a
first engagement, or a very brief marriage, which had involved
a traditional gender contract, which was supported and endorsed by their parents, but which they suddenly skipped out on
– many of them claiming that, at the time, they had not been
able to identify the reasons for their behaviour. Emily James
had been engaged when she was offered two jobs – one in
Chicago, near her fiancé, and one in Washington, DC. All along
she assumed she would take the one in Chicago, but before
sending off the two letters, one to accept the position in Chicago, and one to decline the job in Washington, DC, she carefully read through the job descriptions of each – and hesitated.
During the next few days she found out as much as she could
about the different institutions in the different cities. Still unaware that she had made up her mind, she sent her acceptance
to Washington in what she still described thirteen years later as
a 'whim'.

As women described previous engagements, and how they
had failed to materialize, their descriptions of the marriage and
the associated life pattern that might have been theirs were
remarkably vivid. 'I didn't break off the engagement', Emily
said. 'In fact, the date was still set, and we were simply waiting
for my fiancé to finish law school.' She knew that when he did
take his law degree he would have a position in his father's law
firm. They would be a prominent couple in the small city in
which they both grew up, and she would find a job which would
allow her both some independence and work satisfaction and
the security of not looking further afield. Her life would be
orderly, easily imagined. These women – in their thirties when

I first interviewed them, looking back to their early twenties, and in their forties when I interviewed them again – were startled by the clarity of their previous decisions. The vividness of their potential futures haunted them, and in rejecting the fiancé they were rejecting a gender contract and the life pattern that went with it. Caroline Batcher said that she had been engaged to a fellow student at Oxford, who seemed thrilled by the fact that she was studying law, yet said casually one evening, 'But of course you'll give it up after we're married.' 'Perhaps I should have laughed it off and married him and done what I wanted anyway. He wouldn't really have been able to stop me. But I didn't know that then. I suppose I wasn't sure just how bloody determined I was. You don't know that – do you – at the beginning. You always feel that feminine shadow tickling your neck. Is it going to grip, you wonder. I took what I saw at that time as the lesser risk.' She admires him to this day, and remains a friend, but admits that she 'could never see him in the same way after that. I started hating the way he lifted his chin when he spoke, or moved his shoulders after he said something he thought was frightfully clever. I was desperately lonely after I chucked him, and I kept having visions of our newly-wed happiness and how everyone would be so happy – my Mum, my Dad – my little sister! – and I remember once teasing myself – bolting the door because I hoped that if I wanted to run out to him I just might come to my senses by the time I'd unlocked and unbolted the door.'

When these women did marry, they married with a different contract on the table. And when women who identified strongly with their careers, and their career orientation, decided to cut back on their work or take time out from work (which they usually did not after the first, but after the second or third child) it was usually the woman who came to this decision herself as she reassessed the viability of her lifestyle. Sarah Gyson resigned from a tenured lectureship though she was determined to 'keep in touch' with occasional university teaching when her daughter was three. 'Our family was like a badly managed country – where you just couldn't imagine things getting better because everything seemed so out of control. I felt I was in the nanny's power because she could tell me what the children had done, when they had slept and what they had eaten, and though I often didn't believe her there wasn't much I could do because I had no way of knowing. She could lie to me because I was stupid – I was totally out of touch with what was going on here at home. And there was me thinking I was always doing too much, and my husband was thinking that too much was expected of him, and my kids probably thought that every last one of their friends had better parents than they did. So you have to ask: Do I really want to do this? Do I really want to be this person? Is this what I want to put everything in to? And there are other questions in the background – you know, questions that are more desperate, and make these others seem easy. Because I was really worried whether the whole thing was going to last, and then if it didn't what was going to go first – was it me, or my marriage, or my children?'

Horror stories like these, with their conservative conclusions, are troublesome. On the one hand, women like Sarah have to have their say and be heard. On the other hand, in justifying such a decision and sympathizing with it, one does not want to endorse it as a path for other women. The offence so many women have taken to new conservatism in books and films is that the message is seen to be universal: that it is better for everyone to behave thus, that the attempt to break the traditional moulds is costly, and that wise women discover this and unwise women are punished. It is clear that Sarah has the right to make a decision, and it is a decision which is justified in her circumstances. Yet her conclusion seems to be general: that a family won't run well when the two parents involved are going full steam ahead in their full-time jobs. Part of this is face-saving: a costly decision is easier to accept if it is seen as inevitable. For this reason, too, reconstruction of decisions already made have a much sharper outline than decisions in the making. When I spoke to women who had decided to give up work, or – as was far more common – their previous committed style to work, the story they told of their previous lives as full-time employees was much starker and blacker and bleaker than were the stories told by women who were wondering whether to change from a high career track to more modest working goals – even though some of these women, with their more moderate tales of stresses and drawbacks did eventually go on to make a decision to stop work. And it was then, after the fact, that I heard stories which increased the black side. Some women saw that the descriptions of their lives before the decision to stop work and after the decision to stop (or, what was far more common, to change their job), were very different. 'I didn't realize how awful it was', one woman explained. The shift in emphasis, the darkening and hardening of the boundaries in which they made the decision, was not a matter of drawing a false picture, but part of adapting to and understanding and reinforcing the difficult decisions women have to make, in an environment which does not offer support to the different decisions women have to make: both employed mothers and domestic mothers feel that the other group is critical of and slighting towards them; each group can feel odd and outcast.

Discovered Options

The decision whether to stay at work and to sustain one's workload or to cease employment involve well-known questions. What was surprising, however, was the number of alternatives, the various strategies women had for responding to the crisis without falling back on set patterns. When women confront the dilemma whereby in having it all they are losing out on what they value most, they may indeed decide to give it up and return to being a traditional wifely person, but more often than not women found new ways of dealing with these persistent problems. 'Things can't go on like this' does not necessarily lead to the conclusion that 'Things are better off as people once expected them to be.' It can mean, and has meant for many working women, 'There must be another way of proceeding.'

Because many women who feel this take time out from work to 'take a breather' or 'put things in perspective', and because some of these women return to careers and some do not, it is difficult to name one thing about them that makes the difference. The ability to negotiate a way through this crisis and back into the workplace is the touchstone of maintaining a career track for women, particularly those in their thirties. It is at this stage at which domestic structures, employment structures and concepts of motherhood and career woman and wife tend to clash most definitely. For it is at this stage when a career-oriented man is likely to be putting in more hours at work than ever before. The woman following a masculine career track is expected to do the same, to compete with male colleagues. At this stage, too, her children are usually still young – career mothers often do not have a first child until they are well past thirty. Her concept of herself as a mother, and her ideas of motherhood, are rapidly formed and transformed by her experience, but at the same time she will be drawing on ideas and fears and priorities that are linked to cultural norms and to new personal experiences. Hence many mothers see themselves as gradually changing, as maturing from a more to a less selfish mentality,[2] but they simultaneously guard against becoming selfless.

These changes are not immediate. Meg Weinberg, who had her first child at 32, said that when she came home from the hospital and sat with her young daughter in her arms, she rested a stack of departmental memos from the Treasury Office where she worked on the arm of the sofa and wept with relief. 'I could still make sense of them. My mind was still intact. I was still me. I'd call the office just to hear my familiar work voice.'

Their desire to have children and their love for their children cannot be called into question. Yet what is equally clear is that motherhood posed an enormous threat to identity and determination. The feminine roles which haunted them as they were taking the first steps or making initial plans for their careers, rose up with renewed strength when they became mothers. They were both delighted to be mothers, with a strong sense of the privilege of having children, and terrified by the spectre of 'motherhood' – so much so that the women who during maternity leave felt 'bored' and 'distant' were actually relieved by their lack of immediate maternal passion. This early sense of being withdrawn from a child, of not feeling connected to one's infant, is common enough. Usually women are tremendously disturbed by this; such apathy is supposed both to be a symptom of post-natal depression and a trigger to it. Women are thought to be distressed if their feelings do not match the expectations of falling in love, and they are often too ashamed to speak out. But in the clash between traditional ideology of motherhood and the newer ideology of career fulfilment, many women expressed relief. 'I looked at her and I admired her and I was delighted that she was healthy and normal . . . but I was also pleased as punch that I didn't go gaa-gaa over her and turn into some stupid dribbling idiot full of baby talk. I looked at her and thought "There – that was a job well done. Now I can carry on."'

Different women worried about different things: would they still be able to be the person they had been before? was the most basic concern. Some women were worried about practical arrangements, and some women were worried about other people's view of them as a mother: 'There are two female partners in my law firm,' explained Dana Stein, 'and neither has more than one child.' She saw the birth of her third child as a fact which would say more to others about her than she, her work and her determination would be allowed to say for themselves.

Passivity is not a common characteristic of these women, and many worked hard to counter their doubts. Some women whipped up a manic energy to deal with their fatigue, and the threatened drain upon their energy. The boredom and listlessness that Deborah Pacelli experienced during her maternity leave paved the way for a rapid return to work. 'I began arranging working lunches in my home as soon as I could sit down without wincing. I was tired, but I felt the best thing I could do for my fatigue was to get back the rhythm of my working life. Being tired was like having a muddy brain, and if I could clear that, then I'd get back my energy – I wouldn't get it back by resting. Maternity leave was really torture.'

Negative feelings about motherhood are far more easily acknowledged by women today than they were in previous generations. The openness with which women are able to speak out about their divided or conflicting passions must be healthy, and yet in itself does not offer a solution. But early relief that one's self was still intact, and the fierce retention of one's pre-maternal concentration and identity, were precipitous. For women in professional and managerial jobs still feel that their career prospects are damaged after taking a break to have a child.[3]

Maternal Harassment

> I see myself as competent and independent and well able to do a good job. I know I can find efficient ways of doing things, and that when they are done I can be satisfied. But I've noticed . . . well, something is changing. My daughter wants me to take her ice-skating, and I can't because at weekends I have to catch up with too many other things. There's the Christmas shopping, the accounts, the garden – whatever – I had set aside the weekend for those. I care terribly about my children, and I expect to do well by them. When my daughter wants other things, and I have to refuse, I wonder how good a job I'm doing as a mother. I feel harassed – and that's not me.

It is easy enough, from the outside, to laugh at Emily James's surprised discovery at the clash between one's expectations of using a weekend to become more organized, and a child's expectations that a weekend will be used to entertain her. It is easy to be amused by the way children's demands harass a parent who is accustomed to the calm life a competent person earns for herself. But the dilemmas she feels are hardly funny, insignificant or unrepresentative. She begins with a plan that will help her cope with overwork: she will use her weekend to catch up. This plan in itself becomes a means of coping. Several women spoke about ways of dealing with having too much to do: they would make lists of tasks, which could then be ticked off. In itemizing the things to do they appeared more manageable and more under control, with re-arrangeable priorities. But this simple plan was destroyed by her daughter's expectation that she would be taken ice-skating. The weekend that was seen as problem-solving gave rise to further problems. Then the feelings which these disjointed expectations gave rise to became a further problem which took on two different forms. First, in her empathy with her daughter's disappointment, she felt that she was not doing a sufficiently good job as a mother. Secondly, in her irritation with her daughter's demands she felt that she was feeling something inappropriate to her ideal self. Each twist and turn framed problems of time, management and coping.

New Options – but Who Pays?

Many of the many people who, during the last ten years, have studied working mothers and the problems they face have looked at the division of labour within the household – which usually means that they study what domestic and child care work fathers do and what domestic and child care work mothers do. They ask questions about whether this changes when the mother works, whether this changes when the mother earns more than the father, whether men see themselves as taking on more than they actually do, whether the amount of housework and child care work men do affects the marriage, and whether women themselves work hard to establish equality of domestic labour in the home or whether they protect men and themselves and the marriage from confronting issues of fairness.

These questions are important, and they affect many women in their daily lives, in small ways and in large ways. They may make the daily organization easy, or they may make it fraught. They may make a career possible or impossible. They make one's input in the home a matter of shared appreciation and acknowledged gratitude, or one of drudgery and servitude and insignificance. They make one feel one's child is getting a good deal from her parents, or a raw one. Yet however important the issue is of who does what in the home, it is not the only issue. For the fact is that two full-time career-oriented parents seldom have enough time for their children, however equally their non-work time is allocated in the home. Hence the solution is often for one parent to switch track – and this is virtually always the mother.

This option frees the total sum of parent time, but it has many drawbacks. The woman who switches to 'mommy track' is out of the running for current promotions, and she may find it difficult to return. The persistent disadvantages occur not only at work, they may occur at home too. She may be acutely aware of how she now appears to others, and she may feel that the balance of power within the marriage has changed. But for most women the most immediate fear of stepping out of the workplace is stepping into a mould. The woman who decides to change her career track so that she has more time for her children is caught round the neck by that ghostly shadow of the traditional mother. In so doing her lifestyle is newly confined, and she may be newly isolated. She may feel caught in the domestic structure she has worked so hard to avoid and to change. This 'obvious' solution to the mother's crisis is difficult to sustain. The 'not me' feelings about being a 'bad' or 'poor' mother (minimized and distanced in Emily James's words as not 'doing a very good job as a mother at the moment') and being 'harassed' or unable to manage the current input of demands may simply be replaced by the 'not me' feelings of acting as a housewife, or, in working part-time, taking on much of the housewife's role.

Options on the Horizon

More women are returning to work after having children than ever before, and the women who decide not to return to work have to do work on themselves to manage their difficult decisions. Other researchers have shown the techniques women use to make the decision less momentous: they will 'see how things go', try not working for a while, stay at home for the time being, make a firm decision later.[4] And few women accurately measure the costs to their career of taking a break in their career. This gap in one's work history has been underlined as the most probable cause of the continuing wage gap – or difference in earnings between men and women. Yet when these work breaks are taken life tends to seem long, and one feels one will have many changes. And frequently one does.

When Emily James decided that the two-parent career was not working at home, she refused to fall back on a more traditional structure whereby one parent would stay at home and the other would remain on track. Instead she and her husband came to a decision that they would combine savings and cash in on their investments and take two years off together. 'I knew what it was like staying at home while Jim worked. I'd had that during two maternity leaves, and I was not prepared for more of that. I wanted to do things which we could do together as a family.'

This decision amazed their friends and colleagues. Give up two fine, promising jobs during a recession? Accept a drastic cut in income? Use up all the money they had been fortunate enough to accumulate during the last ten years of work? This was not sensible, but foolhardy. This seemed to invite double jeopardy. In the end it did not, and they returned to their careers with unabated success. The trick behind this apparently doubly risky venture was that in taking a break and consolidating time with their children, neither parent had followed an entrapping pattern, a pattern that could become habit, or that could define them. Each parent knew that at the end of the allotted two years a great effort would be necessary to get back into the business world, and that each would have to accommodate the other's work-search and eventual employment. The drastic measure this couple took indicated an outlook which actually protected the future employment of each. The more traditional domestic patterns are easily reinforced, by habits, by expectations, by simple daily interactions both within and without the home. In escaping the traditional pattern, both Emily and Jim remained in greater control of their futures because at the end of two years change was necessary and no social or family pressures, no gender ghosts pursued them. When we face new problems which arise because we follow patterns which do not accommodate our needs, we need to fashion new solutions. To do so we take risks. At the stage of life at which Emily made her decision to take a break she did not lack confidence as a career woman but as a person who could combine motherhood with a career. The fast track of early adulthood had been easier for her than the transition. But though Emily found this career pattern highly congenial, she was careful to avoid the 'brittle' job devotion which she observed in her colleagues. Many women, rejecting the personal costs of the fast track, find some way of accommodating mommy tracks. But other women work hard to discover new paths that are forged neither by men's dreams, nor by ghostly configurations of women's stereotypes.

When I first interviewed Emily she seemed more exceptional than I now see her – not that I see her as less admirable, but I have seen more women work as hard as she to craft new possibilities. The modern career woman is a special breed.

Late Options

In reading Victorian novels which so often deal with personal choices and their life-long consequences, it often seems that the heroines are outlandishly young. Dorothea Brooke in George Eliot's *Middlemarch* is less than 22 when she first marries and becomes enmeshed in a life that increasingly depresses and constrains her. She is still in her twenties when she is freed of this marriage and able to make a new and better choice. Elizabeth Bennet in Jane Austen's *Pride and Prejudice* gets two chances also, in her very early adulthood, as Darcy's character and her view of him change simultaneously to allow her the best of love, money and society. Jane Eyre, too, has two chances before she is much past 20. She rejects a marriage of love – accompanied by constraint, dishonour and power – but circumstances allow the constraints of male power and dishonour to dissolve, while the love is renewed and reenacted.

When these characters, and many others like them, are making decisions which set the course of their lives, as they resist or succumb to various temptations, as they make mistakes in judgement, as they suffer the consequences, learn from their sufferings, and transcend both consequences and suffering, they are usually around 19 or 20. Of course this is linked to a formula of Victorian fiction, whereby the novel concludes with a marriage, and concludes happily; but it does register the pressure on the adolescent emerging into adulthood to make good decisions and start out on the right track. Youth may excuse poor judgement, but these excuses do not make mistakes less costly. Decisions are not irreversible, and life patterns are not rigid, but change becomes increasingly difficult as we engender attachments and obligations. In human life as we know it reparation for past losses is always possible, but our chances are not endless. Abilities and interests can atrophy. The self-confidence of youth can rapidly diminish, as can our outlook, our belief in possibilities, without which we lose the energy to make our best effort.

Change in adulthood is constant and unremitting, yet is more complicated than in youth. When older characters change they may suffer and inflict suffering on others, so that an impossible dilemma arises between their new awareness and their established attachments. Nora in Ibsen's *A Doll's House* is somewhat like a Jane Eyre who went through with the first marriage contract she had with Rochester, who wanted to create her as a beauty with fine veils, and who wanted to 'encircle' and 'clasp' her with expensive gifts which underlined his power and undermined hers. When Nora comes to realise how her humanity has been undercut by those male heads of households – first in her father's home where she was his pet, and then in her 'own' home where she remains her husband's doll – servicing their domesticity and sustaining their hypocrisy, she is forever changed. But what can she, and only a woman, a married woman with children, change into? She is right to leave. The audience is with her. Bravo! one feels as she rejects her husband's final attempt to cajole, manipulate and bully. But the question of those three children is more than niggling. It isn't that leaving them is unthinkable, but that her leave of them will create a different kind of suffering from that incurred by leaving her husband. Her leave of her husband, too, is far more than a matter of self-discovery. She is still financially dependent, without the 'human capital' to earn her own living. There is more to leaving than just running away. Where will she go? What will she do? How will she survive financially along the way?

Jane Eyre lay on the open moor, drenched, fatigued and starving, as she fled from Rochester's deceit; but all that was absorbed by the romantic plot: of course she was saved and secured by a friendly stranger who turned out to be her cousin and turned into her suitor. The more bourgeois Nora cannot experience this romantic contrivance. Her story is yet unwritten; we only see what she leaves behind.

Today life is more flexible. Women are much better at constructing second chances and repairing mistakes in life patterns that had never suited them, or accommodating new needs which arose with maturity, or accommodating late changes. Women who had not made good choices in early adulthood still found positive ways forward. Few had the luxury of Nora's dramatic insight which bound together both the restricted structure of her domestic life, her husband's customary power, and his hypocrisy. Few had the luxury of being so sure that they were right and their husbands were wrong – and few had the children so separate from the drama. For most women who changed and wanted to change in order to greet the new woman emerging in them and grasp the new options they believed in, had to test and discover and try out and search while sustaining previous commitments, and only gradually, painfully uncoupled from those that no longer worked for them – so that they would have a story to live after they shut the door behind them.

Women's critique of society often starts at the kitchen sink. Change comes as they realize that their daily pattern and daily priorities, though reenacted freely by them, are fashioned according to rules they are just learning to read. Their satisfaction, they may find, has been formed more by constraints which they accept, than by goals which fulfil. The first moves, for most changing women, involve attempts to preserve the attachments they have, but change them to accommodate their emerging plans: 'My husband thought of himself as liberated, but when I changed and started challenging everything, he couldn't take it, and the marriage ended. It was like a second adolescence, with him as parent – you know, because he represented what I'd been taught to think – and did think, and was really happy with even though I eventually knew I wouldn't be happy to continue with all that. So the marriage ended, and I have what I wanted in some way, but I'm also raising three kids on my own and working. I'm free from criticism now. I don't live in the shadow of a man, but I can't say my life is as free as a divorced man's.'

In freeing herself from the marriage which enforced a domestic serving role and a subservient manner, Joelle was free to be herself; but she faced the restrictions of the workplace – of entering the workplace at a later-than-usual phase of life, which is invariably restrictive, however many success stories there are to prove that exceptions are possible. She also faced the pattern of caring for her children as a single parent with all the extra responsibilities and difficulties that entailed. In taking a new option she confronted the restrictions of increased financial and parental obligations within a marketplace that is more restrictive to women and in particular to older women.

For other women, the changes they initiate in themselves and in their families can come to a halt or change course when they see the costs. Many women decide, in their acting-out stage, that adolescent rebellion will cost them dear. If a marriage is threatened they will either return to a domestic track – or, more commonly disguise the track they are taking. They become one person at home and another at work. They may try to run the house as though they were not working. They continue to attend classes, but keep the discussion and the excitement and even the books out of sight. They learn to segregate different parts of themselves.

There are many myths involved in the image of the woman with new options. First, those options have never been as extensive as supposed. Though traditional male professions are now more open to women, they are often uncongenial, and admit women at entry level only to discard them or keep them in a fixed place, or challenge them. When women do rise to high position, they invite difficult and unpleasant challenges, so that women have to be as tough as tough men in order to sustain their 'privileges'. The new options involve greater numbers of women at work – and women often do see many perks of working at even routine jobs. There are social benefits, and the benefit of change, and simply the pleasure of doing something different. But this option is restricted by persistent segregation in the workplace whereby jobs designed for women who sustain responsibility for the home have only these perks, and few others.

Each new option in isolation can be constrained by other structures. For the new woman to have a sure grip on the new options, she has to avoid every other traditional structure – and she may not want to. The new options women face are both disturbing and liberating. They do offer alternatives to the life course which is made good or bad by the choice of a mate, which is enriched or impoverished by marriage, whose boundaries are set and defined by the love choices one is likely to make in very early adulthood. They do suggest that development and change are always possible. They do extend the boundaries of a woman's life. But each extension is restrained by the shapes of adjacent systems of feeling, habit, and expectation.

Free Options

Motherhood is not forever – not, at any rate, in its most binding structure, wherein constant care, constant supervision, and constant attention are required. Women's lives are often sequenced by their families, so that even those women who have taken the traditional burdens of home life upon them still have a chance, later on, to develop their expansive needs, having fulfilled both their affiliative obligations and desires. Perhaps we can have it all, without harming anyone, or cheating anyone, or putting ourselves under stress – if only we have it all consecutively rather than coincidentally. We cannot have it all at once – but perhaps we can manage to have it all during the course of a lifetime?

For many women midlife presents new options, new releases. Many women experience in midlife, as family burdens ease, a sense of opportunity lost or denied to them in the past. The sense of expansion women feel when their children leave home may rush to fill the emptiness and loss which she is expected to experience. Lillian Rubin has exposed the inaccuracy of the empty-nest syndrome, whereby midlife women are expected to suffer depression when their children leave home.[5] Instead, having witnessed the various stages of their children's maturity and independence, they feel the pleasure of completion and the anticipation of new beginnings. They now have time for themselves, and see a wealth of new opportunities.

But women today expect a great deal from themselves. They compare themselves with many other women whose careers have been progressing throughout adulthood. It is sometimes more disheartening to start when so many others are ahead. It is sometimes difficult to take time for self-development when, socially, achievements are perceived as a race.

The challenge of new opportunities is fierce. So for many women the question of 'realising their potential' through a career is addressed when it is too late for them to take straight-forward and obvious steps towards this. Some take action to remedy the situation at a time when most men are well-estab-lished in their work. The women in this enormously varied cohort confront the dual problem of assessing potential in terms of their personal skills, goals and values on the one hand, and in terms of social opportunity on the other.

There are many success stories of late bloomers – of women who suddenly have the time to write or paint or design when their children leave home, and develop the talents and interests that have long niggled and intrigued them. There are women who manage to keep a career ticking over – somewhat like a firm during a recession, maintaining a skeletal staff and work load until opportunities re-emerge. Sometimes a hobby, or very small cottage industry, can develop into a career success. But the exceptions – and so many women today are exceptions – are located in careers which do not have rigid structures, which depend upon talent or contemporary timing or luck. For most of the jobs that most people contemplate, late entries are at a severe disadvantage. There are qualifications that have to be gained, or at least updated. For some midlife women gaining a qualification was an enormous challenge, and a success in and of itself. For some – especially school returners – the road to qualification has pleasures and difficulties in and of itself. For the midlife woman who goes back to work, or back to school, or retrains, still has to deal with a family's expectations. 'My hus-band misses the kids more than I do,' Lee Fernandez explained, 'and I don't like him being alone in the evening, with the house so quiet. I try to arrange my classes and get all my studying done, so I'm home by eight at the latest.' Other women, whose husbands faced redundancy or early retirement, had to con-sider carefully whether they wanted to 'risk putting him down' by retraining and finding a job themselves. They did not want 'to show him up' by having a job when their husbands were unemployed, however much this might improve the family income.

While most midlife women have developed confidence in certain areas and commonly see themselves as competent, many

are still wary of themselves as workers. Retraining schemes sometimes do tap older women's working skills, and people who run
these schemes insist that the most important task is building up
women's confidence as workers, and persuading them that the
skills they have developed in their ordinary lives can be adapted
to their working ones. 'We try to explain that time management, for example, is something they already know a great deal
about. We value their flexibility – which many of them try to
suppress as they think that to do a job properly they have to be
rigid', explained Ruth Aaron who managed a women's returner
programme.

But these programmes, on the whole, deal with entry-level or
low-level jobs – in catering, in secretarial work, in computing.
There is a remarkable split between a midlife woman's personal
self-assessment and her employment expectations. Many women
were delighted simply to have a job. The regular pay check, the
regular hours, the office environment made them feel that they
were entering a mystical world. For many of them success was to
have and to hold a job, however low-paid it might be. They
consider themselves lucky to get a job even at entry level, since
they know that many job opportunities are now closed to them.
Though age restrictions are, in the United States, illegal, they
are easily and widely practised.

Individually midlife women have high self-esteem, and so are
far more likely to shoot ahead in a career which allows individual initiative and patterns. The success stories that are commonly told about midlife women involve the development of
highly individual talents, rather than entry into what remains a
rigid work structure. Careers which are structured simply by
'piecework', by the actual product completed, rather than
through a procedure of progress, building or climbing, provide
far more possibilities for the midlife woman who now has time
for herself, and for self-expansion.

Contemporary midlife women are flexible and determined
and energetic. But they live in a society with rigid career patterns, and in a culture which puts high demands on personal
fulfilment. They want to fulfil their potential, often neglected,
or hedged in; but like women at any other time of life, they

succeed not by following patterns, but by creating them. It is only by being exceptional that they can find the path to commonplace fulfilment.

The idea of the woman with new options is a myth and a puzzle and a reality. She is a reality because women do see themselves as having more opportunities and more options – more opportunities at work, and more options about how to live their lives: whether to marry, whether to stay married, how many children to have and when to have them and how to raise them and who to share their care with. She is a myth because the extension of opportunity at work is not as extensive as it initially seems. This hidden constraint arises partly through prejudice against women in the workplace, especially in regard to promotions; it arises partly from continued job segregation – jobs for women and jobs for men – which invariably means lower pay for women and fewer paths to promotion. She is a myth, too, because as she combines persistent traditional roles at home with her new options in the workplace, the combination leads to stress or to drop-out or cut-back decisions, since the demands of the workplace do not allow for responsibilities for the young, the old and the ill. Hence she is a puzzle, to herself and to others, since it is hard to understand why, when so much has changed, these changes are insufficient to put her on equal career footing with men. The puzzle then becomes a series of questions in which faults in her outlook or determination are suggested as the hidden impediment. Or, some subversive element in society is seen as the condition from which all constraints arise. But the constraints arise from the interlocking of various systems; the links between them give rise to persistent constraints. What we see among women who have made use of the new options, and offered proof that new options can be realized, is avoidance of interlocking points – either through their own personal outlook, or through managed flexibility of a career, or through transformed domestic arrangements. What the new woman, who has it all, does is reformulate a life pattern so that the interlocking of restraints is avoided. She does not do this in one way, but in a variety of ways. Her success is *created*.

5
The Wage Learners: Working as Necessity

At the 1992 Republican national convention Marilyn Quayle stated that though she thought a career was a real option for women 'most of us love being mothers and wives, which gives our lives a richness that few men or women get from their professional accomplishments alone'. The thought-tripping implication here is that the love 'most of us' have for roles as wives and mothers is set in opposition to the rewards of 'professional accomplishments alone'. Women who do take the career option still may value family connections. The decision for most women is how to combine both the personal richness and the professional mastery, and to discover what it is they want as adults while confronting a range of urgent or pressing demands.

The 'hard choices' women make about working and having children involve a range of issues – some real and some spurious. The need to stay at home to see the *first* smile or the first step, seems sentimental, or contrived, though is clearly compelling for some women. But many women who decide not to work after having children and women who decide to work and not have children, share the same decision base: both feel that children demand a great deal of time.[1] Some women wonder whether they are willing to give up the nearly exclusive attachment that a very young child may have to her mother – though few women who work actually do give this up, since even as workers they retain in the home a substantial portion of the traditional maternal functions.

Yet this is not always known at the outset, and our children have only one childhood, and many women who had thought long and hard about having them felt that they had had children in order to value them, and that they were not willing to work in a male fashion, and see as little of their children as did the traditional working father.

The decision as to whether and how much to work after having children seems a crucial one. It is always being discussed – both in public and in private. Contradictions abound, as policy decisions say two things: that women should stay at home and look after the children; and that they should have an equal place in the workforce. Yet many women who are mothers and who also work combine these two jobs by putting child care and domestic work first, and accept only those jobs that can be fitted around school time, partner's work times, child-minder's hours.[2] Work is necessary, but it remains secondary.

For many women these probing decisions, these reflective choices, these determined priorities are luxuries. Many women simply have to work to support themselves, and many of these women are thrown in at the deep end. Having lived as 'wives' who are dependent on a husband's income, they find that this dependency no longer holds. For many women the trauma of divorce is financial: it is the financial decrease in well-being that is divorce's greatest shock;[3] but women do recover, and after several years few regret the divorce, and the only thing they miss about marriage is the financial stability.

Working Mothers: Necessity Sets a Trend

In the United States over half the women of working age do in fact work, and of the women who work, more than a quarter are head of household, responsible for supporting themselves and at least one dependent. Of the women who work, over a third have children under the age of 18, and almost a quarter of working women have children under the age of 4. Among married couples, where both husband and wife work, many cannot meet fixed monthly debt obligations without the wife's salary, and many married couples, where both husband and wife work, would be unable to sustain what they have come to see as a satisfactory lifestyle on one income. Men's real wages have fallen in the past fifteen years, and it is their working wives who have maintained what prosperity the family has.

In Britain the percentage of working mothers is roughly the same, and in fact more women are going back to work after having a family than at any other time in Britain's employment history. In both countries, too, over a third of the women who marry will be divorced and self-supporting by the time they are 35. Yet many policies, of employers and tax and social security authorities and divorce courts, are creating greater difficulties for these women. Alimony or child support payments have always been difficult to ensure and enforce even when they are awarded by a court, and now courts are more and more reluctant to award long-term alimony payments. This change is a result of the increasing awareness that alimony is hard on men, especially on men who who wish to marry again and have more children. It also emerges from the ethos of increased equality: women who wish to be equal to men at work share an equally unprotected financial responsibility. But since women's roles are different in the home, they offer their services to employers under different conditions – not on the whole to perform the macho working hours of the new breed of careerists, but to protect themselves and their children from poverty while they care for them. Though many women do not limit their hours of work, or their career dedication, they often feel that employers look upon them as women in this light and make judgements (or the kind of guesses employers make about an applicant) on this basis. But this statistical prejudice is only one among many impediments breadwinning women face.

Only 12 per cent of newly-divorced mothers live solely on maintenance, and after ten years of divorce only 6 per cent rely on payments by ex-husbands as their main source of income. So the division of labour which has been seen by some economists to be 'rational',[4] and which is experienced by many married women as a choice based upon values and expectations, is a dangerous path. The dependency fostered by this rational decision, this noble preference to stay home and devote oneself to husband, family and home, does not build up what economists call 'human capital' – or the development of a good employable person, someone who is seen by prospective employers to have usable skills, to have pertinent work experience, to be the kind of person an employer chooses. Instead, a woman who has chosen the traditional role of wife and all that it entails is totally unprepared for the shock of divorce or widowhood – or whatever it is that causes a loss of viable financial dependency. They have been doing necessary, essential and 'productive' jobs – which in the end generate no income. For the most part the necessity of earning their own income comes alongside increased domestic and maternal obligations: the sudden pressure to earn one's own living and support one's children oneself goes hand in hand with being a single parent. Women who are forced by financial necessity, through lost financial dependence, to work are also women who have the greatest responsibility as parents.

This responsibility is not recognized by tax laws or benefit laws, and this makes employment particularly difficult for single parents. Women who must pay for child care are permitted tax relief only if they earn a high enough income to pay taxes. The wealthiest families therefore benefit most from tax credit, and poor families do not benefit at all. In Britain, until April 1988, low earners could claim supplementary benefit as an income top-up, and child care costs could be deducted in calculating benefit. The costs of child care then were seen as a necessary expense; yet when income support replaced supplementary benefit, child care costs ceased to be deductible. Recently the nine judges of the European Court in Luxembourg rejected the claim brought by two single mothers that the British Government's refusal to allow child care expenses to be deducted in calculating their benefits breached the European Community's directives on equal access to work. They further denied that this ruling indirectly discriminated against women.[5] Hence the new ethos of equality, wherein it is deemed unfair to assume that children are women's responsibility, comes up against the persistent fact that mothers do take responsibility for their children. The insistence that the assumption of traditional mothering is biased leads to policies which are prejudicial against women. For the vast majority of single parents are single mothers who prefer to work part-time and who, when working part-time, may be worse off financially than they would be solely on state benefits. The woman who is suddenly thrust upon her own resources to support herself and her children, is utterly alone.

Safety and Sorrow

Colette Dowling describes in *The Cinderella Complex* how she nursed an alcoholic husband through his binges until she decided to divorce him. Then she supported herself and her three children as a freelance journalist, working hard, working fast, establishing skills and independence. When she remarried, however, she found that she was turning to domestic occupations. She decorated rooms and made jam rather than pushed forward to complete projects and then seek out new ones. Life became mellow and safe. She was, in her eyes, committing woman's most common sin against herself: she was becoming financially dependent on her husband. Wooed by the roles of homemaker and mother, she was losing grip on her independence. She was selling out, giving into that subversive dependency which had crippled so many fine women throughout the ages.

The early 1980s witnessed a crisis in women's ambivalence about what such dependency needs were, what they meant, and what they were worth. The limitations of women's traditional roles were clear enough, once they were pointed out. What has been a far more difficult task is sifting out what is valuable and what is not. This is very different from the question of what is

145

limiting and constraining, and what is liberating. We live with limits. We define ourselves through attachment and commitment and choice which themselves engender limits. Liberation gives us greater control over our choices, but it does not free us from constraint. Women sought liberation to increase the range of choices; but many writers who speak on behalf of women have had a far more definite view of what those choices should be than do women themselves who daily assess and re-assess the costs and the benefits of new choices against embedded values.

The painstaking attention women themselves give to problems of dependency or attachment and expansiveness in their own lives appears magnified and fixed in many books about women. Dowling presented dependency or affiliative needs as subversive, whereas other writers were at the same time treating them with enormous sympathy, revalidating them, insisting upon a change in that value system in which they were seen to be weak. New interpretations showed that they grounded many women's identity, rather than diminished it.

Indeed, Dowling's determined war against that dependency has been reinterpreted constantly since her once clear and simple message crossed the country. Was she really demeaning herself by turning to domesticity? Was it not enormously difficult to be anything other than domestic, as her new marriage and her new country house demanded nesting practices? Did her children not need, or at least want and deserve, a reprieve from the years of her disintegrating marriage and her fierce (emotional and financial) recovery? Did a good life really involve a continuous battle for achievement? Was she not joining the group of people who seem to speak for women while demeaning their traditional roles, by casting suspicion on the assumption that in being wifely or wife-like they are somehow doing nothing? Do we have to believe that because the skills one develops as a mother and homemaker are not marketable, they are therefore useless? In speaking out for women and women's fulfilment, is she not speaking out against women, telling them to change who they are and what they want and what they value? Is she not imprisoning women in men's most shallow dreams?

What is so disturbing about such cautionary tales is that their hard-core message has much validity. Women are likely to be forced to be self-supporting. They would therefore be well advised to plan their lives with this necessity in mind. If they do not, then they face severe setbacks in the marketplace. Women who take time off to have children suffer severe downgrading in position and income when they return. The more gaps they have in their (marketable) work history, the more downgrading they experience – but the largest downward step is from the first employment gap to the first return. Moreover the higher up in the career ladder women are when they first stop work (which is nearly always to have children), the greater is the downward step when they return.[6] Even small gaps are difficult to close. In a study of women 'returners' some of the women were in their early twenties; these women found that after three years' absence from the workplace they were no longer hirable as new entrants, yet they were not qualified for anything above entry-level. Many of these very young women described themselves as 'too old' to be eligible for a good job.

One difficulty women who want to return to work after a long break have is that they believe they have no idea how to go about things. They face, initially, not so much lack of opportunity, as ignorance of how to discover whether there is any opportunity. The most simple things seem fraught with difficulty. Do I go to a job centre? What do I say? What will happen if he asks me this? What will I say to that? In my study of midlife women who wanted to return to work, this enormous self-doubt seemed the greatest impediment to taking those first steps towards return to employment. They saw the working world like a book in a foreign language, and this could delay their job search or retraining programmes for years. Women who were forced to earn a living, however, were much better at setting these fears to one side. 'I just had to pretend I was someone else. It was like putting on a mask, and just not worrying about who thought what about me. I had to apply for these jobs, and I had to keep applying, and that was that', one women said. Another explained that she imagined her fear 'like something you can just box up. It's there, and I'm going to carry it with me, but I'll just keep it in that little box. When I sit down with people – you know, like the career adviser and then those employers, one after another – I imagine myself looking at the closed lid of this box.' Here was a wonderful metaphor for how she both acknowledged the emotion and contained it. These copers then found themselves in work situations which then could give rise to other opportunities.

It is surprisingly difficult to predict in very early adulthood which women will remain on career track and which will not. Women's early plans are interesting, and they should be encouraged to have work plans, but their plans do not actually determine their future work patterns. Many women with strong domestic orientations nonetheless find themselves, for all sorts of reasons, in high-level employment, which they stick to even as they fulfil their more traditional goals. Many successful career women decline to describe themselves as ambitious not so much because they dislike the term, or fear it, or find it inappropriately unfeminine, but because it really does not describe their motivation. They find themselves presented with challenges which they can meet with confidence and opportunities which they embrace. Their working experience motivates further work. Hence the women who often seem in the worst positions – those who may have no training and who did not plan careers and who are left without any support as they are thrown on their own financial devices with very young children to care for, may in fact thrive, especially if they escape the poverty trap – which is stretching its net ever more widely.

Lessons Unlearned

Once, perhaps, the easiest thing for a mother to do was to give up work. For women today, this does not seem to be so easy. They often do it – but it takes effort. In their study of working mothers on maternity leave, Julia Brannen and Peter Moss traced what they call the *cognitive manoeuvres* women went through in order to make leaving their jobs after having children more acceptable. First, women routinely described their earnings as supplementary to family income: they were for luxuries, for large appliances or holidays. Even when women's earnings were three-quarters of a husband's earnings they were seen as additions rather than essential to household earnings. They marginalized them as they described them. They also modified the expense of giving up work by subtracting child care costs from the woman's earnings. This helped make their earnings seem much less, and provided a way of anticipating and coping with withdrawal from work.

Though deciding to stop work often seems the easy option, it actually involves a great deal of work. Women have to resist their fears, control their regret, justify a decision which may, they know, have enormous repercussions on their future earnings and security. It is hard and women have to work hard to sustain their decisions. This is one reason why working mothers and mothers working full-time at domestic work so often feel hostile and defensive in one another's company. Both the working mother and the non-working mother perform psychological management on themselves to make their positions palatable. They do not want someone else to undo all that psychological work.

Of course, many of the women who stopped paid work after having children eventually returned to work. When I began a study of 'women returners' in Cambridge, I was surprised that my sample included women as young as 21. However young they were, however brief their break in employment, they were very likely to return to a lower-level job than the one they had left. That break – even if only of eighteen months – was seen as a handicap by employers, who were likely to argue that they needed retraining, that equipment, or the market, or policies had changed. But in many cases women who were downwardly mobile when they returned to work after having children were not simply victims of employment systems in which employees are penalized for cutting down or taking time off for domestic duties. Many women who took time off to have children and did not return immediately actually chose, when they did return, to take a less demanding job, with less commitment, fewer promotional opportunities, because they saw themselves as primarily obligated to their children. They chose lower-status jobs in order to maintain their family commitments.

A good start is not enough. A strong start in early adult life, before a working break, does not offer a secure future of employment. Even professional qualifications such as a doctor, lawyer or teacher requires do not make return easy. It is not enough to start a job, or a career, for them to take off. On the whole the marketplace does not permit apparently reasonable human patterns, and this must change if women are to make progress towards equality. Women can succeed now – and women have succeeded in current conditions. There are ways of finding and thriving in careers. Among this sample women succeed by creating a flexibility which was not ready-made. One woman who had followed her husband's mobile career, who had settled in five different countries in the course of 17 years of marriage, who had learned to shop for food in five different languages, established, after her divorce, a flourishing business as an interior decorator. Another woman worked as law clerk and went to law school and after many years became a partner in a law firm. Two things tended to go with success: either being divorced at a very early age, with very young children, when both time and urgency are on one's side, or having a strong, remarkable talent.

Exceptions have a double-edged effect. They may inspire other women, proving that all things are possible; but often they disguise the rigidity of work structures. As some women 'make it' success is proved possible. The working world in our society is friendly enough to allow exceptions; but this often clouds an inflexibility which most women experience as they try to do the best by their children and themselves. Hard messages warning women to take a shrewd measure of the harsh working world, and bend their lives to shape accordingly, are reasonable if one assumes that women's aim is to succeed in the workplace as we know it. Should women think of themselves, as men supposedly do, in terms of what they do (that is, what their job is) rather than whom they are linked to, related to, attached to? Yet in fact many men find this a terrible burden, a denial of their humanity and of the breadth of their worth. Women have long protected men from the alienating conditions of work. Should they now themselves become subject to them?

Life offers no insurance policies, and it is always full of surprises. Women and men who keep to a rigid career path do not always climb high, or even stay on the ladder. Meticulously developed skills can, and do, lose their use. Businesses can, and do, collapse. Partnerships are wound up. Futures which once looked certain can suddenly seem implausible. Ups and downs are experienced by even the most careful players. But a rigid, standard work history is the safest bet. This is the game that most working men play, and this is the game that careful women play. But when women do not play according to these rules it is not because they are being lazy or weak. They are not doing something wrong, or less, which they should be exhorted to snap out of. They are making a different kind of investment.

Misalignments

As social ideas about what women can do and who they should be change, so too do the conditions in which they live. But when aligned structures change individually they move out of alignment. What may be intended as a change to improve women's conditions may make them worse. The family structure has changed: women are increasingly responsible for the financial support of their families. Yet that conventional ceiling on women's wages remains well plastered, as jobs for women are assumed to be jobs for secondary earners. It was men's insistence that they needed a family wage in the nineteenth century that kept women out of the trade unions and out of good jobs,[7] and women have never been able to push a comparable claim with comparable force. Equal pay acts have not been able to ensure this for women, because equality of pay can only be determined for the same job, and women's jobs are constantly hedged in.

The fact that many jobs continue to be designed for women and that women are concentrated in peripheral segments of the market creates enormous hardships for women who have to support their families. During a recession, or period of contraction in the labour market, job security decreases; this change, too, puts women at greater risk, given the usually untenured nature of the part time positions women frequently prefer. Even if women's employment does not fall during a recession,[8] the contraction of the labour market will hedge them into insecure, marginal jobs. During cutbacks women's jobs and men's jobs are treated differently. As firms cut down on money paid to cleaners, which is a job taken by women, pay is cut, but no jobs are cut; whereas refuse workers, who are mostly men, experience no cut in pay – though they may face more redundancies. Women in full-time work may come up against the principle of seniority – since women are more likely to take time off, or start a career later in life.[9] So when a growing appreciation of women's capacity to be financially independent, and financially self-responsible occurs alongside persistent inequalities in women's employments, alongside persistent refusals to provide care for her children so that she can offer employers her services on grounds that might allow her equal opportunity, then the discrepancy between changing attitudes towards women and women's reality will increase women's inequality.

The idea of equal pay for equal work never survives different jobs for men and women. Attempts to create policies of equal pay for jobs of equal value have been ineffective.[10] Repeatedly women's jobs are downgraded in relation to men's. This happens in country after country – and what is remarkable, and grimly amusing, is that the criteria that are used to downgrade women's jobs (so that they are defined as unskilled) differ widely from country to country – but the result is always the same. Heavy manual labour in Russia is seen as 'women's work' and hence is labelled unskilled. Clerical work, too, has become downgraded as it has become feminized – as have certain sections of the computer industry. The jobs women take and the jobs women are given are seen to be less skilled than jobs taken by and given to men.

This has occurred even in countries whose economy has been grounded on ideals of equality between men and women. The Bolshevik revolution had high on its agenda the liberation of women from the demeaning tedium of housework, and to this end state nurseries and equal access to work, training, education and promotion were firm state policies. These policies have allowed women to make enormous strides in the professions; but where Soviet women made strides in the professions their employers took advantage of women's weak bargaining power to lower the salaries of the professions. The shorter working hours of doctors, for example, have made that profession highly attractive to women, and equal education and alternative child care facilities have made women's participation in the professions possible at rates far above those of the west. But the unpaid work of women in the home was a heavy burden where resources were diverted away from consumption. With women shouldering most of the domestic burden, providing an unpaid subsidy to the Soviet growth pattern,[11] their bargaining power in the labour market was weak; the majority of women continued to be employed in jobs described as low-skilled which are hence low-paid. Since part-time work in the Soviet Union was virtually unobtainable, and since women's earnings, even if low, are essential to maintain the household, women were hedged in between the demands of the labour market and domestic obligations. The government's active support of women's paid labour, through child care policies, was not enough to ensure equality.

Most working women in the former Soviet bloc countries are in the poorer-paid and less prestigious occupations. They are also under-presented in the managerial and higher-level positions. Women dominate employment in the service sector, particularly in education, health and social care sectors (where they represent over 70 per cent of all employees in many CEE countries). Women also constitute the majority of workers in the trade, culture and arts, communications, and finance sectors. This occupational concentration reflects a link between the 'feminization' of certain sectors and the related decline in status and hence the average wages of those sectors. So though the stereotyping of certain occupations according to gender may be different in CEE countries and in the West, the effect is the same, and the gap persists.[12] Women coped with the harsh demands at work and in the home by having fewer children. The falling birthrate fostered a backlash against the erosion of traditional notions of femininity.[13] The birthrate fell because women could only manage their lives by having fewer children. The traditional division of labour in the home was never changed, in spite of Lenin's outcry against housework. Housework remained a fact of life, and it remained a female task. These tasks grew enormous as the shopping queues lengthened and the 'labour-saving devices' such as washing machines and vacuum cleaners increased in price and decreased in reliability. Domestic burdens increased. Work demands were rigid. Women began to see liberation as release from paid labour, and felt that the stress of their dual roles undermined their ability to form a resistance.[14] For all the ideological support of equality, embedded bias and habit prohibited it.

Women as Breadwinners

The women who were forced into the position of financial responsibility, after having lived for many years of their adult lives as traditional wives, faced a series of crises and decisions. The overriding query was not 'Should I work?' but 'How can I go about working?' 'How can I do it? 'How do I do it?' The puzzling strategy of finding a job within the constraints of what they perceive as their responsibility for their children and the limited jobs available, and the limited benefits of the available jobs, create an awful helplessness which is largely responsible for what is called the 'low participation rate' of single mothers. Many single mothers do not work. They then become dependent on state benefits which do not lift them out of poverty, but any job they take (which is usually part-time and low-paid) will make them worse off – a syndrome which is known as the poverty trap.

But exceptions to this syndrome are becoming more and more common. Many women who are now single mothers were happy newly-weds when they heard warnings about the ultimate insecurity of marriage. Some of these women may be discovering the persistence of their own 'treacherous hearts' as they made decisions to stick to more traditional roles in spite of initial career tracks. But in the wake of divorce or widowhood their maternal role took on a new aspect: protection of children meant providing for them and sustaining an example of hope and action.

Young Hearts and Hard Times

The experience of being suddenly uncoupled and forced upon

one's own financial resources and lack of resources may feel the same at different life phases, but it yields different results, different dangers, and different possibilities. Bella Warren was a widow with two children at 18, and most unpromising both as mother material and as a woman with strong career orientations. Bella was herself the victim of maternal deprivation. Her mother, divorced by the time she was born, made an informal fostering arrangement whereby a series of families were paid to look after Bella from the age of four months. Recalling a lonely past, Bella described visits from her mother like a visitation from the Queen, and remembers the harsh disappointment when announced visits were cancelled, or cut short.

Many of us, as adults, want to make up for what we lacked as children, and Bella married as soon as she was legally able, and had children immediately thereafter to establish the family she never had. But like many people who anxiously construct dreams, they may be left to reenact their nightmares. Maternal deprivation is often cyclical: the mother who was rejected and uncared for as a child is unable to give her own children the maternal care she herself missed out on. Hence instead of making up for past losses, she may reproduce them. But there are miracles of resilience. What sometimes becomes an excuse for retaliation can become a means of reparation.

Bella's husband was killed in a cycling accident before her unsatisfactory marriage became an issue. A child in charge of children, a single parent with no parents to give her either financial or emotional support, she was perfectly set up for isolation and helplessness. But the self-esteem which was triggered by this desperate situation and her gradual discovery that it could be managed, created situations in which further job opportunities emerged.

In looking back over her early history, Bella declared that one thing that helped her endure her children's makeshift child care arrangements was that she never felt guilty, because she was sure that whatever they went through, as long as they were safe and comfortable, would be less than what she had suffered in being separated from her mother and denied a mother's love. Hence the ordinary structure of motherhood was far more flexible as the 'bottom line' was drawn at actual maternal deprivation rather than the very broad notions of maternal absence that were issues for other mothers making employment decisions in the 1960s. Another structure that failed to hold was the norm of family life to which Bella could not aspire once her husband died.

A young woman who is widowed is unlikely to be financially prepared, but the younger a woman was when she was divorced or widowed, the more recent was her work experience, the more willing employers were to hire her. An 'innocence' of the norm of single motherhood on welfare was also beneficial. Bella had not grown up in an environment of unemployment. She saw makeshift family life and constant paid work as the norm.

As Bella placed herself in employment, she faced a new set of opportunities. The opportunities were of course constrained in some ways: she entered women's employment – as a saleswoman – and she announced as her only stipulation that she would not work on Saturdays. But the work-orientation which was fostered by necessity gave rise to a career-orientation. As with many women, career success did not arise from a prior life plan, but from finding herself in a situation in which further opportunities might occur. It was not as a warrior, but as a scout that she made her way to buyer, and then to manager. 'I then had to work Saturdays,' she laughed, 'but it's one thing to stake your claim when you're a new kid on the block, and another altogether when you're just about king of the castle. I traded my children a good summer holiday for the year of Saturdays – but I knew, really, I was trading even more for it. I wouldn't have stuck it – day in and day out and not going anywhere. Nowhere is hard to work for. I was thrown into the water, and my only hope was learning how to swim. There wasn't any back-up, and no one would've cared if me and my kids had drowned. So I learned, and maybe I set my sights as a mother a little lower while I raised my idea of what I could do in the store. But they turned out all right, so I didn't do too bad.'

Children's Work

Issues of child labour seem like remnants of nineteenth-century mill factories or current horror stories of children hand-knotting carpets. The position of children as aids to mothers' work has virtually been ignored.[15] But not only do children offer a great deal of instrumental work to the running of the home, as they look after younger siblings, do some shopping, help prepare dinner and clean up, they also do strong emotional work to make a mother's employment easier on her. Bella described how one morning, as she was taking her children to the child minder's home before work, her older daughter tripped on the porch steps and tumbled on to the cement pavement. For one moment the brick wall hid the child from view, but a second later the 4-year-old's head appeared, with a gash at the hairline and the eyes blinking as the blood dripped into them. The girl shouted through her tears, 'I'm all right Mommy!'

'You're not allowed to get sick', Bella had told them, resisting the pressure of her son's repeated attacks of vomiting when his mother left him for work. The daughter had taken this to heart in order to insist that she was not hurt even when she was.

Children want their home life to work. They are not merely labour-generating and emotion-taxing beings, but also respondents who see that they make a difference to the people around them. They see that they can help and hinder – and while many very young children find it much easier to change their home environment by hindering other's moments – by crying and screaming and vomiting – as they grow, they are very likely to want to influence their home environment in a more positive way. Some children's descriptions of their work in the home are ingenuously generous. One girl said that when her mother went out to work her grandmother came to look after the children. She then recounted what occurred while her grandmother was 'caring for them': she herself bathed her younger sister and got her ready for bed and read to her until she was asleep.[16] Hence her work at regulating the family and caring for her younger sister was minimized by the grandmother's presence. Her own role was submerged in the more common one of the grandmother looking after the children. Indeed, it was often difficult to find out how much work children did, since when they did a lot of work at home it seemed normal, and hardly worth commenting on, and when they did little, they were proud of what they did and were quick to mention it, since it seemed unusual.

Some mothers believe that children benefit from the responsibility of working in the home, and some mothers believe that it is a hardship their children simply have to live with. And some girls enjoy exercising their competence in this way, while others feel ignored, used or disempowered. Bella's daughter, now 33, said, 'I don't want my daughters to do the same, but it's not the same situation – is it? I tell them their job is going to school, not running the house. But we can manage on that. What do you do in a situation which doesn't work that way?'

Yet when a girl saw herself as doing housework because she was a girl rather than because it was necessary for all to pitch in, she was more likely to be bitter. 'When I was 12 I was suddenly a non-person. My needs didn't count any more. I was just a "big kid" – someone to look after my little brothers. I remember my mother talking to me . . . I remember her voice . . . this monotone, but it got louder if I switched off . . . telling me what to do after school. I'd dread coming down at breakfast. There would just be this on-going conversation about what had to be done. She only had to see me to start giving me some orders.' Petra felt herself working not as part of a family but in opposition to it. She worked for them because her needs no longer mattered. She experienced, early on, the wedge a housewife in crisis draws between participation and subservience.

The Burden of Sharing

Maternal guilt, maternal anxiety is neither a myth nor a neurosis. Women do seem to carry a burden of psychological labour in regard to their children. They have repeatedly been found to be less able to switch off their thoughts, worries and concern for their children when they go to work.[17] This burden has biosocial origins: mothers need to tend their children, to be aware of them and care for their safely, in life's unfriendly environments. But this is enforced by common forms of the 'institution' of motherhood, whereby a woman gets used to seeing herself as responsible for her children. This responsibility leads to the development of maternal skill and confidence. A woman believes she knows when to interfere in a sibling quarrel, when to soothe a child, when to let her cry. As a father, or a child minder, cares in different ways, she may feel critical – and in feeling critical goes back to taking charge herself. Fathers do seem 'better' at switching off that attentiveness (even in the home, with children fighting and crying), and this places a greater sense of responsibility on women to take control. What men see as an acceptable domestic situation, women may not. The issue then becomes one of job definition.

'I'll be trying to work upstairs and he's supposed to be in charge', explained Ann Nuccio who was preparing for an exam to obtain a real estate agent's licence. 'But I hear the children fighting and Gail is crying and Sam is screaming, and he's just sitting there in front of the TV. So I march down and say "What's all this about?" and he says it's okay, they'll be all right. When are they going to be all right? When Sam's nose gets smashed. I say "The boy's crying, it's not all right." Does he think this house is a boxing ring? What's this "all right" business? It's all right for him because he doesn't hear. Just doesn't hear it the way I do.'

Arrangements for sharing, agreements to share the child care often founder on this impasse as the 'off duty' mother is quicker to see the children as needing a parent's input than is the 'on duty' father. Hence the mother either steps in herself, and in taking charge shows the father that he is not doing what they both agreed would be his job, or confronts the father directly, positioning herself as overseer of the job her husband should be doing, and thereby increasing her tasks. Either way, she is no longer free for her 'off duty' work.

In one episode of the television series *Roseanne*, the father declares that he will take over the evening domestic chores because his wife is starting a new job as a waitress. As soon as she comes home she finds that nothing is as it should be – her son is still up, the dishes are done badly. Her sister reminds her that the dishes are badly done when she does them too, but Roseanne finds the control impossible to forgo. The clash between habit and 'possession' of the home and simply different standards and different strategies creates a tension so that giving up control of the home, however burdensome this control is and however it may be resented, is torture. It becomes a habit, and the addict cannot kick it.

The issue of 'guilt' is not just the need to see that one's child is all right, but a prediction and expectation that the responsibility will be one's own. These feelings are not inevitable. Women can change, or the intensity can be modified, and can be managed. But change is difficult, and necessity offers many short cuts.

Women who work because they simply have to – because they are without a male breadwinner in the family – have a few advantages. Surprisingly, single women have advantages over women who are married to men who are unable to be breadwinners themselves. The participation rate in the workforce of women who are married to unemployed men is remarkably low – though this is far more marked in the UK than the US: in the UK 71 per cent of women married to working men work; whereas only 28 per cent of women married to unemployed men work; in the US there is a less startling differential: 67 per cent of women married to working men work, but only 59 per cent of women married to unemployed husbands work.[18] This does not seem to be a sensible financial choice: some social security benefits are badly set out, so that unemployed men lose a lot of benefits if their wives work, but this does not seem to be the cause of women's reluctance to work.[19]

Women often make decisions which jeopardize their financial well-being. Women often retire early, when their husbands retire, though this lowers their already lower pensions. They feel obliged to spend time with a husband, to prevent or waylay loneliness or boredom. Leisure time becomes different for women with a husband at home. They often feel they have less of it. If unemployment is due to illness then the woman is the wife who looks after him. If a husband is depressed by unemployment then they may want to stay home to cheer him up. If a husband is unemployed they may not want to threaten his self-esteem by asking him to do 'wifely' work which might enable them to work. Some women think that it is extremely important not to jolt the traditional division of labour at home when a husband is unemployed. 'He feels bad enough as things are.

I'm not going to ask him to scrub the floor and take in the laundry – am I? – When he's so down like this. People see him and say things, you know, if they see him doing things in the house. I tell him his job is looking for a job and I'll do the rest, even though I know he's doing nothing.' Some women are reluctant to show him up – to get a job when a partner can't. Others feel that they have to be at home to keep him cheerful, and feel that they have less free time with an unemployed husband than with a working one. 'Your time isn't your own any more. You know he's sitting at home all day not knowing what to do with himself.' Another structure or recurrent pattern women come up against when they are married to unemployed men is that unemployment becomes normal, for both men and women, and the chance of getting a job and keeping it for any length of time seems so small that the effort involved in changing one's lifestyle is judged not to be worthwhile.

Few of these impediments hold when a woman has no partner.

Whose Reasons?

The security of marriage is a myth, and yet women do make choices on the assumption that it offers security, and continue to make decisions which undermine their financial independence. Pension plans which might ensure women's financial well-being in later life, are routinely minimized by decisions to retire when husbands retire, to leave a high-track job at midlife because they no longer want to give everything to their work, because they want to have a chance to be more and do more of what they want for themselves and others.

Women in midlife who find their expected financial dependencies dissolved with their marriages face a different set of problems. Many of these women said it was just as difficult to leave older children, who were in practical terms more independent than younger ones but who needed supervision to do their homework (and some needed supervision to make sure they went to school), who needed help with their homework, whose loneliness had a range of potentially damaging consequences. Moreover women at midlife confronted far fewer employment opportunities: it has been calculated that women face greater age discrimination in the US than they do in Britain where there is no law against it. Some women have worked all their married lives, thinking that staying in work would help them in such a predicament, but in fact find that changing their work patterns is very difficult: their more feminized track is changed with difficulty, and with luck.

For some years, and with much justification, psychologists and writers have emphasized the resurgence of energy and the release of free time women have in midlife when, typically, their children are older and older relatives have not yet become dependent on them. Only 3.5 per cent of women provide co-resident care for relatives – that is, have the relatives living with them; and only 16 per cent give non-residential care,[20] so most women are freer of caring tasks when their children leave home. Some women, who were divorced at midlife, did land on their feet, did take control and move forward; but for most this was a painful and painstaking processes. They confront enormous financial uncertainty. They frequently lose pensions, and, in the US, they often lose their medical insurance, when they divorce.

The choices they face, or should be educated to face, are difficult. Given the fact that marriage does not provide security – because men's jobs are not secure, but above all because marriage itself is not secure – they should learn, as part of normal adult life, to take responsibility for their financial position. They should learn that money and power are often linked, that in lacking earning power, they may be depriving themselves of access to money, and the deprivation of this resource can lead to further loss of power.

Yet the decisions women make about their careers are often sensible enough. They are often well-considered and deliberate decisions which take account of their current needs and their family's needs. Many of the women who moved from full-time, fast-track employment to part-time work, judged that working full-time was simply not compatible with good family life. As with many decisions which involve giving up something, the conditions which led to this decision may in hindsight be exaggerated, but the tension was clear: 'It was awful. When I worked full-time I would come home and have time for nothing. Even with someone in to do the housework there was nothing but things to do – piles and piles of things – like letters to open and bills to pay and things to be arranged and school forms to sign and things in the house to pick up, and I didn't know what my kids were doing at school, and all I was doing was shouting at them to try to understand me.' Another woman said simply, 'I was too busy to have any fun, or be any fun for anyone else.'

As she saw the negative impact in her home – her negative emotional input – she chose to change her working patterns, which, given what are acceptable working patterns, led to harsh consequences: her chances of promotion plummeted. Yet women who have persevered through the very difficult years of caring for young children and establishing careers, and keeping two careers on track in spite of long commutes, long hours, relocations, business trips, frequently 'drop out' or change course in midlife, after the rewards of that lifelong work simply require staying on track. They are not the 'prisoners of men's dreams' they have sometimes been described as being; but their liberation from these dreams and their determination to craft new options, make them prisoners of employment systems in which they face severe sanctions for failing to follow traditional male employment tracks.

It has been tempting, as the challenges, securities or excitement of careers have been emphasized, to view women's domestic orientation as worthless because it is unmarketable. A great deal of the resistance to feminism, or backlash against feminism, has stemmed from this downgrading of the human work women are orientated towards. But now many women, among whom are many feminists, do see that the way forward, the way towards liberation comes from creating possibilities for women to balance their distinctive needs. More and more researchers into business and management see that success rests on the ability to change the workplace, to make it far more flexible, so that women are not disadvantaged by their resistance to the high cost of rigid work structures and the new pressures of overwork.[21]

6
Why Women Fail

Achievement versus Ability

In *A Room of One's Own* Virginia Woolf asks the following question: what would have happened to a young woman from Strat-
ford who, in the late sixteenth century, had gone to London
theatres to test out and exhibit her talent? We have a sketchy
knowledge of Shakespeare's life, and a fuller picture of the
social conditions that favoured his dramas, but what would have
happened to a sister of his, should she, as a young provincial
woman, have braved the big city of London to offer her plays to
the theatre? She would have left the only habitation that is safe
for a woman – a father's house. In the pride of her genius she
may have sought achievement and fulfilment, but would have
discovered the peculiar punishments inflicted upon such women.

I have never been completely convinced by the parallel story
Woolf tells. She narrates the tale of Judith Shakespeare as one
of seduction and betrayal, as theatre producers make love to

her with promises of using her work, and then discard both her and her work after the deed is done. Her tale is then one of pregnancy, poverty, humiliation – and finally, wifehood. The would-be dramatist who happens to be female enacts a sentimental soap opera. We are not shown Judith Shakespeare's talent and vision. She remains a bland hypothesis. She has no history outside the history of an ordinary woman's lot – though that, of course, is precisely Woolf's point: woman's individual history is determined by women's common lot.

Woolf presumes that her imagined Judith will be punished and humiliated for her ambition. Though Shakespeare himself experienced the big world of love and betrayal, of rivalry, of lesser talents preferred, of broken promises and contracts, these did not set him back but rather set him alight. He enacted these disappointments in his dramas, for he saw them as normal scenes in the human panorama.

What makes Woolf's parallel story of Judith Shakespeare plausible is that whatever William Shakespeare suffered, and however deceived he was by those he loved and desired, he had endless energy to resist suffering and perceive further possibilities. Life's potential never failed him.

It may be this ability to run with opportunity that makes his story, though not straightforward and easy, distinctly nonfemale. For there is something in the way women experience life which often undermines their talents and distracts their efforts. There is something in the way they experience social and personal prohibitions which allows fewer buried talents to rise to the surface. Ability, in women, is not enough.

About forty years ago, when the lack of women in high career positions began to seem puzzling rather than natural, it was found that though there was a reasonable correlation between a man's IQ and his adult accomplishments, there was no correlation between women's intelligence and their achievements.[1]

A man's intelligence, as it is measured on standard intelligence tests, seems to do good work for him. The tests may be a good measure of intelligence and potential – or, perhaps, as a man comes to learn that his intelligence is rated high, he sets certain goals, and works towards them. Whether it is the intelligence itself, or others' expectations formed by high test results, or his own sense of potential enacted in response to the result or to others' response to the results, men who perform well on intelligence tests tend to do well in their careers.

Not so with women. In this study women with IQs of 170 and more were housewives or office workers. Some were pleased (described as 'tickled') by the idea that they had displayed a high intelligence on a test, but they did not see this as a reason to do anything other than what they were already doing. Whatever linked a high IQ score to high achievement in men, broke among women.

Some research results are highly predictable but nonetheless intriguing. It seems obvious that a hundred and one things work against women realizing the potential measured by their intelligence alone, and that a hundred and one things work for those white male college students (who were once psychologists' only subjects of study) whose IQs and subsequent careers were carefully tracked. What is interesting about this study is that it was done: that it questioned whether adult achievement bore the same relation to intelligence among men and among women.

Elsewhere we have looked at many of the many obvious reasons for the discrepancy between women's and men's career achievement: the structures which marriage and motherhood tend to build in their lives; the structures built into the workplace, so that the jobs that suit women's lives as mothers do not foster high flying careers; the sense of exclusion and discomfort many career women experience which makes the personal costs of career dedication less likely to be paid; the new rise in working hours which makes career success difficult to achieve alongside family commitments. But here a somewhat different issue is highlighted. The question is not why so few women manage to win competition for the jobs and promotions and positions men aim for and get – at least over women – but why women fail: why they fail to try, why they fail to compete, why they fail to persist. For the true tragedy suggested by the story of a female counterpart to Shakespeare is not that she goes to seek her fortune in London and is cheated of success by men who take advantage of her womanhood, but that in all probability she fails to leave her father's house. The real tragedy is not thwarted ambition, but the failure to develop ambition. She may fail to notice her talent, as it is experienced more as deviance than as insight. She may try to suppress her talent, as it threatens the easy relationships with those who expect her compliance. She already knows the rules which sanction women who try, who aim high and above all, who aim to go in a different direction, along a male-trodden path. The setting-off might have been the battle won. A willingness to declare her vision would have fired her pride and her strength. She might then have been a survivor, rather than a victim of rape, and seduction would have been no more than experience. Pregnancy would not have forced the end of her story, but instead would have provided a twist or a turn. If she had acknowledged her needs and set her sights high, then she would at least have had a chance. The real tragedy is that her defeat, though not self-inflicted, is self-assured. She does not have even a single chance, because she does not give herself a chance.

Becoming a Woman

The discrepancies between girls' intelligence and achievement have puzzled educators and educational psychologists for some time. When the handpicked women in the Harvard Business School Class of 1975, the first class in which a full 10 per cent of women participated, failed to thrive as much as expected in the business world, the Dean explained that at that time they had not been able to assess the women applicant's drive, but only their ability.[2] Whether or not the Harvard Business School is now 'better' at choosing among applicants, women still leave management and management track careers at a staggering rate: they are highly visible as they enter, and then they seem simply to disappear.[3] Is there a kind of dedication or determination that intelligent or capable women lack, so that training and (apparent) opportunity do not do for them what they do for men?

Sigmund Freud noted, as he studied psychological development in children, the initial, but deteriorating, intelligence of girls. He marvelled at the fact that in early childhood girls were bright, curious, vivacious, that their intelligence had energy, that they were eager to try out new things and exercise their wit. Yet the vision of the mature woman chilled him: at thirty, whereas a man's future lay before him, a woman seemed set and rigid, with no paths to future development.

Freud believed that the demoralizing task of becoming a woman drained intellect and vitality. In his opinion this task was a necessary part of psychological development. Men and women simply had to accept and adapt to their sexual and social roles. For women, this involved accepting their sexual inferiority, their terrible status as non-male. The absence of a penis was conceived as a wound – and the humiliation and anger of this involved a network of suppressed self-esteem and compensation.

Few psychologists now accept that the inevitable conclusion of psychological development involves an awareness of women's inferiority to men. Yet since Freud's time, more and more psychologists have become aware of how girls' social experience constrains them in special ways. Recently Carol Gilligan and her colleagues have tracked the break between the eager, easily accessible intelligence of 9-year-old girls, and the carefully suppressed voice of adolescent girls whose intelligence goes 'underground' in resistance to the social realities which inform their relationships.[4] Girls may receive messages from teachers and parents and friends that they, as girls, must not aim too high or compete too hard. As more people have begun to reconsider the rights and wrongs of women's education, training and socialization, the inconsistencies of women's success motivation have been emphasized. Do women learn to avoid success as they are taught what is appropriate for them as girls and women? Do their responses to challenges and competitions in which a successful outcome is possible arise from the belief that success-seeking behaviour is socially unacceptable?[5] What is it that holds girls back?

The observation Freud made about girls' eclipsed precocity continues today, and has been more rigorously tracked. In primary school, girls are far ahead of boys. In reading, writing, English and spelling, the average 11-year-old girl beats the average 11-year-old boy but, in secondary school, girls fall behind the boys in other subjects – particularly arithmetic, geography and science.[6] What happens?

Some accounts avoid a social or psychological focus. These discrepancies arise, it is claimed, because boys and girls simply develop at different rates. Girls are quicker in early childhood, but boys develop more quickly in early adolescence. Some believe that this difference is one of brain maturity; and that the fact that teachers' expectations in the first years of school suit girls more than boys means that boys have to develop a tolerance for frustration in learning that girls do not. Hence when subjects such as science and higher mathematics are taught at puberty, boys not only enjoy the rush of new abilities but also have mastered a tolerance of frustration so that they can keep at it when the going is rough. Girls, with their easy headstart, fall back because they are no longer developing mentally at such a rate and because they have not learned how to keep going when things are hard. In this view, teaching methods which do not account for the different rates of brain maturity in boys and in girls, give boys a rough ride in early childhood, and leave girls out in the cold in early adolescence.

Other explanations convincingly show the masculine ways in which maths and sciences are taught, and how more feminine examples in problems invite stronger and better responses from girls.[7] Some common practices in scientific teaching would not appeal to anyone unhappy in highly competitive situations: many women are turned off by competitive teaching methods which involve students racing to solve problems; even women scientists seem to show more initiative in the laboratory when working with women than they show when working with men.[8] More subtly, it has been suggested that in adolescence girls notice that their way of thinking and seeing is not the accepted way, the way acknowledged by academic authority and by the male dominant culture; so their own voices go 'underground' as they silence the thoughts that they are rapidly learning are unacceptable. With this silencing goes a plummeting in self-esteem, self-confidence and achievement.[9]

It is at this stage that important decisions are being made about a girl's future, and it is at this stage that girls' and boys' visions of their futures tend to diverge completely: boys see their working futures, girls see their domestic ones – at least this is what has been found,[10] among children 11 to 15. It seems especially hard, too, to bolster the self-confidence of girls. When they do well – in an exam, or a school task – they are far more likely than boys to say that they have done well because the task was easy, or they were lucky, or the teacher happened to feel kindly towards them. In attributing their success to ease or luck, their success does not indicate to them they are capable, or intelligent or talented – and hence their success does not lead to self-confidence. Boys, however, are far more likely to say that they did well because they are clever or able. Hence for boys success is more likely to foster self-confidence. Similar differences have been found to persist between women and men scientists. In a study of authors of frequently-cited scientific papers the psychologist Helen Astin found that men tend to credit themselves with motivating research whereas women credit others. Astin believes that women fail to see the connection between their ability and their achievement because others are far less likely to praise their achievements.[11] Instead of giving credit where credit is due, they may follow others' practice of giving credit elsewhere.

Times are changing, and more girls expect they will work; but this expectation is not enough to see them through, for as they expect to work they also seem to minimize the demands domesticity will make upon their time, and they minimize the forces against them in the workplace – forces which are as often embedded as overt, due not to clear malevolence or intent, but to the persistent structure of employment and family life. Girls' achievement orientation is supposed to be made or broken before they become adults. But women's lives, with their zigzag courses, have many setbacks and many second chances. Women are far less susceptible to burn out in middle age than are men,[12] yet women's plans often go awry. In fact, it is impossible to predict, in early adulthood, who among women will sustain a career track throughout adulthood and who will not.

170

Success and Punishment

Success is something we normally think is desirable. We are expected to aim for it, and welcome it. But few things in life, even simple goods and goals, are straightforward. We perceive our environment, and the opportunities or impediments it presents, in many different ways, and see aspects of good things that make them seem, to us, not so good.

For example, what if we think that we are bound to fail? What if we see the goal as good, but are certain we will not reach it? Not only does the attempt then seem futile, but it also incurs other costs. We will be seen (by ourselves and others) to have tried and failed. We may avoid loss in self-esteem (and 'save face') by not trying, because we therefore avoid putting ourselves in positions in which we are seen to fail. By not trying we protect – or see ourselves as protecting – ourselves from humiliation and disappointment. Failure is so unpleasant that we would rather not try, because by refusing to make the attempt, we avoid confronting the experience of failure.

This strategy among people who strangely refuse to make the last-ditch effort has been found among men and women alike. There are many variations of this strategy, wherein distorted perspective seeks both to ensure and excuse failure. Sometimes one can try, but so half-heartedly that the attempt is clearly meant to fall short of its apparent aim. Sometimes a person develops a deliberate handicap, so that this can be blamed for failure. If a person, confronting failure in a career, begins to drink heavily, then whatever failure he or she goes on to experience is likely to be attributed to alcohol. A handicap is sought which will excuse failure, but this means of establishing an 'alibi' for one's true talents is of course self-defeating because it makes failure inevitable. Or, someone may believe that he does not deserve success, and so trips himself up. Guilt twists efforts into knots, and failure is greeted with relief, just as success would be greeted with anxiety at having got more than was deserved. Success is avoided because it would disturb one's conscience.

The motive to succeed clashes with the motive to avoid failure. People who want very much to avoid failure will avoid situations in which failure is likely – or even possible. But of course where success is possible, failure is possible, and so people who are orientated by a fear of failure will avoid the types of careers and efforts which are constantly evaluated and tested for success (and failure).[13] They will be less successful, because they are determined to avoid failure.

Fear of Success

But something a little different, and more puzzling, has been observed in some women, which could not be seen as fear of failure, or self-defeat or self-punishment, but straightforward fear of success. How could anyone make sense of that?

In 1969 the Harvard psychologist Matina Horner reported the results of her research on fear of, or anxiety about success among bright, high-achieving women.[14] The research project was triggered by her observation that in certain situations in which achievement is measured, and measured in a graded, competitive way, women became anxious far more often and more easily than did men. She tried to track and measure these differences by asking a group of men to complete a story which began 'At the end of first term finals, John finds himself at the top of his medical school class'. She also asked a group of women to complete a story which began: 'At the end of first term finals, Anne finds herself at the top of her medical school class.'

The men's stories were fairly predictable, or at least unremarkable. In their allotted four minutes the men described happiness and career success, self-satisfaction and a sense of earned achievement. 'John is a conscientious young man who worked hard,' was the uninspired comment of one subject. Another explained, 'John has always wanted to go into medicine and is very dedicated . . . . He continues working hard and eventually graduates at the top of his class.' Coming top of one's medical school class was a simple good thing, indicating hard work done and its rewards.

The women's stories, in contrast, contained bizarre references to unhappiness, anger and rejection. 'Anne starts proclaiming her surprise and joy', one story read. 'Her fellow classmates are so disgusted with her behaviour that they jump on her in a body and beat her. She is maimed for life.' The imagery was often violent, though descriptions of physical harm were not as common as those of social and personal rejection: 'Anne is an acne-faced bookworm. She runs to the bulletin board and finds she's at the top. As usual she smarts off. A chorus of groans is the rest of the class's reply . . .'. Some stories suggested that this first-term success threatened future happiness, and evasive action should be taken: 'Anne no longer feels certain she wants to be a doctor . . . she decides not to continue with her medical work but to take courses which have a deeper personal meaning for her.' In some instances, Anne's success was simply denied: one woman's story suggested that it was not Anne but her boyfriend who had come top of the class, and another said that 'Anne' was the code name for a non-existent person constructed by medical students who took turns writing exams for 'Anne'.

The difference in results was astounding. A full 65 per cent of the women in Horner's study exhibited what could easily be coded as 'fear of success' imagery, or ideas which signalled a negative response to 'Anne's' success, in contrast to 10 per cent of the men. But these were after all, only stories, and it had yet to be shown that there was any indication that these peculiar narratives had any bearing whatsoever on how either men or women behaved. So Horner went on to see whether there was any relation between the use of fear-of-success imagery in the written stories and actual behaviour which reflected this. Were women more inclined to avoid success than were men?

Indeed, women who showed marked fear of success imagery in the stories they told about Anne's success did get lower scores on activities they were asked to perform in a competitive setting – especially when they were tested with men. They could not achieve a good score when they were told that their performance would be graded against others who were working alongside them; but they were able to do much better when they were alone. Yet the women in Horner's study who in their own lives had the highest goals expressed no violence towards 'Anne' and her good exam result. Instead, having less to envy, perhaps, they had less to fear. More in touch with their own expansive needs they did not resent the expression of those aims in other women. Horner concluded that 'femininity and individual achievements which reflect intellectual competence or leadership potential are desirable but mutually exclusive goals'.[15] Women believed they could not be achievers, while remaining acceptable to others.

When these results were published in *Psychology Today* under the title 'Fail! Bright Woman' it seemed as though a bombshell had fallen on women's call for equality. It was women themselves who sabotaged their chances, and women who kept themselves back. But this leaps over a lot of bumpy ground. If women do find femininity incompatible with a wide range of individual achievement, then they recognize this incompatibility in the context of their social realities. They may be accurately measuring the costs of success to them, and to others.

Yet some groups of women are more resistant to this type of conflict. Fear of success is not found in all women, and not found in uniform rates among different classes, types and races of women. African-American women showed less evidence of fear of success than did African-American men. Perhaps these women have had the dubious advantage of learning that they cannot expect to depend on other people to finance themselves and their children, and that other people – at least those in the wide world of work – do not tend to see them as 'nice' and 'harmless'. The double jeopardy of being black and being a woman may make them stronger, more positive – and less afraid of sanctions against success. African-American men, on the other hand, may fear success because success will make them different from their peers, because they may have more to lose by playing the dominant race's rules for success. But more recent studies show that Caucasian middle-class men too are more frequently displaying fear-of-success imagery as they are learning to see the costs of success. Men, too, fear being alone; they fear missing out on the good things of a good personal life, and of being bereft of their children's childhood.

'Failure' is a Nice Girl

The impulse to be nice rather than sharp and intelligent was caught off guard by Virginia Woolf as she began writing reviews. She experienced a constraint as she began to write. After some reflection on this impediment between herself and her writing, she discovered that she 'should need to do battle with a certain phantom'. Woolf named this phantom 'The Angel in the House' – a representation of the sweetly accommodating, selfless feminine servant who brightens the homes of men and is forever at their bidding, forever transfixed by admiration. In a metaphor describing her deliberate determination she turns upon this phantom and 'catches her by the throat'. Woolf explains, 'Had I not killed her she would have killed me. She would have plucked the heart out of my writing.'[16]

Reviewing books involves many success-oriented poses. It involves taking a stand, having a say, speaking with authority and judgement, and therefore may involve a critical (not nice) voice, a separate (not connected) response. All these involve what women see as power, and power of a kind women often feel they lack. But what Woolf's description of her strengthening voice and determination show is not only the impulse to succumb to the angel in the house, but also the ability to throttle it. This is a tendency, a habit, rather than a fixed characteristic, and women are increasing their ability to overcome it.

Success Reconsidered

The image of femininity which has haunted this generation of women as they try to balance their needs and change the patterns which make balance so difficult, is one of trying to please, being careful to be nice, to be liked, to be accepted. Women have set themselves the task of reeducating, resocializing and rethinking themselves. This task, initially, may have made some women suspicious of all traditional female roles and characteristics; but the real difficulty lies in sifting the good bits from various female roles and responses and putting these together in new ways.

Fear of success is not purely negative, and what sometimes looks like a self-inflicted failure may well reveal an intelligent, reasoned, honest choice. The repudiation of Anne's success may have been a rejection not of effort and achievement, but of the trappings in which it was displayed: the publicly-displayed list of examination results, the emphasis on achievement as doing better than others, the definition of 'Anne' as 'coming top' of the class – rather than having done something skilful or useful, or having made some contribution – may have been implicitly criticized in those bizarre answers.[17]

Women are changing. Far fewer women now do seem to exhibit fear of success in any psychological study that has been done recently.[18] Changes in trends like this often invite concern. Have women worked for equality in their careers only to adapt to men's terms, and to adopt less attractive male traits? Have they adapted to male, aggressive, competitive strategies? Are they learning to be ambitious like men only to lose the good they had as women? The connectedness, the ethic of care, the tendency to nurture – are these all now to be left behind as women value their careers, and value themselves according to success in their careers?

Nearly 20 years after exposing the feminine mystique which controlled and limited women, making them into 'contented' housewives who were prone to depression and boredom and low self-esteem, Betty Friedan made a plea in *The Second Stage* for recovering and reaffirming the values women have traditionally held and exhibited and represented. For one consequence of feminism did seem to be that women's traditional roles were devalued – that a worthwhile life could no longer be seen as wife, mother and community worker. Change always triggers doubts and fears, along with the question: what other changes will accompany this change? And in questioning the 'damage' that might be done to the home and to children, women's own health also seems vulnerable. Does not the stress of being ambitious in a man's world damage women in new ways? Researchers at the Institute of Psychiatry in London have found that working women in the Home Office drink more with each step up the career ladder. Those who entered the Home Office as executive officers drank an average of eleven units of alcohol a week. Six years later eight of the women who had not yet been promoted drank only seven units a week, whereas those who been promoted (two steps up) to executive office level drank almost twenty units a week.[19] Whatever this finding may mean, it is seen as a danger signal, a warning to women of the costs of promotion.

Along with the increase in alcohol-related problems is thought to be an increase in other previously male-dominated diseases such as heart-attacks and ulcers. There have also been predictions that the rate of violent crime among women might increase. On a more common plane, it is feared that women, once victims of male aggression, are now gaining and maintaining status by identifying with their aggressors. 'We have entered the male kingdom – and yet we have been forced to play by the king's rules', Suzanne Gordon declares as she sees successful women trapped 'in gilded cages – unhappy with their lot but too fearful of losing what they've gained for the promise of a richer life or the fulfilment of a common morality'.[20]

As in many aspects of women's lives, each advance has a twist. Some women reach a compromise between the notion that they should not be competitive and ambitious, with the knowledge that they are ambitious, by redefining, and honing the term 'ambition' with its implications of ruthlessness: 'I'm ambitious, yes, but I don't like it being said about me that I am tough'; 'I'm ambitious for my project, but not for myself'; 'I'm ambitious, but not manipulative'. These redefinitions, which may sound like face-saving devices to maintain a feminine guise and yet do what one wants, are actually enacted in the decisions women make in the course of their careers. Interviews with women managers and with midlife women undergoing career changes show that they constantly reassess their goals in light of the personal costs of pursuing their goals.[21] They seek ways of fulfilling their achievement goals without being in every sense of the word 'ambitious' or 'competitive'.

Some of what has been seen as 'backlash' culture – or attempts by the dominant culture to stall women's advance at work – has really been expressing anxiety about what women will lose as they overcome that 'fear of success' to gain 'courage' to behave like ambitious men. The character Faye Dunaway played in the film *Network* was successful, ambitious, and therefore mean and lonely. The obsessed pregnant lover in the film *Fatal Attraction* has been rewritten as an independent woman punished by the failure of 'feminine social clock pattern'[22] which gives priority to family formations. In giving priority to her independence she becomes a psychospinster preying on more traditional women's husbands.[23] These anxieties obscure the real question virtually every woman asks: How can I succeed as myself?

Once I believed that a woman's success hinged on issues of true and false independence – how some young women seemed determined and dedicated, yet their ambition eroded as they married and had children. This labelling strongly suggested that some character flaw made the difference. I no longer believe that this tells a coherent story. Many young women are fierce in their determination to combine motherhood and a career. Surprisingly, many of these women, having fought all these battles – of fatigue, of domestic management, of marital stress, of maternal guilt – decided in midlife to cut down or pull back or change direction, as they criticize their lives for a lack of balance.[24] The unpredictability of women's career lives cannot be explained by an internal flaw, but by the contexts in which they make decisions.

When we look at women's 'failure', or what may appear as fear of success, we are really looking at compromises and negotiations among desires. Both in the refusal to perform under highly competitive circumstances and the rejection of notions of success in terms of coming top of a pecking order may be a symptom of sound judgement rather than fear of success. The demands of marriage and children may be chosen over unwholesome conditions at work, though these demands do not necessarily make women less productive. Women with children are frequently observed to produce as much and publish as much – even in the still heavily male-dominated sciences – as women who are not mothers.[25] But they are still held back by competitive culture in the workplace.

In the 'failure' to keep on career track, and in the 'failure' to thrive in competitive corporate conditions, or in masculine corporate cultures wherein women are seen as outsiders, women are refusing to buy into certain means of gaining certain ends.

Victims and Agents

The question as to whether women fear success may be a bogus one. Women avoid success as they judge its consequences to be punishing, costly or worthless. Fear of success involves a judged decision, and a compromise, rather than self-sabotage.

Yet, in making decisions which demand frequent and repetitive compromises, women do feel frustrated. We feel frustrated too as we sense ourselves working within a constraining system rather than empowered by self-determination. The circumstances in which people act, and make choices, often seem to take away the power of choice. When we feel the enormous weight of social and political influence, we sometimes see ourselves as oppressed. Sometimes oppression is really a metaphor; sometimes it is literal. Sometimes we feel it immediately and experience it directly; sometimes we realize it through various descriptions of our actions. As we tread the tricky path between constraint and choice, as we interact with a society which influences and informs our behaviour, as we feel ourselves to be agents acting, we are also bound by social realities. What we must do to escape frustrating systems is to see how they affect us, how we respond to them – and indeed how we collude with them. This understanding may then empower us. For we are part of those systems which disadvantage us.

Seeing how women are contributing to the system which they want to change does not involve blaming them: it involves understanding how structures work. This is different from spotting the flaw within them – like hidden needs for dependency or fears of success which have previously been thought to 'explain' their slow progress towards equality. It points to circuits and feedbacks and actions which maintain or inhibit, rather than to perpetrators.

Choice has both voluntary and structured aspects; choices are made in circumstances we ourselves do not choose. The outcomes of choices are not fully predictable; consequences accumulate and interact with one another. We have to be aware of both aspects of choice, to make sense both of ourselves as agents, as people who make choices and decisions, and as people living amid conditions which are 'ruled' by institutions, assumptions, laws and expectations. In this way, we can make sense of our feelings of constraint, and our awareness of our power.

When Vaclav Havel wrote, in 'The Power of the Powerless', 'individuals confirm the system, fulfil the system, are the system',[26] he was trying both to redeem an oppressed people's self-esteem and to mobilize them. By insisting that they colluded with their oppressors to maintain the oppressive structure, he was showing that they could take control and could take power. By seeing the constraints upon them in alternative ways, they could gain power; they could alter expectations and action would follow. The work towards women's equality requires a similar persuasiveness. Women need to understand the constraints against them, and to recognise their power to change.

For the 'powerless' reinforce the oppressive system if they do not actively reject it, because they act in accord with it. This new view of power grants us agency. When women refuse to deny what they have seen and what they know, they free themselves individually of complicity in such a system. Together they can destabilize apparently impregnable power. Ways of seeing become ways of gaining power.

Systemic Examples

Women can often be seen to sustain the patterns that constrain them. How the powerful and the powerless take part in circuits of power is a frequent theme in literature and film which explore women's collusion, as the 'powerless' render effective the power of others. As women accept the rules of a patriarchal society, they constrain – even cripple – their daughters, 'in the daughter's best interests'; for they know the dangers in wait for women and try to protect their daughters who, they believe, must live within the endangering patriarchal structures. In Emily Prager's story *A Visit from the Footbinder* a young girl is subject to pain and disfigurement by the mother and aunt who love her. Keeping the men of the house away because they should not know of such things, they invite the footbinder to break the arches of the girl's feet and bind them back because they believe that only a tiny foot, the mark of privilege, can attract a superior husband. The dangers of insecurity – penury, prostitution, slavery – lurk all too near for women in societies where patriarchy and privilege are interwoven. The mother who believes that her daughter needs a good husband to avoid these ills and that a good husband will only be had by a footbound daughter, puts her daughter through this suffering for what she sees as her daughter's good. The footbinding practice, so often perceived as male power inflicted on women, is here shown as a practice in which women increase constraints in their attempts to protect themselves against their worst effects. A complete change of mind-set, perhaps requiring circumstances of upheaval, may be required to enable women to see their role in sustaining these constraints, and hence their power to change them.

In the 1991 Chinese film directed by Zhang Yimou, *Raise the Red Lantern*, one wife introduces her child to her husband's new wife as 'a girl – how useless', thus accepting the patriarchy which oppresses her. Believing that power lies with men, she plots against other women who threaten her attachment to a man, rather than plotting alongside women to take their own power. In failing to see how male power is supported by her belief in it, she reinforces men's power, and loses her sanity and integrity.

Far more simple examples show women working within constraints and sustaining those constraints. In trying to understand how inequality is stabilized, industrial sociologist Elizabeth Garnsey gives an example of the ways in which both the woman and her employer mutually reinforce the status quo. The 'powerless' woman gives feedback to the 'powerful' employer, as she fulfils his expectations and makes choices within her minimal opportunities. When an employer running a printing press recruits a woman to a job as an 'unskilled bookbinder', Garnsey explains, offering the market rate for the job, this is normally viewed as an exchange freely entered into by both parties. But the employer has combined the range of tasks called for in the production process of the printing works in such a way as to create a bookbinding job which is designed for a worker drawn from a specific social background. The hours of work, the labelling of the skill, the combination of particular tasks, the exclusion of other tasks of machine operation – all these (as well as the implicit expectations of the employer) imply that the work is destined for a certain category of unqualified married woman living locally. The woman in turn is not seeking work further afield because of her conception of her family responsibilities. Her choices can only be understood in relation to her role in the household as a social system in which there is a domestic division of labour and earnings are pooled. She may have other qualifications for which no employment is available, or which is compatible with her child care duties. She settles for unskilled bookbinding because she needs to contribute income to the household and so fails to improve her qualifications which might enhance her future bargaining position. 'The norms of the community, the power of the employer, the dependence of the woman have set the stage within which the market mechanism can be seen to operate as promoting exchange, but in a highly structured setting'.[27]

In this example what emerges is how the two open systems of the family and the market interact and 'give rise to and maintain persisting patterns of segregation and pay disparity'. But if social institutions are so closely interconnected and mutually reinforcing of power and disadvantage, Garnsey asks,[28] how can human agents effect change in their own institutions?

Though the micro-expressions of attitude and power help maintain and reproduce social forms, these relations are not fully determining in human society. We are able to reflect upon the systems which our own actions and those of our fellows maintain and reproduce throughout our day-to-day actions. We are able to see, to judge and to change. A social system is reproduced by the day-to-day actions of its participants, and it can be transformed by individual, day-to-day behaviour. We can see scope for purposeful change alongside the natural trend towards continuity. As we change our understanding of what we are doing, as we change our outlook, we may, together, change the power relations in the wider society through influence of public opinion and legislation.

But the changes are gradual, and often discouraging for the

individual. There is a difference between changing something when one can see some effect of one's efforts (even if they are unsuccessful) and refusing to 'join' a structure when the only effect is to miss out. The woman who refuses to apply for a part-time job that make assumptions about (and hence 'exploits') her immobility and domestic responsibilities, finds that some-one else applies for it and someone else is given the job. For some actions, individual acts will only count when there are many of them. To move forward, women and men will have to move together. Yet from this perspective we can see that power is not a commodity to be owned, seized or exerted, but some-thing which emerges through relationships with others. Anyone within that relationship has power to change it.[29]

7
Depression: A Female Ailment?

The link between women and mental illness is notoriously problematic. As women's lives change, so does the nature of this link; but however much women's lives change, the link remains strong. Both hysteria and depression are far more common in women than in men. The *Oxford English Dictionary*, in explaining that the origin of the term 'hysteria' is from 'wandering womb', or some unspecified disturbance in the uterus, remarks that 'Women being more liable than men to this disorder, it was originally thought to be due to a disturbance in the uterus' (*OED*). The incidence of depression in women is twice as high as depression in men. Maggie Scarf, researching this puzzling fact, embarked on a book about the problem of women and depression, but then discovered her book was to be simply about women.[1] The story about depression became a story about women.

Depression is usually considered to be an illness. Some failed function, some infection of the soul, causes a condition of which one must be cured by experts, who 'relieve' the patient of these emotional difficulties. To be well is to adapt more or less cheerfully to what is accepted as ordinary life.

Though we view depression as an illness, which often prevents its victim from functioning, and certainly from thriving, in ordinary life, this view raises special questions. Are women more prone to depression because there is something wrong with them, or is there something wrong with the conditions in which they live? Could it be that women's 'normal' conditions are unhealthy conditions? In curing women of depression, do psychological professionals not run the risk of persuading them to adapt to conditions in which they cannot thrive? For perhaps depression is a rational, reasonable response to the constraints women face and the manipulations they experience as they buck those restraints. Perhaps depressed women are working towards health as they protest against 'normal' functioning.

Research into depressed women reveals common facts and failings in ordinary women's lives. It also seems to be an ordinary part of ordinary women's lives. In a classic study of depression among urban women, Brown and Harris found that a third of all women could either be classified clinically as suffering from a psychiatric disorder, or as borderline in terms of accepted clinical criteria.[2] Why was depression so widespread among women? Were doctors simply more likely to call them depressed? Were women genetically more prone to it? Was their experience more likely to stimulate it?

What is Depression?

Depression is different from unhappiness. It is different from anxiety, frustration or anger. These are emotions which focus on a problem that can be named. We are unhappy about a boss's behaviour or our failure to be promoted. We are unhappy with the pressures upon us or on other family members. We are unhappy about a child's performance at school. Or, more generally, we are unhappy in a marriage that involves recriminations and quarrels. We are anxious about the outcome of an application. We are frustrated with a job in which we cannot achieve our goals. On a day to day basis we face problems that make us feel less than happy, but we deal with these as part of the rough and tumble of life. These are all very different from depression.

Unhappiness about specific issues can become more generalized. It spreads out from a problem and hangs like a cloud over our lives. It colours our mood and our outlook. We may be so concerned about something that we cannot concentrate on anything else. But this is still a problem-focused issue, and however unpleasant it is, it is not an illness, but confrontation with a real difficulty which we can name. Sometimes we have moods, however, which cannot be so simply defined. We feel 'down' or 'blue' or simply sad. But these usually pass. We can help them pass. We can cheer ourselves up with a good film or a favourite meal, or distract ourselves with exercise. Hence we control our feelings, at least to some extent, and learn how to pass in and out of such moods. We continue to function well enough. The normal framework of our day still hangs in place. We can 'cope', we can manage. Things keep ticking over until the mood passes.

The depressed person, however, does not simply feel down or blue or sad. She suffers profound disruption in the normal rhythms of her life – in eating, sleeping, sexual activity and concentration. She may want to sleep all the time to escape stress and awareness, by avoiding all stimulation, by seeking the simple comforts of a stupor. Or, she may be too anxious, too 'up tight' to sleep, and pace through the city streets at night. She may fall asleep regularly, but awake in the dark mornings, where she confronts the cold isolation of her impasse. Some women, when depressed, cannot eat; the activity seems grossly physical and revolting; other women eat constantly, seeking the comfort and distraction of food. Whereas one woman may feel that she does not deserve nourishment, another woman may take vicious delight in her weight gain, wanting to show the ungainly person she sees lurking inside her. Usually depressed people lack interest in sex, though for some women physical contact and stimulation offer temporary relief and support. 'The problem with that', one woman explained to me, 'is how awful I feel afterwards, coming back to this locked cupboard I live in.'

Depression is characterised by loss of energy. One feels sluggish and enervated because one sees no point to action. Whereas
the person who is unhappy about something knows what to
change and has some idea of what might make her happy, or at
least relieve her unhappiness, the depressed person can barely
envisage circumstances that would improve her condition. For
the depressed person sees not so much the world, but her self at
fault. For her, the 'way out', the 'solution' is usually seen as
death. Dead, she will no longer have to suffer and endure this
hopeless, changeless, endless emptiness. This 'logic' is usually
not directly confronted, because in depression thoughts become slow and confused. Recurrent thoughts of death or suicide, recurrent self-reproaches and self-mocking, pass in and
out of one's mind, like kites that are flown by someone else, at
whose strings one grabs for mere convenience. In this state of
despair, the depressed person is rarely seriously aggressive. She
may shout at her children, but these efforts push her to tears
rather than blows: the shouting hurts her more than her children. She may throw china and glass, but aims at a wall rather
than people, and finds a bemused horror rather than vindica-
tion from her release. The depressed person is not aggressive
because, on the whole, she sees no point in attacking anyone
else. She sees the fault as hers, as lying within her crippled soul.
She sees herself as the rightful victim of her own anger.

Women's Illness

To see depression as a woman's disease, and to see depressed
women as having some relevance to women's general condition, involves far more than noting its more frequent occurrence among women than among men. What does this variation
mean? Does the difference indicate a different response to the
same feelings: do men become violent when angry or frustrated,
while women become depressed? Does it indicate a difference
in how women are seen: are other people more likely to describe women as depressed than they are likely to describe men
as depressed? Does it indicate a difference in how women begin
to deal with their feelings: are women likely to seek expert help
for problematic feelings more readily than do men, and so put

themselves in the position of being diagnosed as depressed more than men do? Or do women actually experience depressed feelings and exhibit depressed symptoms more commonly than do men? If so, what does this mean? Why are they more likely to suffer this condition? Is it genetic, carried by an X chromosome, of which women have two and men one, thus making women genetically twice as likely to suffer depression as men, with their single X, and single Y chromosomes? Does women's psychology, with that connected sense of self, make them more vulnerable to depression, as relationships change and weaken, and are lost? Or do doctors treat women for depression more readily and more drastically? Seeing women as more emotionally volatile and dependent, do they assume that women require chemical, drug-induced help in sustaining a mature adult life? Does drug treatment then lead to further problems, presenting further impediments to self-esteem and self-direction which might make depression a passing mood rather than a debilitating illness? Or does women's inability to 'adjust' to life indicate some flaw within the conditions they are supposed to adjust to?

In her book on women's madness Dr Jane Ussher asks whether 'women's madness' is misogyny or mental illness – whether women are controlled and rejected by this term, or whether women actually experience an illness which itself requires medical treatment. This question has been asked repeatedly during the past fifteen years, as women have become more aware of the constraints upon them, and as they have asked themselves how they must change both themselves and the social conditions in which they live. But what is so striking about Ussher's account is that in the first two pages she narrates the experience of women's depression from all these angles – a position she then goes on to justify in a more scholarly fashion in the rest of the book. And like so many women of today trying to understand women's experience, the life she draws on is her mother's.

'When I was an adolescent my mother was mad', Ussher writes, and throws us into the world of women's madness which in her mother's case was 'termed depression'.[3] After a laconic list of the common symptoms ('Sometimes she cried. Sometimes she was angry . . . She didn't eat a lot.') Ussher's child's view combines with the now adult psychologist's. She recalls how she and her siblings were delighted by the absurdity of their mother going out into the garden to throw 'cracked cups and saucers set aside specifically for this purpose.' There was both relief – for this potty garden party was preferable to the mother's tears – and, eventually, shame, when the mother was hospitalized after a suicide attempt, and they 'weren't allowed to tell our friends, or our relatives and we didn't talk about it ourselves'. The experts 'cured' her mother when she was in hospital with ECT (Electro-convulsive Therapy, better known as shock treatment) and a cocktail of drugs that made her forget everything – her pain as well as her children's names.

Though today Ussher's mother is 'healthy, happy and independent', the adolescent witnessing of her mother's 'madness' and of the medical establishment's crude treatments marked out her future career. First, was the loyal conviction that her mother was *not* mad, and second was the awareness that the anger, pain and despair which had been diagnosed as madness, were shared by many women, especially those 'trapped in unhappy marriages, isolated, lonely, with young, demanding children, no money and no friends'.[4]

These, indeed, were the conditions that Brown and Harris's startling study uncovered. They found depression in women extremely common, and they found much of it hidden. Half of the women whose symptoms and outlook clearly defined a psychiatric disorder were not being treated for it, and two-thirds of those who were assessed as borderline – at the very edge of clinical depression – had not even brought their symptoms to the attention of a doctor. And because depression among housewives was found to be so common, it was reasonably supposed that being a housewife made one – anyone – depressed. Women were more prone to depression because women were far more likely than men to be housewives.

Four things in particular make women more likely than others to be depressed: first, having three or more children at home under the age of 14; second, lacking a close, open relationship with a spouse or other adult; third, the loss of one's own mother before the age of 11; and fourth, not having employment outside the home. Only among one group of men was the incidence of depression nearly as high as in women, and these men were unemployed. Women who were poor were far more likely to be depressed than women who were not (23 per cent of the working-class sample were depressed as opposed to 6 per cent of the middle-class sample of women). Depression could no longer be seen as a simple genetic tendency in women, or a product of female hormones. Even depression after childbirth, which still (described as 'post-natal depression') is thought to be caused by hormonal changes, or some 'internal breakdown',[5] can easily be seen as a response to new routines, extreme demands, and implacable constraints. It now is thought that the hormones which are secreted by depressed people are secreted *because* those people are depressed. Depression, whatever else it is, and however else it may be described, is a response to the social conditions in which someone lives, to stress they experience, to lack of support and to past grief.

What now probably seems like common sense was, less than 15 years ago, a startling result. It seems reasonable enough that someone who is poor, lonely, stressed, and confined should react by becoming depressed; but this was not observed because women's lives were not understood in those terms.

Mastering the Treatment

As Jane Ussher linked her mother's depression to the common experiences of being a woman, she determined that she would escape the 'common fate' of a dead-end job and an early marriage. Like many women committed to professional success, she saw her adult task as one of rewriting the feminine script she as a child looking at her mother had learned would be hers. She would escape the feminine lot through education and professionalism. She would escape dependency through mastery. But she found as she mastered clinical psychology, that she was helping women like her mother 'adjust' to the roles which had given rise to their depression. The task of the therapist, whether clinical psychologist or general practitioner, is to help the patient 'readjust' to their roles – usually to their domestic role.[6]

Depression: A Female Ailment?

Therapy may not cure depression, but offer a further means of controlling women so that their depression is contained, while they continue in their minimal roles. In a study of people taking Valium – a common tranquillizer, or psychotropic drug – it was found that this was prescribed to help people tolerate roles they 'found difficult or intolerable without the drug'. This drug would assist women not in changing their roles, but in adjusting to them. A mother of four teenage children explained why she felt she needed this drug: 'I take it to protect the family from my irritability', she said. She saw her children as 'normal' and herself as yelling at them 'because their normal activity is bothering me'. She went on to say that the Valium kept her calm and 'That's what my husband wants . . .'. She also believed that one day she would leave them, and perhaps then no longer need Valium.[7]

Why didn't she leave now? one is inclined to ask; or if that were too difficult, too complicated, or too drastic, then why did she not change things so that she did not need medication to stay calm? I pose these questions not to persuade someone to answer. I do not pose them in a rhetorical mode either, expecting that no answer is possible. I pose them to indicate a problem many people have in understanding the impasse a depressed person feels. Whereas others may be impatient with the ways a depressed person reinforces her depression with negative thoughts, these recurring negative thoughts are so much a part of the depression that a sufferer cannot simply 'snap out' of them or begin to 'think positive'. If she could do that, she would not be depressed.

As one sees that women who are isolated, lonely and unemployed outside the home tend to be depressed, one may ask why they do not take steps to improve those conditions. The response many people have to a depressed person is, 'Well, why don't you do something about it?' Depressed people often alienate others, further isolating themselves, because of their persistent gloomy outlook which is both unpleasant and, in others' opinion, unnecessary. The depressed person always has some negative response to, 'Well why don't you do something?' This can be irritating and frustrating, leading others to con-

191

clude, 'She wants to be that way.' But the greatest challenge to a depressed person is to learn how to (re)identify the problem, and to see that something (anything) might be done about it.

Learned Helplessness

When a team of psychologists at the University of Pennsylvania were working on learning theories they discovered a strange condition in which animals subjected to series of punishments which they could not avoid, eventually ceased to make any effort to avoid them even when the physical constraints were removed.[8] The excruciating and not very subtle experiment involves two phases. During the first phase a dog, restrained in a harness, is subjected to repeated electric shocks. During the second phase the animal is subjected to the same series of electric shocks, though this time it is not restrained. Normally of course a dog would jump immediately away from the electrified part of the cage and search frantically for a part of the cage which was not electrified. But when a dog who, harnessed, had been subjected to repeated electrical shocks was subjected to same shocks unharnessed, it did not move away and made no attempt to avoid the shock. The psychologists watching the result of their experiment called this condition *learned helplessness*. The dog, having experienced this discomfort while restrained, learned that it could not avoid the shocks. What the first phase of the experiment had taught the animal was that it was helpless, that it could not avoid pain. Having become passive while harnessed, it remains passive while unharnessed. It can only unlearn this helplessness by being dragged to the safe part of the cage.

Further experiments revealed that humans responded to similar conditions in a similar way. Human subjects were presented with noises that they could not control and with problems they could not solve. They then seemed to perceive themselves as unable to control their environment or to understand it in a positive way. They no longer saw themselves as agents, able to act upon and change their circumstances. Even when, subsequently, they were presented with noises they could in practice control and with problems they ordinarily would have been able to solve, they made no attempt to exercise their abilities. Having experienced powerlessness they 'learned' that they were powerless: they therefore lost the power they might have had. Moreover, when the people in these experiments had learned that they were helpless they also became passive, sad, anxious. Their appetite – both for food and sex – was reduced. Their self-esteem decreased – as did their ability to learn. Chemical changes in their bodies, too, were noted – the same chemical changes that have been known to accompany depression.

It was in this way that the link between learned helplessness and depression was drawn, and since then some therapies for depression involve an unlearning of powerlessness. The therapy includes a series of graded tasks which serve to undercut the patient's negative views. It may involve something a simple as proving to the patient that she can, after all, get out of bed: she will be instructed to sit up, then to put her legs over to the side, then to take one step, and then another. Simple techniques, gradually increasing in challenge, are designed to convince the patient that she does after all have the power to act effectively, that she can avoid circumstances that hurt her, that what she does can effect how she lives.

Gaining the Self: How Much Do We Need?

The sense of powerlessness in depression is very much like the loss of interest and aim and energy that is experienced in grief. In mourning someone we have lost, we not only feel loss of the loved person but a loss of interest in everything around us, as though our love for that person provided a direction and energy. In recovering from such a personal loss we gradually are able to link up with outside interests. The central sense of loss may lessen, or it may remain, but 'recovery' involves not so much the obliteration of sad feelings as an ability to engage actively in the world around one.

Depression has a similar structure to mourning. Like mourning, 'melancholia', as depression is sometimes called, is characterized by loss of interest in the world, loss of one's sense of connection to it, loss of goals and direction. The puzzling thing about the similarity between mourning and depression, however, is that in mourning it is clear what or whom one has lost. Depression may set in after what is called an 'exit-type event', or loss of an important relationship, but not in the clear, distinct manner of mourning which is defined as a response to loss.

New perspectives on depression see that it too is a response to loss, but the loss one is mourning is a loss of one's self. In her eloquent and searching book *Unfinished Business: Pressure points in the lives of women,* Maggie Scarf traces the special sense of loss women are prone to at different phases in their lives: the loss of the comfort of parents in early adulthood, the loss of first love, the loss of a husband's love, the loss of children, or the loss of youthful capacity to inspire a certain kind of love as one ages. These losses link up in each individual to earlier, unresolved losses or separations which trigger a fissure in the self that leads to depression. Women, she believes, are more prone to depression because they are more dependent on others for structuring their sense of self. Though Scarf does suggest that women need to protect themselves from their susceptibility to depression by improving their ability to survive on their own emotional resources, her work has been criticized for its emphasis on women's dependence, while their protection from depression is seen as mastery.[9]

Recently, Dana Crawley Jack[10] has built on a somewhat different theory of how women's true voices are submerged – often by the masculine cultures which make one type of discourse more acceptable than women's own,[11] or by the greater power which men often do have in relationships, as they have greater power in the world outside the relationship and greater assurance as to what they want and how to go about getting it. What a depressed woman loses, however, is not actually the self, but a means of expressing and gaining access to her own feelings. She may be so caught up in the question of pleasing others, or accommodating others, or preserving others' goodwill, that she lacks a direct line to her own wishes and needs. The path out of depression then is found by tracing new paths to her own voice.

Finding oneself involves a fine balance between self-discovery and self-creation. We create our daily lives not in isolation, but through our responses and circumstances. The enormous problem women face is having to construct new circumstances while discovering what circumstances suit them. They have to decide what they want to do, fight for it, all the while they evaluate the point and purpose of the struggle. The more research that is done on women and depression, the more it seems that the problem is aligned to the balance of affiliative and expansive needs. Mastery – or the development of expansive needs – is needed to counterbalance the strong dependency that arises from being predominantly (or merely) oriented towards others. It also helps, in our society, to find further paths to self-expression and further ways of exercising mastery. This breaks the financial dependence which women's traditional emotional dependence has traditionally bred.

When cases of depression in men and women are compared, men who are unmarried appear to be at greater risk of depression than unmarried women. Women are particularly good at adapting to being alone – though, irrationally perhaps, they seem to fear it more. Women who are married and work are less prone to depression than married women who are not employed. In fact, there is only one condition under which married men are as prone to depression as married women – and that is when they are unemployed.

Men are thought to be prone to depression when they are unemployed because their identities are linked to their role as breadwinner, but this is not the only problem. Women are today far more aware of the perks of employment than they were twenty years ago. Even women whose identities are not bound up in their work, and who think of employment in terms of a simple job, without tremendous work satisfaction, still understand how the sociability of work, the reprieve from the domestic routine ('a change is as good as a rest') alleviate the restraint and isolation they are likely to feel at home with only children as companions. Many people who feel depressed – perhaps those borderline subjects in the Brown and Harris study – are surprised at how little things can lighten their mood. Achievement in one area can spread like soft butter. The discovery that one can meet a challenge in one area reduces conflict and fear in other areas. A person who stutters, for example, may experience an alleviation of speech difficulties after a successful parachute jump. Personal rejections, previously found humiliating, may be shrugged off after meeting a successful challenge.[12]

Domestic Depression

Housework may be the sort of job which prevents those little successes and triumphs which light up one's day. In Ann Oakley's study of housework[13] she found that three-quarters of women found housework monotonous; 90 per cent complained about its fragmentation – the fact that tasks were never completed, never finally finished, and always being interrupted by another more immediate or urgent task, or a task with more irritable demands. No task required the worker's full attention, and yet no task allowed the worker's attention to be satisfactorily engaged elsewhere. Alongside this endless unsatisfying routine came isolation from adult company and the stress of coping with young children. The 'protected' conditions of housewife were a breeding ground for illness.

The question about marriage, housewifery and women's satisfaction is really a jumble of questions. At the most simple level it is about whether anyone is happier fulfilling one role or one job well, or whether people are happier doing lots of different things, where they will experience different reinforcements, where a disappointment in one area can be mollified by success in another, where they will have a greater chance of feeling successful, and so spreading around the general confidence that success brings. Women have already experienced the drawbacks of limited and confined roles. What they face now are the consequences of limited energy, for they expect themselves to combine many roles which neither women nor men have combined before. They are hence caught with the trick of both deciding which roles they want to keep, and to what degree they want to keep or to change them, at the same time as they work hard to break into roles to which access has previously been denied. They have to discover within themselves several perspectives: they have to discover what is involved in professional success, how to obtain it, how to manage their family lives, what to give up and what to keep, and how to organize the things which still have to be done but which they do not want to do.

It is not surprising in view of this balancing act – which involves a simultaneous discovery of the world outside the home and how one functions in it – that few women had the straightforward career patterns that men typically have. These women followed traditional patterns, side-stepped into a professional world, charged full steam ahead, then took time off, then went back, then changed their jobs. Shadowed by traditional roles and trying out new ones, women still often feel isolated and uncertain of their future. They trade in role-restriction for role-overload. They step out of the breeding ground of depression – but often with only one foot. They often feel angry and frustrated as they remain in the conditions which they intended to leave behind.

Depression: The Newest Models

The stresses of working mothers are complex and piecemeal, and there is always a fight for balance. They want to be fair to their families. They want to succeed at work. They want to be fair to their colleagues and clients or patients. The problem of role scarcity – as the housewife does not have enough challenges and enough variety – quickly becomes one of role-overload, whereby she simply cannot complete all the tasks she sets herself. The stress of the working mother, and the depression that threatens her, is a sense that all this effort is not paying off, that her goals have been somewhat misdirected, her energy misspent.

The most recent studies of women and depression have found that though housewives are still more depressed than working wives, and working wives are still more depressed than working husbands, women who have children and who work part-time are significantly less prone to depression than are married women with children who work full-time.[14] Though it does seem that employed married women experience somewhat less distress than housewives, the presence of dependent children in the household – especially very young children – is stressful, and this stress counteracts the effects of employment.[15] So the good effects of paid employment on women's morale are offset, or undone, by the stresses of young children, so that when a woman has young children in her home, there are – statistically – no positive effects of paid employment. In fact, 'the age of the youngest child is the major factor associated with a woman's mental well-being. Women with children under school age show the highest prevalence of psychiatric symptoms. This effect appears to be exacerbated if they are in paid employment, particularly full-time employment.'[16]

The problems women face which are likely to give rise to depression have changed as the condition of their lives change. The greatest threat to women's well-being is no longer the isolation and tedium of being a housewife. Women are now threatened by the stress of imbalance as they try to love and to work in a society which traditionally separates private and public lives, and which prevents women from doing both, according either to their sense of balance or to others' expectations of them. For employers expect that women must do work equal to men's, while in the home women are expected to do women's work. The stress they face then is not simple overload. The stress persuades a woman that she is failing to come up to standard. It leads to a new sense of isolation as her stress is ignored, or criticized. She may feel puzzled at finding her life so difficult because she does not see how her circumstances make her life so difficult. Or, she may resent others' failure to appreciate the difficulty of her circumstances. Her efforts and her achievements become invisible, and only the wrinkles of her day show.

It is in this context that the ease or the difficulty with which child care can be arranged[17] becomes an obsession, when a nanny's resignation or a child minder's brusque manner loom with metaphysical import. The 'gifts of exchange'[18] which become so important to a woman – her gifts of domestic work, and the exchanges her family offer or deny her – become essential to the quality of her marriage.[19] Her sense of disappointment in marriage is very closely linked to the trivia of dirty dishes and soiled diapers. Does her partner share the work? If not, does he help her? If not, does he appreciate what she does? The demands of very young children at home, the stress of feeling the burden of ultimate responsibility and the stress of care which love breeds, create a psychological world wherein the fabric of one's life depends upon minute, mundane details which from the outside seem insignificant, and from the inside seem momentous.

The emotional and instrumental support of those around her are crucial to her well-being. A husband's instrumental support – his practical involvement with children and the home – takes on a deeper meaning. It gives the domestic and family work a visibility and reality, so that her actual life is not only less stressful in terms of work but also in terms of isolation. Women with high standards and strong goals may be more prone than others to depression,[20] but these women are less at risk when they have husbands who take an equal share in child care. When a woman has young children her husband's participation is important to her sense of a good marriage and to her overall well-being.[21]

Depression arises from confusion as to how to proceed, in not seeing how anything one does will make one's life more reasonable. But a woman's sense of power and her belief that her life is manageable may rest on others' responsiveness. When she feels that she has pushed herself to the limits, it is an enormous boost to discover that those around her are willing to change and respond. When they fail to back her up, she may be not merely disappointed but devastated.

A whole new set of issues about stress and depression are besetting women of today, at different phases of their lives. In young adulthood women often worry that traditional female roles will swamp them, that traditional expectations and traditional feelings will take from them the goals which are so important to their identity. As working mothers the idea of these traditional roles is less strong than the reality of the division of their time between their work and their children, and this time/energy issue spills over into their marriage, as the partner is seen as the potential helper or easer of stress, who may not fulfil his expected role. In midlife women often become disillusioned with the goals that may have driven them to career success. They may feel that they have been successful in another's terms, and are no longer willing to give quite so much towards the goals that once seemed essential. Many of these women are seen to 'drop out', or shift course as they find other ways of achieving once they have modified their goals.

These are the new life phases of the working woman, and each of these carries its own risks of depression.

Depressed Visions

Depression seems to grow out of the destructive ways people view their experiences. It is a response to repeated failures in controlling the reinforcers of one's environment, when one gets no satisfactory response from the significant people and institutions in one's life. It often seems to occur when there is insufficient reciprocity, or confirmation, or positive self-discovery. One's own needs and wishes seem futile, and one no longer acts on them – or, sometimes, one loses contact with them. Failure is the expected outcome, and when failure is expected no effort is made, and so the outcome remains static. Helplessness, once learned, is not confined to the situation in which one learned it, but becomes an outlook on oneself and the conditions in which one lives. Learning helplessness, one concludes that one is not the sort of person who is able to control or influence anything. It is not merely a state – like a state of shock one can snap out of. It becomes a personality trait, a stable pattern of response. As one sees oneself as ineffectual one becomes ineffectual. What might ordinarily reinforce one's sense of agency and power, now fails to have any effect.

A depressed person is likely to say that she did poorly on a test because she is not smart enough, rather than because she did not spend enough time studying. She is more likely to say that a relationship failed because she did something wrong, or because she is not good at maintaining relationships. Instead of managing a failure, as most people do, by seeing it as a specific setback, a depressed person will see it as a general trend. She sees her whole world within a single failure. Her experience of failure reinforces her low self-esteem. Yet she will respond quite differently to a success. This, she is sure, is a stroke of luck. Or perhaps the task was easy, so easy that the success casts no reflection on her ability. The way in which a depressed person perceives both her successes and her failures reinforces her low self-esteem.

The negative self-image which accompanies depression dominates everything else about depression. The sense of loss one feels, the link between depression and mourning, is loss of a positive and active view of the self. This negative view often isolates the depressed person further, as people shy away from such persistent negativism, which the depressed person insists is plausible, and which others know is unhealthy, however 'irrational' healthy optimism may also be.

Those who suffer depression are usually in touch with both their expansive and affiliative needs, but have difficulty in seeing how both can be met. They see themselves as caught up in circumstances they can neither change nor manage. They have low self-esteem – and high standards, which they believe must be met if they are to be acceptable to themselves and to others. Often they feel they are not good enough – that their problems cannot be managed because they themselves are not performing well enough, or cleverly enough, or efficiently enough. They continually strive to be better, hoping that in improving they will come up to their standards and the expectations that they believe others have of them. This approach leads to achievements, but it can be an essentially negative attitude as it leads them, too, to take on too much responsibility. They then blame themselves inappropriately and feel their world falling apart when life, and their own contribution to it, fails to meet their expectations.[22]

A new difficulty arises, then, with the treatment of depression. For it now commonly arises as women try to balance their goals – as they feel the pressure of suppressing their affiliative needs at the behest of their expansive needs, or as they suffer more traditional forms of depression from a suppression of their expansive needs. Self-esteem is enforced not simply by doing a lot, but by managing one's life, and the contemporary version of depression stems from being unable to manage – in circumstances which indeed are often unmanageable.

Clinical work on women and depression often emphasizes the inability to deal with costs and benefits. Once again therapists are expected to help women come to terms with the conflicts and constraints they face in society. Therapists working with women discuss the difficulty of treating patients whose emotional difficulties they try to heal, but whose circumstances they cannot change.[23] The paths through depression for women today often depend on changing their circumstances rather than changing selves.

Changing Outlooks

Depression and the problems that women have with depression, and the continuing questions about how to overcome it and how to treat it, focus those questions raised at the beginning of this book about social structures and women acting in them. They also focus questions about expansive needs and affiliative needs, about mastery and dependency.

Even the best writers and researchers looking into this problem can slip between seeing one aspect of the problem as the ultimate cause, and then another aspect of the problem as pointing to the ultimate solution. One moment the fault lies with women's dependence on others, and the next it seems to lies in the way others perceive her. Hence Ann Oakley said that 'it is the very *sensitivity* of women to other people's needs that is likely to produce the appearance and the consequence of mental instability – women's instability stabilizes the world'; yet in the next sentence she says 'Depression and oppression are thus linked. Feminine hysteria and depression are reflections and projects of a sex-divided society.'[24] There is a slide from saying women's psychology makes them susceptible to depression, to saying women are depressed because they are oppressed, to saying that women are seen as depressed in a society dominated by male values. But this slide from cause to cause, from effect and back to cause, is not the result of poor argument or sloppy thinking. It is part of the strange puzzle that is being considered.

Any description of the conditions under which women are more likely to become depressed can also be explained in terms of their greater sensitivity to others' needs and the greater alacrity of their response to others, their greater sense of being connected to others and their general willingness to suppress expansive needs on behalf of those affiliative needs.

Modern-day depression arises not so much from the restrictions of the traditional role or the difficulty career-oriented women have in 'accepting' or adjusting to traditional roles. Modern-day depression arises from the stress of finding a way to combine very different needs and desires – of wanting to give a great deal to one's work, and wanting to retain what is best in women's lives, and finding that in general career dedication is measured against a gauge of people whose domestic and family lives are serviced by wives.

8
Dressed for Success

The Managerial Woman

That still rare person – the female executive – was first studied when she was very rare indeed. Two people from the Harvard Business School, Margaret Hennig and Anne Jardim, found a consistent family history among those women who had reached top management positions by 1970.[1] She was the oldest daughter, usually in a family with only daughters and no more than three children. She was closer to her father than to her mother, who tended to be a traditional housewife. She either did not marry, or, if she did marry, she married in what would be considered late by a traditional 'feminine social clock'.[2] If she had children, they were not her biological children, but children of the man she married in her mid-thirties.

These similarities were significant, and played similar roles in the development of the different women. As the oldest child, and as a child in a family without sons, she was often given by her father the time and attention that he might otherwise have directed towards a son. Hennig and Jardim noticed how slow women were to see the configurations of a game played, how little experience they had with team sports. When this type of manoeuvre occurred in work, women therefore tended to be out-manoeuvred, and male colleagues were more likely to see women as outsiders simply because they were not team players. The closer association women executives had with their fathers during childhood and adolescence gave them some insight into the male world of games, with its rugged competition, its rapidly organized cooperation, its rough acceptance of wins and losses. But such a tie was not merely instrumental. The close emotional bond with the father changed the developing girl's orientation to gender roles. Feeling more comfortable with the fun her father offered, she was less comfortable with her mother. Judging the mother's vision to be limited and her skills to be minimal, these became a barrier to intimacy.

The vast majority of the generation into which Hennig and Jardim's women were born saw marriage as a necessity, and envisaged a marriageless state as heavily sanctioned. It was seen as a lonely, insecure, even ugly state. The career woman was that by default: she succeeded in a career because she failed in her femininity. Yet what many of these women were to understand later, what they were stimulated to realize, was that this failure in femininity was a success. For the women who played it safe, and bonded with mothers rather than fathers, and learned their mother's rather than their father's skills, were sold a raw deal. What deal were these very different women of the same generation sold? And what deals do the corporate women of today make?

The similarities among executive women, and the differences between executive women and women at large, did not determine success in careers, but paved the way for it. They were not women of the new generation who pursued careers *en masse*, in conditions which purported to be more friendly to women. Instead, they pursued careers in unchanged, blatantly masculine institutions. Their success rested on outlook – on changes in how they saw the world, how they saw themselves, how they became determined agents, fashioning their success in an unprepared and unexpectant society. They described themselves as being trained, and training themselves to think like men in the workplace, and to avoid personal commitments that might undermine their ambitions, or their ability to pursue their goals. Hence, they become like men at work, but developed greater rigidity in their personal life than ambitious men are expected to develop, since they saw personal attachments as threatening rather than supporting them. This avoidance acknowledged the danger of feminine roles. They did not believe that they could have it all: they believed that they could have what they wanted by giving up what other women had. They were modern in deliberately counting the cost of marriage – which women are far more likely to do today than they were in their generation, when marriage seemed both 'natural' and necessary, and where endangering one's chances was an unacceptable risk, both in women's own eyes and in their parents'.

For these women the task was to keep guard on themselves and to change, to learn in more and more detail how to think like men: that was their path to success. They criticized themselves for failing to see the overall picture of their career progress, as an ambitious man would. They criticized themselves for paying too much attention to detail – for fussing over a simple task, rather than learning how to pinch time on one task in order to pursue a more distant goal. They spoke about their triumph over that niggling desire to be 'nice', and their battle against their fear of quarrels and confrontations. They learned to assert themselves without feeling ridiculous. They remoulded their doubts into certainties and their fears into determination. They were the forerunners of the new woman, because they proved that a woman in the male corporate world could be as good as man, and could – at work – be just like a man.

Unexpected Types

In Mary McCarthy's novel *The Group* a somewhat different group of women, of roughly the same generation, is described. These women are very different from each other, but they too hope to become the new woman, as has every generation of women in

America this century. For them the ticket to liberation was education – which they had attained. The book opens one week after Vassar Commencement, with a wedding, but a wedding which is special, different, as the couple forgo a honeymoon and think about work. The different characters who form 'the group' have very different lives in early adulthood – some of them married men with good careers who support them, some of them married men who have to be supported, some of them were unmarried. All of them value their intelligence and see their education as a door to opportunity. But what they all discover, in various ways, is that after the dawn of early adulthood, they have become typical women: they are individuals, with individual worries and disappointments and triumphs and frustrations but they are enacting women's typical lot. They slot into typical feminine positions – as wife afraid of her husband, as mother terrorized by a child's needs, as wife demoralized by her husband's infidelity, as woman ashamed of her confused sexuality. Both author and her characters feel disappointed and puzzled. The author registers things going wrong as men become authoritarian over their wives and children, as women follow careers and find promotions in women's jobs. Education gave these women high self-esteem, high ideals, and high goals. As they set out to fulfil their potential they repeat old patterns. The novel ends with a funeral of the woman who, in the opening scene, was married. There is nothing different about this funeral: it is a 'regular burial in the ground'. A decade on, these once-eager women are now ready to bury the expectation that they can, in their society, be the individuals they had set out to be.

In contrast, Hennig and Jardim's sample were success stories. These women did escape old patterns. Their success was built upon rigid determination and rigid self-education. These pioneering women executives are certainly not to be pitied. They made deliberate, albeit hard choices about what they wanted to achieve and what they were willing to do to achieve it. They deliberately crafted their lives so that they would not be sidetracked or sabotaged – either by others or by themselves. They learned the rules of the game and played them as well as they could. Their lives are success stories. And yet it is difficult, at least for me, not to be angry on their behalf. They fought so thoroughly against the roles and relationships and responses that might put them at risk. They conceived of success in the male fashion. They did not aim to have it all or to do it all, but to have what men had and do what men do – except that because they were women they had to watch themselves more closely, guard themselves more carefully, and give up – at least until midlife – the family life that men had. They assessed the cost accurately, and had few regrets themselves, but it does seem unfair that they had to do all the reshaping work, while the companies in which they became executives remained the same.

New Managerial Women

The managerial world has changed, as has the nature of competition, as has the volume of work, as have corporate structures, since the first women executives were studied. But we still ask why so few women, in spite of business school training and equal opportunity legislation and vastly different outlook and expectation, thrive and succeed in corporate life. As we ask this we have to be sure we are asking the right questions about women's rises, falls and stasis. For corporate organizations have changed – and have to change – in order to survive in very different market conditions. We have to ask whether the changes which organizations have undergone in the last two decades have made it more difficult for women to enter them, survive in them, and thrive in them.

As corporations seek ways of dealing with the competition they now face throughout the world, they find ways of changing to work more efficiently and profitably. In what Rosabeth Moss Kanter calls the 'global corporate Olympics' companies have to seek new means of survival. The leaner and meaner policy of many corporations makes life tough for everyone. It means that employees have to work harder, under greater pressure both from a sense of competition and from a sense of job insecurity. These conditions are precisely the conditions which many women feel unable to work well in. These are precisely the conditions in which their behaviour seems like 'fear of success' as they remain immune to a daggered motivation. As the atmosphere at work becomes highly competitive, the intrinsic pleasures of the job and attention to meeting one's own standards are ignored. It is an atmosphere which can be highly inefficient, as others try to run alongside every other runner, rather than find their own means to their own ends. Women who see themselves as having a choice, cannot see the point.

As companies step up the competitive atmosphere they also step up the working hours. The overworked American does not have time to be the parent she usually wants to be. And the policies of 'doing more with less' lock these longer hours into place. In tandem with 'streamlining' employees, or constantly making employees redundant, has been an enormous proliferation of activity, especially in stock exchanges and financial markets whereby different time zones are accommodated – another symptom of the pressure of global competition and the changing (decreasing) power of American companies. The Chicago Board of Trade recently launched night-time hours to accommodate Japanese interested in US bond futures. As the Japanese trade during their daytime hours, the workers in Chicago lose sleep.[3]

Rosabeth Moss Kanter vividly describes what restructuring feels like for *any* employee of the firm: it can make people feel 'helpless, anxious, startled, embarrassed, dumb, overworked, cynical, hostile or hurt'.[4] Restructuring, which has become necessary for all firms, is not a one-off event, a crisis which then settles, but a continuing processes, shaking the foundations and the past certainties as severely as a divorce may upset a child's vision of adult stability. The effects, which can easily persist for three years, are 'bizarre': 'Some people come to work in an almost catatonic state, starting no new programs; others who have been let go continue to come to the office.'[5] In these conditions everyone feels that membership is in question – and women, as newcomers, as people sensitive to bias, are likely to suffer more from this common threat of exclusion.

Women in corporate life are not simply trying to enter a man's world. They are trying to enter what was previously a male domain, but which is rapidly changing and casting doubt upon men's membership in it too. Everyone's career expectations have changed, and that makes everyone wary of membership. The corporate ladder is no longer as stable as it once was. It also has fewer rungs.[6] A common organizational policy known as 'demassing' eliminates middle management positions, so that there are simply fewer places a woman can climb up from. The new opportunities of women have come up against the narrowing opportunities of corporate men. Hence even as women's position in general may be expanding,[7] it is only the very determined, the willing sacrificers, who remain as competitors in the corporate world.

New Profiles

Recent profiles of managerial women are surprisingly similar to those of the women of two generations before. The female executive who was expected to be representative of the 1980s bears a close resemblance to the exceptional women executives of the 1960s. When Korn/Ferry commissioned research into the life history of senior executive women,[8] it was found, among 600 subjects, that the 'composite woman senior executive' is still the first-born child in her family – though she is not as uniformly as was her predecessor from a family of girls only. She is likely to have one younger sister and one younger brother. Her average work week is 53 hours, which she considers to be comparable to her male colleagues – but, given the way in which structures interlock to women's disadvantage, the home life possible for her male peers is not possible for her. She does not have a 'non-working' wife as her male peer is likely to have. More than half of the women senior executives were unmarried, either because they had never married (28 per cent) or because they were widowed (4 per cent) or because they were divorced (21 per cent), while 95 per cent of their male peers were currently married and had children, and of these between two-thirds and three-quarters had wives at home who did not work. The women who had never married explained that they saw marriage at odds with their career commitments. Those who were divorced or separated said that their career commitment had been an important factor in the breakdown of the marriage.

The newer generation of corporate women was more varied than the women of Hennig and Jardim's sample, none of whom had children biologically their own; yet, still, the majority of women did not have children. And of the 39 per cent who did have children, most took primary responsibility for their children's care. Where a partner did share child care and domestic tasks, the share was never more than half. The partners of these women did not become wives. The women who did share child care and domestic tasks, moreover, put a lot of effort with their partner into minimizing the amount of time this would involve. They had nannies, gardeners and housekeepers and sometimes even personal secretaries to deal with domestic matters. The key to sharing was to minimize the total amount that needed doing by parents. Domestic chores could be shared equally only when the whole was vastly reduced.

Two aspects of this profile of senior executive women's lives remain disturbing. First, their acceptance of what they give up; and second, the way that whatever they achieve in their personal lives, they cut back on family life; and, since few fathers give more time to families than do their wives, this usually means that parental time is cut. Their willingness to do this may be symptomatic of the new work culture: the idea that we are what our job is, that the value of our job is what we earn along with the perks that trail in the wake of a high salary. Have women not fallen prey to the feminist mystique, whereby they put careers first, and either forgo family life, or treat it as an aside?[9] Has women's liberation not led to a devaluation of women's traditional input into future generations, and into the community, and into the home? In the workplace too, are women's traditional jobs in the caring professions not being devalued because they do not offer high-profile platforms for success, because they are not fast-track, because they are not highly paid? Are women losing the best of themselves in the fight for equality, and as they fight for equality have they not mimicked men and made themselves into masculine beings who see themselves as separate, who prove themselves in competitive situations, who shine rather than connect? Have women become prisoners of men's dreams?[10] Should they not transform the world to accommodate their various needs and abilities rather than change themselves to succeed in the man-made world? Have we not heard far too much about how responsiveness and connection are self-defeating, when they are after all, so clearly essential to a society in which people can live comfortably and happily? Has the desire for liberation not minimized the essential task of caring for children, which is after all time-consuming, which does require labour as well as love, which does require a great quantity of time which cannot be substituted for some desperate fiction of quality time? Have these women misconceived success, thinking that their personal rise in a corporation or profession is a political good for women, whereas in reality it puts personal above the collective good? In aiming for equality with men, are they not contributing to the devaluation of women?

The managerial women I interviewed for this study, and the managerial women whose voices are emerging from other studies[11] are very different from the executive women who were tracked earlier. The women I spoke to – and here, to get my numbers up, to avoid too small a sample, I spoke to non-mothering women as well as women who had children – were aware that to succeed they had to learn some of the dominant culture's games of corporate life. They had to adapt to men's rules in order to be equal; but they also saw that these rules were not, quite, written in stone, and they were determined to use them as a tool kit, from which to pick and choose, to use in one case and discard in another, to use but only after modification.

When I first interviewed Sandra Gillginham she was a vice-president of a commercial New York bank. We spoke about the practical problems she had when she started work, how much help she had from her husband – from whom she was now divorced. She spoke about control, about how many of her friends were in one or other stage of divorce but seemed lost and frightened, whereas she felt in greater control after the divorce, when life once again, with her two sons, became simple. So the story I told about her – what was meant to be her story – in the 1985 study *Why Women Don't Have Wives*, was about domestic organization, about the tension between her success and her increasing impatience with what she saw as her husband's weak will. When I contacted her again a decade later, her story about stresses and impediments was very different.

The issues behind the practical and organization difficulties were more clear to her, and the energy that she had so generously exuded during the first interview sessions was now redescribed as 'a kind of manic bravado'.

'It's hard to admit while you're going through with everything just how hard it is. Say you've just had a baby and people ask you how you are, and you say. "Fine, everything's fine" and you say that because you managed to get a few hours' unbroken sleep and the woman who comes in to help you is pretty regular, pretty reliable, and you think you can get through the next few weeks all right. You say things are fine because you know things are going to be tough, but you feel you're managing. Well, I knew that working my way up and staying up as Vice-President was not going to be easy. So the fact that I was doing it and was more or less holding my ground, was pretty good. You get used to being divided. I mean when I look back now I see how much I hated some things, but didn't think of it at the time as hating it, just learning how things were. There was that aspect that we focused on when we last talked. Kids and work and how you managed. But there's a deeper level of managing, of getting used to things, so that you're coping, but with a bad taste in your mouth. Something was really divided in me, which I – well, I'm not sure I understand even to this day – but it was like moving really fast towards a target, and knowing that in order to move you really have to keep your eye on that target, so you refuse to see what might distract you. All the things that make you feel bad about work seem kind of – well, kind of subversive, I guess. You just keep your sights on that target and keep moving, and it's only when you stop that you see that maybe all those things you only half-saw were really important after all.'

Then Sandra explained a very different drama of management in which she had daily dealt with the incongruity between her sense of self and her job, a task of maintaining a persona that would work for her at work on the one hand, and of minimizing the sense of alienation this aroused on the other.

Who Constructs the Glass Ceiling?

When we look at the conflicts confronting women who reach

executive status, we can also understand why so many women who are trained to think like men, to succeed like men, to work like men, do not stay in an executive-track career, but are shunted off to a different track, with a different, more modest ladder. For the moment I brush aside the huge and important question of real, confirmed, overt prejudice against women in specific corporations or institutions. The culpability of individual men may be less significant, and less subversive, and less harmful to women's equality than are the embedded constraints on women which flourish in spite of the best intentions of the people who in their daily lives support and reproduce them.

It has been apparent for many years that though women have more opportunities in senior positions than they did a generation ago, and though much has changed since senior women executives were first studied, there is some stalling factor in the expansion of opportunity and the growth towards equality. Some have declared that the stall in the revolution of equality is domestic: men do not share household and child care tasks, and the work women do to accommodate their men reduces their chances outside the home. And there is little doubt that most people who attain senior positions in business and in the professions have a 'dense' curriculum vitae: their work history has no gaps, there was no time off for children or other family reasons. Without wives, women cannot compete on the same terms as men. But all this is less important than the discomfort they experience at work. In a recent study of 1500 women managers, 43 per cent said they experienced the effect of male networks and male prejudice which enabled men to help one another, gain the best jobs, and exclude women from promotion and influence. Yet only 9 per cent of these women believed their careers had suffered from lack of child care. Those who had battled against prejudice, the study concluded, 'appeared to have done so at considerable personal cost'.[12] Undermining their determination to change things in the home, making mommy-track decisions more appealing, is the stalled revolution in the workplace where 'masculine cultures' persist.

The 'trick' to spotting the importance of work atmosphere over domestic atmosphere is to look at women in midlife and beyond. Many women who have stuck at their careers throughout the most pressured domestic times – when male partners were, typically, working hardest, when their children were, typically, the most demanding, when their own jobs required extreme input, when their own commitment and perseverance were most likely to be challenged by their colleagues and employers, decide in midlife, when these demands are reduced, that the battles of surviving in this 'alien' culture are not worth the gains.

These observations take place in the context of women's apparent retreat from managerial careers. This exodus is constantly noted – recently in Canada, Australia, the United Kingdom and the United States. The women I interviewed who had left, or who, like Sandra, had stuck it out to retirement but like many women retired early, laughed at my question 'why?'. In their opinion the answer was 'blindingly obvious'. But what is obvious still needs to be explored.

Dominant Cultures

In dealing with women in management and in senior levels of the professions, I want to shift the focus from the special challenges all women face in combining work and motherhood, and focus on the inhospitable conditions in which many women have to work. Here the emphasis is not on the pull towards child care or the demands of domesticity or the impact of seeing relationships as prior to career achievements. Though these should never be brushed aside in issues of women and work, they will now be in the background as the issues these women face bring to the foreground the problem of being women in a man's world.

The positions in which they were employed – or, in two cases, elected – placed them within a man's world, where the 'dominant culture' was masculine, and this set down the conditions in which they operated. When I speak of a dominant culture in work, or when I refer to 'masculine cultures', I am using a term that has been used in describing the experience and socialization of minority groups. When a dominant culture is experienced by a minority group, the members of that group may have very little direct access to that dominant culture. Toni Morrison in her novel *The Bluest Eye* describes beautifully how black children are aware of living within a white society, while they have only the slightest knowledge of who whites are and what they do. They already know, as very young children, that whites have power which they as blacks lack, but gradually they discover too, through more indirect means (such as dolls and films) that whites enforce a standard of beauty which is death for them to adopt since they can never meet it. Yet at the same time as these developing children see the dangers, they are entrapped by them. Admiring the standard that excludes them they suffer a deadly envy. They adopt the ideals of a culture in which they are invisible, or discounted, and as they do so they lose that innocent self-delight which is every child's birthright.

The dominant culture of male versus female standards is somewhat different. Women have daily contact with men, and daily access to them. Normally, traditionally, differences between them have been acknowledged. The puzzling and frequently frustrating fact is that there are often appearances of equality – either equality of value (though with different areas of expertise supposed) or equality of abilities – yet there remain differences in power and differences of understanding from which differences in power often emerge, and as these differences emerge, the men, or the male views, seem to emerge as the stronger. It is by seeing conflict in action, and by seeing women adapt to the standards they perceive at their workplace, that the notion of 'dominant culture' becomes linked to masculine culture.

Corporate Cultures

Now partially retired, and working as a consultant from her home, Sandra at 63 was not making a statement against women's advance in the managerial or corporate world, but she was highlighting what is often – and often for very good reasons – ignored.

What many career women wish to emphasize is that their abilities are similar to those of men. In this way they feel better-equipped to compete with them and to work alongside them. This is an obvious point to make when making demands for equal opportunities for women: women deserve equal employment opportunities, it is argued, because they have equal abilities.

Early studies of women managers and executives assumed that organizations were masculine, and that to thrive in them women had to learn their rules and act according to those rules. This assumption has now come into question. And among those who have first raised the question are the women who have experienced these masculine organizations and have worked within them.

Women working the sciences face similar problems. According to current reports from the National Science Foundation, women's salaries remain lower than men's. They have lower rates of tenure, lower rates of promotion, and higher rates of unemployment. Sue Rosser found that among the 1647 scientists elected into the National Academy of Sciences only 70 are women, and of the tenured faculty in the top ten mathematics departments in the United States there are 288 men and just five women.[13] Here the methods of competitive teaching, the environment of others' expectations, the persistence with which others see women's scientific achievement as the result of hard work or 'slog' rather than intelligence and inspiration, tend to keep out all but the exceptionally talented and exceptionally determined women.

Women's equality with men based on their similar intelligence and ability and energy levels is only half the story. Women have to break away from common expectations about what they can do in order to enter corporations and scientific fields. When they do so, they then may discover that they have entered worlds which they dislike, which do not suit them, so, painstakingly, they try to change themselves to suit their environment, or leave the unfriendly environment or – the greatest, most complex task of all – they try to change the environment. To change it, however, they have to identify what they do not like and discover what is possible. In these circumstances, their greatest support will come from other women who contribute to their vision and confirm their goals. But in an environment in which there are so few women, these positive steps are very hard to take. In the meantime, women who want to change dominant cultures have to communicate and negotiate with the men alongside whom they work.

While some writers describe men and women as learning a different language[14] or speaking a different language[15] or inhabiting different worlds[16] they have also underlined the conflicts that arise as men and women communicate with the same language, follow similar moral rules, and inhabit the same world. It is the huge similarities between them, and the amount that they share which make the differences problematic. The differences between men and women have been highlighted more and frequently, with increasing vividness, as women's expectations of equality at work and in the home have also increased, because it is this extended sharing of ground and boundaries that forces differences to emerge. The differences become more problematic for women because they are entering men's worlds and finding men resistant to sharing theirs. They see the masculine cultures of the workplace as dictating rules which should be followed, and they see themselves as unable to change them. They feel marginalized, or sanctioned or dismissed when they try.

Marginal Managers

'It is significant how repetitive the story of women managers as marginal is', writes Judi Marshall[17] who, for the past ten years, has been studying women managers in Britain – though work in Canada[18] and the United States[19] has produced similar findings. 'Women managers . . . hear a positive message – that of equal opportunities – undermined by a covert negative message – that of the repression of female values.'[20] These 'values' are not simply beliefs about how people should be treated. These are not a novice's inability to distinguish between business and personal norms. These differences are often both more extensive and more evanescent. Everything feminine seems 'wrong' or out of place, and women's speech is discounted, and women's agenda are brushed aside in a multitude of ways which are both ruthless and not necessarily intentional. As a result, many women in management and in the professions expend a lot of energy trying to 'assert their legitimacy and maintain their membership'.[21] They know they are vulnerable to other people's definitions – and for this reason they put effort into refashioning and controlling their image.

As women pursue their careers they feel that they are motivated by their own individual goals, needs and perspectives – yet in their workplace they often feel that they are in a hostile environment. Hence women often begin to do work on themselves – to monitor their own behaviour, to mask their femininity – not only in styles of dress, but also in tone of voice, in facial expressions, in laughter. Women described how they took voice lessons, how they practised new, less giggly laughs, how they had videos of themselves taken at work whereby they 'corrected' feminine posture, and tried to appear alert and interested without interjecting 'all those little nods and mmhmms which I mean as sort of "Yes, I'm following you" but my colleagues used to see as agreement, like I was too easily led by others'.

In this new, more reflective story, Sandra was describing how to uphold the norms at work by changing herself to suit them. The increase in the number of women working alongside her in the bank did not change things, since they too changed themselves to fit in. As Judi Marshall wrote, after studying women managers: 'Despite larger numbers of women around and equal opportunity policies, fundamental patterns of values and behaviour seem highly resistant to change. Women are not defining, influencing, and changing cultures as significantly as many people had expected or hoped.'[22] But as more and more women believe corporations should change, more and more women express dissatisfaction.

Different information often comes up at different interview sessions – even those which are not separated by a decade. Assessments of our lives are complicated and often changed by the decisions we make to change them. We look back, and construct a reasonable account of why we did what we did. Reasons for leaving a job may become clearer after we have left than they were while we we trying to come a decision. In 1983 Sandra accepted the constraints in her job because she believed she had no choice. She was satisfied with her work because she believed there were things she could not change, and saw her task as one of adaptation to reality. When I spoke to her again, in 1992, her reassessment was based on the belief that the constraints she had accepted as inevitable or constant should be changed. Her new dissatisfaction registered her protest. Her earlier account now sounded more like attempts to work on herself and change herself to adapt to her situation. Coping was not a matter of thriving but of surviving,[23] and managing was a means of changing or disguising incompatibility with her work circumstances. Gradually she had become less critical of herself, and more critical of her environment.

Patterns of Awareness

Shelley Freeman, whom I first interviewed in 1981 when she was 33, was still working in the same communication corporation in 1992. She insisted that the company was not male-dominated, merely professional, merely business-like. 'There are women who come in here like they want to do battle because every man's trying to get in their way. Little things become big issues. You can see them making an issue out of everything. They create the sex war as they go along. If you just do your job and assume that everyone will be fair, you become a person rather than a woman.'

She then went on to describe how she ensured this personal – as opposed to feminine – identity. She, as do many women managers, reported consistent and elaborate strategies to avoid sex stereotyping.[24] 'As long as you behave professionally, and keep a business-like demeanour, you're all right. You learn not to show what you're feeling, and you don't start chatting to the secretaries about make-up and movies, and you avoid sitting right next to the one other woman who happens to be in a meeting, because then you'll be seen as forming a cosy little group. You learn when to send a memo rather than make a phone call, so people don't think that you just love to while away your time gossiping. You learn to make your point sharp and quick at a meeting. You can see the others wriggling when a woman keeps going on and on and looking around the room with puppy-dog eyes, pleading with everyone to nod their head just like she's nodding it. And you don't flirt or snip or start accusing your colleagues of being sexist.'

This litany of 'don'ts' took me aback. Here she was saying that her work environment was not sexist, and at the same time she was saying that in order to make it non-sexist a woman had to be very careful about what she did, how she spoke, lest she appear as a woman. There is a sharp contradiction between believing that one will not be discriminated against because one is a woman and taking such pains not to draw attention to the fact that one is a woman. If one has to non-womanize oneself to be a person, then surely one at least believes one is living in discriminatory circumstances.

Many researchers have noticed in their studies of women in management a simple process of denial whereby women de-scribe their jobs as less crowded by gender issues than they really are. The denial of discrimination is a way of managing it. If one assumes the conditions in which one lives are not preju-dicial, then one is more likely to feel in control, and more likely to avoid anger, which can be creative and energizing, but which is often frustrating, debilitating and humiliating.[25] Hence Shelley was managing her environment by learning to control the dis-crimination she in one sense clearly perceived, but in being determined to control it, she could deny that it would affect her.

Since Shelley's description was so like Sandra's account of her past beliefs, I wondered whether Sandra had at the time been aware of this discrepancy between her stated beliefs and the beliefs that emerged in her self-managed image. She felt her case was different, because she had believed that the work environment was potentially very unfriendly to women. 'But what I did think then – well, I really thought it was a phase – maybe not when I was 50, but early, before I was [Vice-President], I thought that when I did get to the top, things would change, and I could change things. And I think many women then did think things would just gradually improve, part of that progress we all believed in. But you start by learning how to fit in, and you stay in by fitting in, and by the time you're really somebody, it still somehow comes down to a question of doing what fits in – and no matter how high up you are, you are rapidly told when you're not doing what fits in. Vice-Presidents come and go, and no one is sorry to see someone in that position go, and can a woman who is a Vice-President really say that the men are discriminating against her – when she climbed over so many of them to get where she was?'

So the dilemma Sandra was expressing was the impasse someone faces who has colluded in a set of norms in order to sustain membership. In failing to challenge the expectations of what is businesslike and what is professional, one then helps define them, so that even when one is in a position of ostensible power, one remains bound by the rules one has helped enforce. Hence the power women often hope to have in organizations – to change the norms, to increase flexibility of work atmosphere and even working hours – does not emerge even when the individual woman gains a powerful position, because the power she has is based on her willingness to confirm and enforce the current norms. Shelley was expressing her awareness of this in the enormous amount of work she did on herself in order to be included, or feel included. The strain of these efforts, and the knowledge that the terms on which they are engaging in battle means that they will never win the battle, accounts for much of the 'wastage' among women in corporations. They may leave, rather than lose themselves to the battle.

Protesting Dominance

But many women in such positions do not opt for this muted control, whereby they see the task of achieving membership and fair treatment as carving their feminine impulses into masculine forms. Instead, some women face the difficulty as a battle, and become the woman with the 'feminist' label which the first group of women are so keen to avoid. They are highly aware of the masculine culture of the workplace, and they see this as means of exclusion. This woman is unlikely to leave[26] because she sees the battle as her task. This can be seen as one early phase in a developmental scale of coping with the masculine cultures which emerge in many careers and professions. This may be, Judi Marshall thinks, 'inevitable in individual consciousness-raising. Its heat and passion become a way of life, but are demanding to sustain. They make the individual continually vulnerable and volatile.'[27]

222

I found that embattled women also feel strong in their certainty that they are doing something with their anger. Whether or not they also feel vulnerable depends very much on their support network, and their ability to have their anger validated by others who also see them as doing a good job with their anger and with their skills. They may be vulnerable, especially since other people perceive them as tough and willing to engage in conflict, whereas they more often see themselves as embattled not because they enjoy confrontation but because they must defend themselves. Yet they assess in different ways the effectiveness of showing their anger. One woman complained, 'No one hears me when I shout,' whereas another demanded, 'Why do I have to become such a bitch before anyone listens to me?' What is so exhausting about being embattled is that though one's position, to the distant observer, may seem simple and simply principled, the embattled woman's responses themselves are volatile and complex.

Simple reminders that the workplace is dominated by a masculine culture are easy to find. Some of them seem a little archaic, but management seminars still refer to how you would handle 'this guy' who comes to you with a problem, or draw parallels between negotiations with other firms and negotiations 'with your wife'. 'I feel like an honorary man in those workshops', Liz admitted after a day's conference among consultant engineers. More significantly, informal networks through which crucial information is passed often exclude women. Hence these are known as 'the men's room', since they tend to occur in places and at times women are absent. Women often feel left out of the decision-making process, and denied access to information which would allow them to understand and influence the context in which decisions are made. Some women, too, spoke of small ways in which they were not heard at meetings. 'It's as though the others are waiting for me to quit talking so that the real meeting can continue. I've said this before, and everyone says – you know, I'm imagining it. So I watch them, and there are these fixed smiles or wonderful pencil tricks performed while I'm talking, and when I finish the flow's completely different, all smooth and natural again.' Another woman explained that she could have a say only when she deliberately took the floor, as it were, and offered a set piece; she did not feel she was heard alongside men when the remarks were informal and brief and overlapping.

These indicators, some of them minor, take on symbolic importance. One woman described her response when the conference organizer closed a session in which she had participated with the following comment: 'I would like to thank Mrs Bellows for her contribution to this panel. She is certainly the most attractive speaker here.'

'I was blushing before I knew it – smiling, like you do at a compliment. And then I heard that little chorus of chuckles, which were uncomfortable, perfunctory, just like the compliment was. Look at me – I'm not attractive, and that doesn't bother me, but somehow everyone thought that because I was the only woman speaker that afternoon, they had to make a deal of it. And saying I was attractive when I'm not – because I guess that's what you have to say to a woman to be polite – is that what they think? – it made me feel I wasn't the sort of woman they wanted there. And then I just felt angry. There I was biting my lip, and what am I going to do? Stand up and say, "Now wait a minute here!" But no one would hear me – you know, take the point I'm making – it would just be a feminist on her high horse, slapping someone in the face for being nice – and then I'd really be out of things. I should have come back with a quip – some throwaway remark, like . . . well, the best thing would have been to come back with some compliment that would cut him down to size, like how nice it is to be complimented by someone who knows so much about women – something like that, leaving it hanging there where I'm being ironic. But I had to sit tight and control that blushing. You can't seem smart when you're blushing . . . You see what this does to me! I'm brooding on it still like a self-conscious teenager, and that's not what I am . . . I'm a 36-year-old woman who's had fifteen years' experience in sales and management and who has come out on top of every reshuffle.'

Kari began by criticizing her own responses – she regretted her blushes. Only secondarily did she go on to criticize the unwarranted remark that causes her embarrassment. But even this anger is complicated by responses which push towards what she thinks of as liberation and those which pull her back. She is angry because her appearance becomes relevant through the organizer's gratuitous remark. The righteous anger that such a comment is deemed appropriate comes up against her wish to be worthy of the 'compliment': she wishes for a moment that she were an attractive woman. She is (nearly) sorry to disappoint them, sorry that she is not what they say she is. Then she feels confusion and anger at her own response, since she sees that it plays into the culture she wishes to reject. And at the same time she is dealing with these vacillating responses, she has been wondering what to do, how to handle the situation, and each protest that occurs to her is immediately blocked by her assessment of its outcome. If she states her objection to this compliment then she will embarrass herself and the audience more; by protesting she will emphasize it and prolong its effect. Because of her paralysis the idea stays with her, and she keeps wondering what response might have been effective. But even the best response she could imagine is not one she believes she could have carried off even if she had thought of it at the time. 'You can't look smart while your blushing.' Her queries about what she might have done or said then return full circle to criticism of how she appears presently, as she speaks to me: 'I'm brooding on it still, like a self-conscious teenager', and she reminds us both that she is not what she fears she now seems, and concludes by listing her credits.

The cumulative effect of such responses is exhaustion. Women in management and in the professions may deal with them daily – not because men are evil or nasty (and Kari Bellows' understanding that the speaker does not mean to insult her confounds her protest) but because they are embedded in expectations and habits, and are often unconscious. Marshall refers to 'the amazing redundancy in cultural symbolism and messages'[28] that occurs in corporations to remind women that they do not belong. Hence the protest that feminists take things so seriously and are such fascists in what they see as acceptable[29] both undermines and arouses anger. As one is told one's anger is unnecessary, one feels it all the more.

Others see the protesting woman as starting the fight, as twisting a light-hearted, good-willed remark into an affront, as taking everything too seriously, as making mountains out of molehills, as taking the fun out of relationships between men and women, as militarizing something which should be a playful dance. Unaware of the assumptions underlying these playfully meant, 'friendly' quips, they attack and undermine women, but are unaware of the attacks they make. Being unaware of the hostile and humiliating implications, they are then surprised, abashed or outraged by a woman's counterattack. Because their behaviour, their examples, their compliments, seem normal, and are not perceived as hostile, the response of these women as to hostility seems unnecessary. Women are often aware that in fighting back, they are losing yet another battle, for in fighting back they may be 'proving' that women – especially feminist women – are unreasonable.

Women who do their best to be one of the boys fare little better. Gail May, who had made a career in a midwest city fire department, described the 'hoops' she had to jump through in the beginning of her career to show that she was a good co-worker. But being one of the boys became far more difficult when she was promoted. Though her male colleagues could have one drink and still judge themselves fit for action, they judged that alcohol had a greater effect on her as a woman, and found it inappropriate for her to join them in any rule-breaking behaviour. She felt under constraint to be as 'tough and reckless' as the men, but as soon as she was, 'they drew a circle around me and laughed at the fool in the middle'. The scene which has become a stereotype in films and stories, wherein the boys taunt a girl who then proves herself more able than any boy and hence wins acceptance, is counter to the experience of women who have tried to enact this scenario. In meeting the men's challenge to be 'as tough and reckless' as the boys, women often find that instead of gaining acceptance they are underlining their exclusion. 'Masculine cultures' judge 'tough and reckless' women to be 'asking for trouble'.

The ability to cope as an embattled woman depends very much on the support a woman has either from someone at work or outside it. This can change drastically. Younger women who were entering corporate life had better access to the experiences and difficulties of their peers. They exchanged stories and compared notes because these were new enough to be interesting and they were young enough to be heartened by their anger. As women got older and became more senior, they were more and more isolated. Their families and partners offered emotional support in the form of kind words and cups of tea, but many partners also encouraged an exit approach. 'If it makes you feel like this, you should be doing something else', Elsbeth's husband proclaimed after she described how she felt continuously out-manoeuvred in board meetings. 'I know he means to tell me I'm too good for all this, but what I've decided to do is just keep quiet. Things aren't great at work, but I don't want to leave – not after all the time I've put into it, and everything I've achieved. It does make me feel awful, sometimes even about myself, because I know I don't handle things in the best possible way, but I want to stick with it, even though I'm not sure I can justify that position. So I try at home to grumble a little less often.' As her partner's sympathy urged her towards an exit decision, she decided to suppress her complaints.

Several embattled women had changed firms several times during the past ten or twelve years, each time hoping that the working atmosphere would be better in the new firm – and indeed, five out of nine of the women who made job moves were much happier, though when they changed jobs they often looked for a different kind of position, with less power over others, and greater opportunity to work either on their own projects or alongside others.

The discussion of women in management and women in the professions treads a difficult course. There are today increased opportunities. There is also a high drop-out rate among women, or disappearance rate, which has been widely observed and reported, yet which no one has satisfactorily accounted for. It is tempting to 'blame' either the men who keep women out or the women who fail to sustain their will and determination. The causes are seen either as male malice or female weakness. Instead, what occurs is an opening of opportunities to women within institutions which are persistently male in orientation and assumption and procedure. The working hours of senior members of corporations and professions have increased in the past decade. The narrowing of opportunities and the pressure of redundancies have made employees at all levels more anxious to be seen to work hard. In large corporations and firms it is often difficult to gauge the productivity of individuals, and in absence of some clear measure, the hours of attendance become more important – a proof of one's commitment and one's input, a strong suggestion that one's input in turning to good output. So the working style itself has become more hostile to women's overall life patterns even as there may be attempts to introduce women into previously all-male positions. And while there have been gestures of welcome in business and the professions, there has on the whole been little effort to extend the cultures in which employees operate. Though there has been surface agreement that equality should be attained, action taken by management is often ineffective simply because the masculine cultures are taken as the norm. From this perspective it is impossible to see what needs correction. Views from outside that perspective do not emerge within it, because they are labelled as feminist, and hence radical. What is masculine and rigid and hostile to women is seen as businesslike and professional and practical and 'fair'.

Success in Management

Yet many women do thrive in executive positions – not because they are especially tough, or have a masculine love of power, not because they have successfully unwomanized themselves, but because they develop a set of effective strategies which they exercise in a place of work which is muted in masculine cultures. Some women believe that they are 'lucky' in their working atmosphere. They praise their colleagues, both at the junior and the senior level, for being 'welcoming' or 'tolerant' or 'understanding'. These women often have flexible hours. 'If I come in late because I had to take my son to the orthodontist, no one questions me. They all know I'll make up the time – either by staying late or taking my work home.' These women see themselves as having a great deal in common with the

228

women who find corporate life inhospitable, but view their different situation as a result of the particularly friendly circumstances of their corporation. Such women speak about their 'luck' with companies the way other women speak about their 'luck' in having partners who share the household tasks. Their appreciation registers their knowledge that such circumstances are unusual.

To some women who thrive in management, in the professions, in politics, the difficulties other women have in similar conditions seem manufactured, or even hysterical. A few successful women take a highly individualistic view: they succeeded so why cannot other women succeed? The common cause of women is not high on their agenda. The clarity of their vision and purpose has served them well, and the fact they are women, and engage in gender-ordered relationships such as marriage and motherhood, does not seem to make the differences to them that it does to others. For these women, at home in the 'normality' of corporate management, the demands women as a group make seem excessive. These women do not see themselves as succeeding through luck, but through their own abilities and efforts. They believe that women who complain about masculine cultures and structural prejudice are seeking special favours. Hence they do not wish to associate with feminism, and many women, feminist or otherwise, feel alienated from them. These successful women often fulfil the strange position of representing women's potential while remaining exceptions. Margaret Thatcher proved that a woman could become Prime Minister and sustain power in office, yet she deftly eschewed both commitments to an old-boy network and to female solidarity. The workplace is ready to accommodate exceptional women, but at the top of the ladder only exceptional corporations accommodate representative women.

New generations of women in business, the professions and politics are becoming increasingly aware of the need for cultural change within organizations.[30] New styles of work and managements must be negotiated. In the meantime women's voices remain guarded. After a year as managing editor of a large publishing house, Amy Lint reflected 'I know I can't brush aside the fact that I'm a woman. It's there – in everything I do, and sometimes it becomes an excuse to reject what I say and to override a decision, but most of the time it just chugs along beside what I'm doing. I never know how things are going to switch on me. One day things are fair and the next day there I am again trapped in their image of me. But it's better than it was. I'm here after all, and more women come into the firm – though like I said, that doesn't always help, because they can be glazed over too – they're suddenly typecast, so what they do becomes female more than anything else. You can see it happening – a gentle disappointment, men sadly shaking their heads: "We thought she'd be fair, but alas, she's taking *this* line." And when I deal with these women it isn't any easier. I don't want to play mother hen or easy woman. So I sometimes have to act cooler than I'd like, but I keep hanging in there.'

As Lynn Aggie spoke of settling into her new position as executive administrator of a large hospital, she admitted that her vision of change was 'minimal'.

> I do my 'man act' from time to time, being tough and biting back, but I also remember that I sometimes won't be heard so I sometimes shut up. But things like that are sometimes important and sometimes not. When you think what this job is – what hangs on it, and how many things we all have to fight – well, you don't have to be a woman to see that society is narrow and stupid and bigoted and that a mountain of inefficient bureaucracy has to be climbed even though your aim is clear and simple. I work with men on that score. I work alongside them – we've got the same feelings and very similar outlooks. So I bring it up because you ask – not because it's what I focus on day to day. If I did, I would leave. This isn't a 'me' sort of job – there's no glitz or power high from it. Whatever I achieve, it's with a lot of other people, and we all feel we're working against 'the system' – lots of systems, and some of those systems are internal, but we're working at those too. For example, the macho doctor image of a lot of these guys – and the gals too – just doesn't work with patients. We're trying to teach the more senior doctors how to listen to what the patients say, and how to find out whether the patients have taken on board the information the doctor gives

them. You'd think that was basic training, but it's not, and experience seems to make some worse, not better. So we're working on that. Communication is a big part of this business after all, and I guess I'm more aware – maybe as a woman – of how things which have gone on for so long and are accepted because they're common practice really don't work so well.

The shifting ground of Lynn's aims and acceptance and dissatisfaction show the momentum and vacillation of change, even among the 'lucky' ones. She had to concentrate on her job, rather on the implications and complications of a woman doing that job. Simultaneously, she would find that being a woman did make a difference or 'intrude' in the day-to-day tasks; but she would manage this in a variety of ways. Sometimes – but not always – she kept silent. Sometimes – but not often – she performed her 'man act'. For her it was something that cropped up rather than dominated her position. Membership was defined as a common effort, which she identified (and no doubt inspired) in many of her colleagues. Lynn, as a woman administrator, utilized a strongly female value system to enforce her own sense of membership. When she achieved something, she did it alongside others, who together saw the impediments to their work as 'the system' against which they joined forces.

9
Looking Ahead

Women continue to find ways to overcome the odds against them. Whether these are overt prejudices or embedded biases, career-oriented women who also mother confront them and, with one another or with their families, restructure their lives and restructure their work. Both the women I interviewed in the early 1980s and those I interviewed in 1992 felt that in orienting themselves towards career achievement they were offering their daughters a positive image. They were showing their daughters not only what women could do, but what a mother could be.

But children do not always interpret our behaviour as we think they should. They may construct examples from our behaviour which we do not mean to set. Very young girls whose mothers worked full-time were quick to see that their mothers were tired and tense. They, in contrast, wanted a more relaxed life – a desire enforced by their belief that it would be nice for them to have a mother who was always available, always at home.

It seems unfair that this image of the mother at home is still available to children, for them to take as normal. It seems unfair that children should remain so conservative in their expectations. Why do they not speak of their desire to see more of fathers, and wish that their fathers would stay home, and feel deprived when their fathers work full-time?

It is not merely cultural images that determine these expectations, but also the activity in the home. For the father is more likely to treat the home as a place in which he should be allowed to rest, as a retreat from labour and stress; whereas a mother is more likely to see the home as a place for a different kind of work, as a place in which there are things to be done, things to put right. Home for the woman presents organizational and emotional tasks, in ways that it still does not, generally, seem to do for men. As children see their mother's divided responses to the home and to work, they fashion images of their futures. 'When I grow up I want to be an at-home mommy,' 4-year-old Joanna explained to me, and as she spoke, her mother's body sagged with humorous defeat.

Daughters learn a great deal from their mothers' lives. They learn both positive and negative lessons. They learn surprising things, and pick up messages that the mother had no idea she was sending. They learn through their sympathy with their mothers and through conflict with her and through hostility towards her. Mothers provide 'role models', but their children also construct negative examples from a parent's behaviour: children see in their parents both what they might become and what they choose not to become. Daughters then go on to use these positive and negative models, which may be reformulated at different phases and in different contexts of their own lives. Girls pick and choose and change their choices about what to take from their mothers and what to discard. Role models are not mapped out like a builder's drawing. They are used in highly individual ways by those who are attracted – or repelled – by various aspects of them.

Change occurs not only in what a daughter needs or wants from a mother, but also in how she sees her mother. As daughters mature, they see their mother more as a person with her own needs. They are better at seeing how things are from her perspective. They also learn to take her working for granted.

The younger children I interviewed were dealing with their own needs at the time, when they never had enough of their mothers – a 'deficit' which most young children feel, whether or not their mothers work. Young girls' sense of their mothers' options has also changed. Women's working lives are now a reality. Ten years on, the child who at the age of 4 had confounded her mother with her own adult goals, said she did not now know what she wanted to do, but she expected that she too would work throughout her adult life. But the issue was still rife with conflict.

> I don't like it when people ask, 'What are you going to be when you grow up?' I don't like thinking about it because I don't know – like what's going to happen . . . I can't remember what I said then [when I first asked her whether she wanted to work, ten years before], and what does it matter? I was four! Like what I say now won't make any difference in ten years . . . so why bother asking? My 9-year-old sister wastes hours every day worrying about this sort of thing. She makes lists of all the pets she's going to have, and then worries how she's going to find a job where she can spend time with them too. You know she really wastes time worrying about this, and there are my parents saying, 'Well, you could be a vet' or 'You could study agriculture or forestry or biology'. She doesn't even know what those things are, and my parents think they're helping her, giving her ideas, that sort of thing. There's not a whole lot of option in this family. You have to do something – I don't know – hard. I love sewing and making clothes, but they're not going to let me do fashion or design – which might sort of more fit it – I don't know! – it's more what I like doing. But *apparently* that's no way to earn a living. It'll be physics or math or something like that. Anyway, I know my mother has to work . . . it's not an issue, like maybe it was when I was a kid.

Joanna's petulance at the question was partly an adolescent's irritation with my intrusion, and impatience, too, with the recitation of her 'ancient' but recorded remark as a 4-year-old; but she was also registering her awareness of an unknown future in which many things would have to be resolved before anything could fall into place. My questions about her future plans were annoying because she knew enough about uncertain outcomes to see that a confident answer would be a pretence. She felt anxious, too, as she perceived the clash between what she wanted to do, and what her parents would persuade her to do.

Whatever 4-year-olds say about what they would like to be as adults, girls of 14 see a complex future in which parents' expectations will have to be balanced against their own interests, and both of these will eventually have to find some niche in the workplace, which in turn will have to accommodate or be accommodated by their children (or their pets), their partners, their ageing parents, and their continuing need to have a job and to do what they like doing. Though Joanna clearly saw that solutions would be difficult, and rest upon circumstances so highly specific that prediction would be either fraudulent or illusory, many girls, looking towards their adult futures as mothers or as wives and as workers, blur the sharp edges and blend contradictions. Girls of 18 and 19 commonly minimize the demands of child care, and the costs of 'time out' on their careers.[1] In Carol Tavris's survey of 10 000 women between the ages of 17 and 30 (87 per cent of whom were under 25) only 2 per cent did not intend to work at all. Women saw the increasing trend: they understood that they might have to be self-supporting, or significant contributors to family income, at least for some periods of their lives. But these young women also wanted to have children, and not merely to have them, but to stay at home with them for between two and six years. A full 60 per cent planned to take extensive time out to spend raising their children. A similar proportion also expected to earn in excess of $25 000 a year at the peak of their careers – which may seem high, but it is only the average salary in the US for men.

Women's expectations are often based more on a general belief in fairness and new opportunities for women than on reality. The time off they plan to take will almost certainly affect their career, just as their knowledge that they want to have children and invest time in them, will affect their outlook, so that they will see certain jobs as suitable and certain jobs as unsuitable. They will not be offering their services to employers on the same terms as do men, and this will affect their working paths and their working futures.

Young women, and girls developing into women, express their awareness of the contradictions that confound the successes they have learned to expect. When I visited the Harvard Medical School twelve years ago, and spent three days with six women approaching graduation, they expressed anxiety about the costs their ambitions had already incurred and the costs they were likely to incur in the future. As they spoke about their medical careers with self-conscious seriousness, they seemed, well into their twenties, still emotionally young and uncertain, still nervously sharing and swapping ideas with one another. They discussed figures and diets with the same intensity that they discussed their applications for internships. But for whom were they preening themselves?

The girls' bond to one another was partly based on the assumption that the young men who studied alongside them looked down at them and avoided them.

> I've always felt – well, a bit different, which is kind of isolating – except maybe for a wonderful reprieve in my first year in college. But in high school – well, all of high school was a road to the discovery that I wasn't like other girls. I was smarter. I was bored by what thrilled them. And the boys they were mad about were jerks. It was great to get to Barnard, and realize I wasn't the only smart girl, and that others could talk to me. I don't know what happened then, but the beginning was the best, and I guess I expected something much better here. We'd all come so far – just to get here. But again . . . there's this – well, it's like you're odd again. Somehow not what people expect, what you're supposed to be. Not only the guys? Is it mainly the guys? [Heather McNeil wondered].

'We're too ambitious for them', Jenny Lau explained. A male colleague concurred, though from a different angle: 'The women around here are always telling us how important their work is. They think about their work all the time, They always tell us that their work comes first. Always them and their work first. I'm happy to have a wife who works, I expect to have a wife who works. But I don't want to be to told all the time that I come second.'

The vehemence with which these young women asserted their professional orientation signalled their knowledge of what they were up against: the expectation that in becoming a wife they would have to put someone else first; the awareness of others' ability to manipulate them or influence them through those expectations; the fear of finding themselves in situations in which they would become a different kind of person, with different priorities; the concern lest their own responses would leave their hard-won achievements behind. Heather felt 'odd' in her high-powered medical school, just as she had in her rural high school, as she saw the split between her hopes and others' expectations. She and her friends felt they could not be 'just another medical student', but had 'to work on it' because they were women whose orientations were more likely to change than were men's, however similar their training and their achievements. They actively battled against their needs for closeness.

'It's not so much sex I feel in need of,' Natalie, 25, said, 'but physical closeness. Sometimes when I'm studying I just close my eyes and imagine someone stroking my hair. It's not easy to be alone, but the guys around here expect me to support them, and find ways of making their lives easier. I'm not going to trade a boyfriend for the freedom to work as hard as I want.'

They presented a steely exterior to protect the ambitions that felt so strong but which they knew might fail to thrive in the open air of real life. The clash between a romantic involvement and ambition was perceived not in terms of the time spent with a boyfriend, but in terms of the distraction and distress when things went wrong, and the possibility of compromises in the future. 'You get real friendly, and they're suddenly expecting clean matched socks to appear every Saturday morning. Do you realize,' Natalie demanded, 'when I was a Freshman someone would ask me what I wanted to do, and when I didn't know there'd be this "Yeah, Yeah, you want to get married and have four children and live in a house with a white picket fence"? This was me – you know, some silly girl – they were cracking down on for being stuck with little feminine clichés. But these guys . . . one sweet night out and they're making you into their *hausfrau.*'

The challenge was to appear certain, to shut out others' expectations with their own certainty. In creating a simple and strongly directed persona, they could make career decisions without reference to the complications most women ultimately face.

Each of these medical students admitted that she might – perhaps – one day want a child, though it was always 'a child', never 'children': the image was of a contained, manageable commitment. Even though they were aged between 24 and 27, this event seemed distant. Recently, I was able to make contact with three of these women, who are now in their mid to late thirties. Two had three children, and one had two. Two were married, and one was divorced. They were all working, yet only one worked full-time, and each had changed her career track after having children. One gave up her plans to become a neurologist and became a paediatrician instead, working three-quarters time, now, in a small practice, which she hoped would not get any larger. One worked for Kaiser, after spending five years working half-time in a private practice which she decided to leave after facing a suit for wrongful death. 'I went into dermatology because I thought it was safe. There wouldn't be emergencies in the middle of the night, and there wouldn't be malpractice suits over cancer. Now no one I know isn't being sued, and it just feels a whole lot better with an organization behind you, even though that sounds a little dull.'

The only woman working full-time was on an academic schedule as a professor of psychiatry, and she had returned to full-time work only eighteen months before I contacted her. Each had made use of her training. Each had developed further the skills acquired during medical school. Yet each also had accommodated a partner and her children more than she had planned, and more than she had expected. The working patterns of each woman had been cut and fashioned by both marriage and its demands, and – in one case – by the distress of its dissolution. Career commitments and advances were made with reference to the birth of their children and their changing needs. These determined professional medical students matured into doctors who were pegged to a woman's life.

This small sample of women may not be representative of women doctors, or even of their class of Harvard Medical School. Nor are all the problems they have faced linked to being women. All doctors face high risks of malpractice or wrongful death suits (which is what a malpractice suit downgrades to if the patient treated has died), and many of them are opting for more protected employment from a health group rather than face the high risk and high insurance premiums of private practice. Many male doctors have changed track, finding fields such as gynaecology too vulnerable to litigation. The pleasure they expected from such fields was overshadowed by its tensions. Both men and women graduating medical school in 1982 believed that they would be wealthy and respected, and many have found the going very tough indeed. But what these women shared was the interference of 'women's business' in their career and the constant negotiations of family commitments. The oldest of the three women had just had her second child, and was still negotiating the discovery of her husband's ability to switch off at home, and his assumption, which then became hers, that she would take on the task of finding a child minder to replace the child minder whom she had recently hired, and subsequently fired when she failed to meet her son at the agreed time. The litany of complaints was almost too familiar to be interesting, and yet it remains a central impediment to women's successful, equal integration in the workplace.

When I began writing up the earlier research project I believed that the women I was interviewing, women who were advancing into strong positions along male career patterns, represented an expanding trend. I discovered, through working women's voices, that this trend, though real, has no obvious trajectory. Many women do enjoy greater degrees of opportunity than did women a generation before them, but these opportunities are complex, to say the least, and commonly costly, as they are enacted in 'organizational cultures' or conditions which prohibit or deny women's lives as mothers, and as relationship-prioritizing people. It is still difficult to compete with men at work because women have children – apparently in a way men do not. Work patterns are not becoming more flexible, nor are day care places expanding. In Britain and America there are, at present, fewer day care facilities than there were in 1945, when wartime conditions made women's work economically necessary. Nor is the cost of child care (which even in two-parent, two-earning families is usually perceived as coming from the wife's income) viewed as a necessary business expense. In Britain, when child care facilities are provided by an employer, this service is calculated as a benefit in kind, and therefore taxable. The piecemeal process of policymaking positions women as responsible for child care in terms of time and attention; yet as fewer courts award or enforce child support payments from fathers, and as fewer women wish to be financially dependent on their children's fathers, they become more and more hedged in by social expectations and policies at odds with one another. In the United States dependent care tax credit has increased recently, and is a significant type of federal support for child care – though it is also the only type of federal support. By means of this tax credit families who pay taxes can offset a portion of their tax bill with the expenses they have incurred from paying others to look after their children; yet since this benefit is only for those families who pay tax, low-income families paying little or no tax do not benefit, and those who benefit most are the high-income, high-taxpaying families. Again, the changes in policies fail to help the women who are solely responsible for both their children's care and control, and their family finances. As the family structure changes, the bills and policies which are meant to 'liberate' women, severely disadvantage many women. In her recent book on how changes in divorce policies which are ostensibly advances towards equality actually enforce the poverty of mother and child, Sylvia Hewlett cites Lenore Weitzman's and Ruth Dixon's analysis of what has gone wrong: 'Most judges appear to view the law's goal of equality as a mandate for placing an *equal burden* of support on men and women whose position and capacity for support are, by virtue of their experience in marriage, typically *unequal.*'[2]

Divisions and Contradictions

Women, it seems, remain responsible for their children. This responsibility takes time. This time is not allocated in work time. Parenting is not seen as a real job which the workplace should accommodate. As women have emphasized equality with men, they have tended to slight 'women's' work. The real demands, the real jobs, of parenting and household organization tend to be treated as residual aspects of adult life. This began with Betty Freidan's *cri de coeur*, as she found the condition of being a housewife a means of emptying out one's soul, creating 'a sense of . . . non-existence, nothingness, in women'.[3] This acutely depressed angle of her vision narrows the meaning of 'housewife' into one who does housework only. In seeing that this life did not offer enough choice, the depth of this role was minimized: it could, she wrote, be 'capably handled by an eight year old child.'

In England, Ann Oakley began a study of housework and housewives for her doctorate thesis which evolved into three books, which have become classic sociological views of what housework is and how it affects women who engage in it. Like Betty Freidan in America a decade before, Oakley found that housework was drudgery. The tasks were endless, but they were also repetitive. They were menial and mindless, and yet subject to constant interruption, which itself caused fatigue and frustration. Housework was isolating and demeaning. It turned women into servants of their husbands and children, and slaves of social norms.

Recently, at a conference in Cambridge, a paper was presented in which Oakley's account of housework was criticized as out-of-date and inaccurate.[4] First, Oakley described the housewife as someone primarily responsible for the domestic organization of her home and the care of the children within it. As such, the majority of working women, too, are housewives, which is not the picture either Friedan or Oakley drew. Moreover, according to data available, more than 60 per cent of women who are housewives, as we use the term today – women who do not work outside the home and who are primarily and virtually solely responsible for the domestic organization and child care

– claim to be satisfied with their lives. Hence, the argument of this paper ran, being a housewife was not demeaning and degrading, and the majority of women who did it were happy doing it.

What was most interesting about this paper was the response which arose from it. The academic audience, committed apparently to truth, was highly disturbed by the implications of these findings. 'Have you thought about how these results will affect the position of women?' one member of the conference demanded. To say the housewife is satisfied now, apparently, threatens the status quo. Housewifery remains a highly-charged political topic – like topics about the family and motherhood, it is largely emotive, and yet we need to understand it objectively in order to assess our reality. It seems virtually impossible to come out with a balanced and fair view of domestic organization and child care. It is either vilified or valorized. The 1983 role reversal film, *Wait Till Your Mother Gets Home*, shows a gym teacher, deprived by education cuts of his usual summer job, taking over the household work while his wife returns to work, after many years as a housewife, to a secretarial job. The man first approaches his job in a logical fashion. He will master the difficulties. He will get things done. But he discovers that, however efficient he is in cleaning the bathroom and doing the laundry, his efficiency is undone by his three children. The bathroom that he cleans so splendidly is cleaned only to be made dirty again. His children's clothes are laundered only to be soiled as they wear them. Yet the frustration turns to something deeper as he discovers that washing his children's socks becomes a stimulus and a symptom of his love for them.

Housework is often seen by women – or said to be seen by them – as an expression of love. Their arguments or dissatisfactions with husbands then become arguments over gratitude and responsiveness – rather than over the division of labour. But this film combines each and every aspect of housewifery, so that it seems to take away the housewife's identity – whether the housewife is a man or a woman. For the wife, before she returns to work, feels that she has lost her identity, that she is merely her husband's wife, not herself. Her husband, taking over her domestic role, feels that he is 'nothinged' by the demands and tasks of the day. The wife, taking a job, feels she is gaining a self – and yet the job she takes is a woman's job in a patriarchal workplace, a secretary of demanding and patronizing men, who help her accommodate male demands with female support of female assistants. Yet the message of the film is: work gives one identity, and housewifery takes it away, yet gives one a great deal, and the ideal compromise is to share. How this sharing is achieved is not described – nor is the question answered as to whether the wife retains her job when her husband returns to his. The practical details of these high principles remain vague. Specific answers would be too emotionally charged to be handled in such a nice, polite film; and, in any case, however general the problems, there may be no general resolution.

As each woman's view about domestic life and work life changes with her experience, she may leave unsolved problems behind only to approach new ones. The complex problems of the housewife have changed in complex ways. The women's movement continues to address the needs of a generation of women who came to adulthood with high expectations and found themselves confounded by the strength of norms which inhibited their potential. In speaking from her own experience, and on behalf of others, Betty Friedan spoke of the essential emptiness of housework. Twenty-five years later, as the persistence of women as domestic organizers became more puzzling, Arlie Hochschild has spoken out for the overload of housework alongside employment. The problem of housework is no longer that it empties women's lives of meaning and challenge. The problem now is that it fills their life with too much to do.

The women in this study were not like the tired women of Hochschild's sample, who spoke of sleep the way a hungry person speaks of food. They were not like the women of Suzanne Gordon's sample who have adopted men's ideals and follow men's career tracks. They are not like the women of whom Sylvia Hewlett speaks, who contribute to the famine of family time; there were not 'co-dependent' workaholics *à deux* who keep in step with their fast-track husbands and neglect their children. Instead, these were women who confronted the problems of balance, and tried to fashion ways out of these patterns

243

which were so clearly unsatisfactory. What these women tried to fashion was a new flexibility, and new standards in the workplace. Their personal and professional success depended on the ability to create patterns, and to avoid ready-made ones.

Bleak Futures

The continued rapid growth in the number of working women will be the most significant change in the workforce this century. The US Department of Labor estimates that from now until the turn of the century, two-thirds of all new American workers will be women. 'Home-related problems' – or problems involving women's wifely roles, such as child care – are estimated to be costing US industry $137.6 billion every year as women stay away from work to fulfil domestic and maternal demands, to train new employees when women, for personal reasons, decided to leave. Low-paid, often illegal, aliens are so attractive as household labourers because, with little choice in employment, they will do the never-ending wifely tasks. Both the government and corporations remain blind to the reality of their workers' domestic concerns. Those workers without domestic concerns – those who have wives to take on those concerns for them – are those who continue to advance more rapidly and more easily and hence gain positions in which these patterns are reinforced.

The trend of workers and the culture of work are diverging. Workers are wives, yet workers are still assumed to have wives. Not only will more women work, but they will work for longer, and may bring more qualifications with them. This change and its permanence are not ensured merely by changing ideas and attitudes, but by changing economic needs. The sense of job security and the ability of one adult's income to support an entire family paved the way for the possibility of the wife as some may still, however erroneously, envisage as typical: the non-employed woman who stays at home, supported by her husband, while she manages his domestic life and his children. Changing economic realities since the mid-1970s have fostered ideas of the new woman, her new independence, the advantages of working and staying in work while simultaneously raising a family. Whereas the median income of men grew steadily and substantially between 1955 and 1973 (in the US from $15 056 to $24 621) the growth stopped, and by 1987 had dropped 19 per cent.[5] As inflation was accompanied by job insecurity and high unemployment, the average family income in 1988 crept only 6 per cent higher than in 1973 even though twice as many married women were working.[6] The high profile yuppie generation – couples consisting of two high earners – was a blip in economic and social history, as some very lucky or highly-qualified couples began to have a great deal of spending power earlier on in their lives, with more time in which to spend their money than had young couples of previous generations, because the opportunities for both men and women in early adulthood were good and because these men and women were having children later.

Opportunities are diminishing for both men and women. Fewer job opportunities do not as a rule lead to men's greater participation in home life, or to men's greater sharing of domestic tasks. Women of unemployed men seem particularly reluctant to instigate changes in their domestic arrangements. To insist that the unemployed husband engage in more child care and domestic work strikes the woman as unfair or unkind or insensitive, or insulting: 'Too much of that would get him down – you know, on top of everything else. It would be like throwing it up in his face. I couldn't do that', explained Janet, whose husband had been made redundant five months before. She kept her voice low as her husband watched television in the next room. 'I don't want to make him feel a failure', she concluded. This response is not isolated, but part of a trend: fewer wives of unemployed men work than do wives of employed men. Such women also feel that they should stay at home to 'keep him company' or to 'keep up his courage, you know, until he finds his feet again'.

Reduced job opportunities mean that women and men both need to work to ease their financial vulnerability. Two jobs may be harder to lose than one. The narrowing market also means that employers can demand more of their employees, that they can expect to increase working hours, and that employees rise to this challenge because they do not want to put themselves to any disadvantage. It can mean that a partner's more demanding job may be accepted, because the risks are perceived as greater and the options are perceived to be fewer. It also means that women at work compete with more men, for in conditions of high unemployment, even those inferior 'women's' jobs may seem attractive to men looking for work.

When men and women compete, men tend to do better. Both in Europe and America this is getting worse, not better. Not only has the gap between the wages of women and the wages of men widened, but the old division between men's work and women's work remains – and where there is job segregation, there is job inequality, for the work that is designated women's work is less well-paid, with less status, with fewer paths to promotion. According to the latest Census Bureau report, nearly 80 per cent of women are still in clerical sales, service technical, factory or plant jobs. Lawyers, judges and engineers account for less than 1 per cent of all employed women. The sexual integration of the workplace is occurring more as a result of men turning to occupations such as nursing, receptionist and telephone operator, than as a result of women entering male employment. Women's employment does not fall rapidly in a recession simply because the services they offer – part-time, short-term, unskilled, non-unionized – appeal to employers more during a recession when demands for productivity are unknown and likely to diminish.

Women have made gains by investing more in their training and experience, through legislation against certain restrictive customs, through suppression of some prejudice, through increased bargaining power. But the advances women have made are slowing down. While women represented nearly 20 per cent of all employed managers and administrators in 1982 – a rise of 16 per cent since 1970 – that progress was, until very recently, at a standstill. This is not a deliberate backlash, as much as a mess of mismatches, of assumptions that equality is available alongside prejudicial habits and practices which sustain inequality.

The interlocking and locking-in of unfriendly structures is neither inevitable nor permanent. What is needed, quite simply, is greater flexibility – which is what all women seek, and which has worked for the women who have succeeded. They have found ways of taking a flexible course that happens to work. Most women aim for flexibility – but most women are disadvantaged by those aims.

Work Flexibility: The Challenge Defeated

Throughout the past twenty years women have sought new ways of working. The most obvious solution was to accommodate their orientation to the home by making the home their place of work. The advantages for women of working from home are clear. It allows them to rest easy with all those emergencies which play havoc with women's more rigid work schedules. It allows them to be available and accessible if an emergency should occur during the day – and emergencies in a family with young children, are not things which occur occasionally, but events which are expected, and which occur regularly. It allows them to arrange each day's time to fit each day's demands, to work late, to rise early, to work efficiently, with real measures of productivity, hence avoiding the control, the intrusion and the frequent senselessness of clock time.

The advantages of home work signal its dangers. The clear advantages mean that many women are willing to take it at disadvantageous rates. Hence lower rates of pay are frequently offered. Because it can be done in one's own time, the time done is often not properly paid for. Because it is so convenient for women who want to offer their services to employers, home work becomes segregated. It becomes women's work, and as such becomes low-paid and without promotion prospects, without security of tenure and without benefits. Because it allows one to be available and accessible in case of need, women who work at home are constantly interrupted. Their work is not seen as real work because it lacks the trappings of office space and workplace aura. One remains the wife and the mother in the home even as one tries to define oneself as the home worker. In fact the most common complaint among women who did work at home was that people always felt free, apparently, to interrupt them, nor did they get whatever kudos they thought they deserved from working, since there was no official aura about their work. Children of course were the main source of interruption, but by no means the only source. Interruption came in several ways. First, there was the presumption of an emergency. I remember knocking on the closed door of my mother's study as she was preparing for specialist exams in ophthalmology, 'Is it important?' she demanded coldly from the other side of the door. After a few moments' consideration, I assured her, 'Yes.' For the ribbon on my toy kangaroo had come undone. It was a beautiful bow, thin and blue and silky, and we had admired it together, and she had warned me that the only way to keep it so beautiful was never to untie it. I needed it retied, by an expert, before the creases which marked its tied pattern were lost. This was clearly an emergency.

Other women find that interruptions come in process of minimization. Mary Hoffman, the children's writer, found that her mother-in-law, who lived in a ground floor flat in her building, would 'pop up' either for a 'quick chat' or 'to check up' on something. In the mother-in-law's view, these interruptions were 'nothing' since they 'took no time at all', yet to the writer, hoarding her time while her three young children were at school, the interruptions were exasperating. Another minimizing technique was described by Daniella Hyde, who would work at home in the evenings, while her husband would look after the children and the post-dinner domestic tasks. 'He puts his head around the door and starts mouthing words – as though as long as he doesn't actually speak he's not really disturbing me, yet it takes longer – for me to guess what he's saying, or why he wants me, and then I start shouting and he backs away, but since I didn't know what he wanted in the first place I start worrying, so I go back to him and with apologies and queries – and the whole thing is utterly exhausting.'

Another source of interruption arises from the politeness factor. Again, for a woman who was setting up an information processing service in her home computer, the mornings were a 'rich time' for work. She would walk her 3-year-old to nursery school, and then march rapidly home to settle down to work. But for many of the women she met on the walk home, this time was reprieve from the demands of a child, and it was time to talk, to connect, to share. 'You can say "I have to rush off to work" but when they know you're just going home they think it's rude. The mothers who drive off to work don't link up with them either, but they're seen as different. I once explained I just couldn't go to a coffee morning, that's just not the way I can use my mornings. They took it as a real rejection, like I was setting up a difference between me and them that really didn't exist.' For women who worked at home the definition of themselves as workers, and as working, became a problem both of identity and relationship.

In *How to Survive as a Working Mother* Lesley Garner's terse advice about home work is that it simply should not be done. It is, she believes, a 'trap', a way of gaining pin-money without any benefits of employment. It is simply a means of sheer exploitation at its most depressing and degrading. Home work can indeed be made into exploitative work, but it need not be. In fact, it is a growing area of employment which has environmental advantages, since it releases workers from the necessity of transport, and financial ones, since it decreases the cost to firms of office space. It is also becoming increasingly viable, through computers, telephones and faxes. It has also been found to be extremely efficient – in terms of productivity. When Rank Xerox, under the pressure of office space, allowed a pilot scheme whereby 5 per cent of its office staff ran small businesses from home, it was found that the productivity of this group – some of whom wanted to reduce their working week, some of whom wanted to increase their earnings – virtually doubled.[7]

When Juliet Schor exposed the human cost and corporate cruelty of overwork, she saw that people poured time into their work to protect their jobs and their image as good workers.[8] Time is particularly cruel to women who are mothers, most of whom continue to feel a special need to spend time with their children, as they see the time their children require. The ideals of equality were formed when the future was expected to be less rushed than the present. Yet the ideals of equality at work have been pursued while time demands increased. As equality was so high on the agenda of so many women – and in particular on the agenda of the women who were entering masculine organizations, their emphasis was on equality. Anything a man could do they could do too – maybe better, maybe with children as well.

These women were not imprisoned by men's dreams, though they have been kept under a different kind of house arrest. Their mothers were confined to the home, and they have more or less been confined to a masculinized workplace, one which developed, and which proceeds, on the assumption that the workers therein have a wife at home to attend to domestic concerns.

Yet men as well as women would prefer to work fewer hours. What seems to differentiate the women from the men is that women's incentives to decrease their working days or working weeks or working years materialize into motive and action, whereas men's on the whole remain wishful thinking. The part-time work women seek, however, constrains their careers, even as it makes them and their children much happier. The depression which was found to plague the housewife in studies conducted in the 1960s and 1970s, has been found, in somewhat different forms, to shadow the woman who works full-time – either in terms of stress from doing too much, or from feeling she must compensate her husband or her children for the time spent away from them, or from being unable to do herself as much as she would like of what she values. It is the married woman who works part-time that, today, has been found to be the least prone to depression;[9] and it is the infants of part-time working mothers who best tolerate group child care.[10]

Women continue to confront the problems remaining from a division between work and home, where work is part of the public domain, inhabited by creatures whose private lives are lived elsewhere, and on different terms. Their sense that this is wrong comes into conflict with their goals of equality: they want to be equal and yet they know that in order to thrive, they must make things different; for they cannot thrive, as people and as workers and as parents, in the established working climate.

Many changes have been effected to make work possible for women. Twenty-five years ago women who entered the diplomatic corps in Britain had to resign from their jobs when they married. Now they can get joint postings, and up to five years' unpaid leave – quite apart from maternity leave. In America many companies have established crèches. Day care centres were carefully designed at IBM, Proctor and Gamble, Campbell's

Soup, Polaroid, Johnson and Johnson, Eastman Kodak, and some Government Centers. The family leave bill, passed in the US in 1993, ensures that companies with 50 or more employees must provide up to 12 weeks' unpaid leave to allow a worker to care for a relative in need. Awareness of the problems has increased, while their extent remains daunting.

There have been other innovative ways of dealing with the problems of full-time employment. Jobs can officially be shared. A person – virtually always a woman – finds a 'twin', that is, someone whose qualifications and skills and ideas match hers sufficiently so that together they can act as a single worker. Hence they can divide their time, working part-time, but at one good full-time job. Alternatively, one can find someone to complement one's skills – a civil servant who has a strong political background may choose as a partner someone who has a firm economic background. Some academic couples who work in the same field, get over the difficulty of finding two jobs for their speciality by offering their services as one job. Employers remain sceptical. Will they have to train two people, at twice the investment? Will they have to brief two people? Will they have to keep saying the same thing twice? For the employer, as well as the time-sharing employees, time is the issue, the highest commodity, the resource not to be invested unwisely, and not to be given away.

The flexibility that exists is made use of by many women, but they are sanctioned for it. People who work in job shares or who opt for more flexible time are rarely promoted, and are the first to be made redundant. Men, who seem to have a greater choice, who can fall back on old habits and patterns when the going gets rough, who can cut down on family work when the work pressure increases, learn rapidly not to make the mistake women make who need more flexible time, and often put family first.

Escaping the Design

The women I discuss in this book were initially careful to avoid part-time jobs, knowing well that part-time work is work designed for women and as such is poorly paid. The norm of a strong career involves full-time uninterrupted employment. It involves the devotion of the bulk of one's life to work. These women spotted the prejudicial structures of traditional female work, but their efforts sometimes came up against other structures. Flexible, part-time jobs clearly offer one solution to women's domestic commitment. Flexible or part-time jobs would then leave this system of domestic commitments basically unchanged. What women want most is good, challenging, responsible jobs, but with reasonable work hours. Work hours for good, responsible, challenging full-time jobs are often, by any standards, unreasonable. They most certainly do not allow for a balanced life.

But flexible working hours, which even the most determined women longed for, and which many women opted for, inhibit occupational advance and enforce women's lower occupational status. The norm of full-time employment is possible only for those in good health, who can avoid such responsibilities as care for the old, the young and the ill. Full-time employment depends on social arrangements which release workers from outside commitments.

Though many men would like to work fewer hours, few men work part-time. Part-time rates of pay are drastically reduced: two half-time incomes would not support a family, or offer the insurance and pension benefits that one full-time job does. Moreover, men with young children tend to work longer hours – getting over four times as much paid overtime as childless married men of the same age.[11] The structure of their jobs encourages overtime, and hence increases women's domestic responsibilities. Part-time work is presumed inefficient, whereas the deleterious effects of prolonged work – through fatigue, and 'burn out' – are ignored. Yet many men at the very top of the occupational pyramid do several 'part-time' jobs: for though employers often insist that jobs with high responsibility cannot be part-time, the jobs on the highest pay scale, and the highest rank, are often a series of part-time jobs. Directors and managers do many different things – administrative, personnel work, personal relations work, management of specific departments. Many executive jobs can be analyzed into three or four or five different jobs – all as it were, part-time; but it remains very difficult to break the assumption that high levels of responsibility are compatible with part-time hours.

Among this sample of women, who were also mothers and who did not have wives, were many who were so concerned to maintain a career on a part-time level that they had to create new careers – as cottage industries, or self-employed artists, or family businesses. Some, too, were able to construct job shares and some, once their expertise as full-time workers was recognized, were able to sustain credibility with an employer as part-time workers. Some did overwork for a stretch of time – as they complete a book or run for an election – but this is a response to a specific challenge. Employment practices are difficult to break, but they are not immutable.

Living in Time

The ethos in the workplace still seems to assume that workers will have wives at home. In this respect organizational culture – in particular, corporate culture – has not changed. As Kathleen Hirsch notes, 'It still works best for the entrenched elite: white men with few family obligations.'[12]

Women's progress is slow because domestic and work structures interlock to constrain them. This interlocking is not a gridlock: change is possible, but it is slow because ways have to be found round the ready-made patterns. Both women and men have been trying, with varying degrees of success, to change the division of labour in the home. This remains difficult to change as men tend to be paid more, and rewarded more for their work-time while more work-time is demanded of them. The next wave of change depends upon making working schedules and working cultures more flexible and more forgiving.

There have recently been passionate pleas for kinder, gentler norms – not only because as a society we need a different kind of care, and different mode of responsibility towards our future, both the future of our environment and the future of our children, but also because this would generate a more productive and competitive economy.[13] Without flexible time, without regard for family time, women will remain burdened by traditional women's roles and will be 'overextended and desperate'[14] as they try to compete in the modern, demanding workforce.

Time bullies workers, and most women refuse to sacrifice their need *both* to work and to love on behalf of their need to work. It is through time that women are now constrained to make choices which often act against them or against their families, and it is through time that they can progress. 'The control over time is absolutely critical, in terms of what one wants to do with one's life,' says Lotte Bailyn. What so many of us experience is now being highlighted: time is the scarce resource. Employers are now asking more of it from their employees. It is a badge, a proof, a token of commitment. Many feel its demands, and its costs, yet few realize what a useless token it is. Increased hours at work do not necessarily increase production, but often – especially over the long term – decrease it, with burn-out, with ill health, with stress. The link between time and productivity is outmoded, based on a simple model of the production line, wherein longer working hours lead to more things produced. Yet companies continue to be 'manned' 24 hours a day, seven days a week as they respond to the increased volume of work and the manufactured belief that it is necessary to remain in continuous contact with every other country, whatever its time difference. Time becomes 'a proxy indicator for performance, based on some crazy assumption that the more time, the better'.[15]

And alongside this 'bully time' run notions of female rates of pay, based on the mistaken assumption that women do not need to earn a 'family wage'. Andrea Dupress, an astrophysicist in the Harvard–Smithsonian Center for Astrophysics, once protested that her salary was lower than that of her male colleagues, but was told, 'Well, we knew you had a husband who could support you, so we didn't see anything wrong with keeping your salary down at this low level.'[16] But while low, or lower, wages continue to be seen as fair for women, on the assumption that women do not need to support a family, more and more women need to do so.

While women's lives may not be changing within the home, the finances of the family are changing so that most women need to work to sustain family income, and increasingly more women are sole supporters of their family. Yet women continue to make different decisions, partly through habit and example, partly because 'female' occupations provide friendlier working conditions, and partly because some women simply value the work of traditional female caring and service professions. Yet the need to ensure that women are entitled to equal pay for work of equal value comes up against common ideas of how employment and pay should be determined. Women's jobs continue to be seen as less skilled, less important than men's jobs, however much skill and value they clearly have. And while losing one's job is an increasingly high risk for men, for many women there remains the certainty that if they wish to have children they will have to leave or change their current job, for there is no 'right to return' on a time basis that suits mothering women. As they leave they face enormous consequences for reduction in long-term career opportunities.

It is against these odds that the women of today are creating new patterns of working and family lives. These odds are increasing, but so too is the number of women involved in the effort against them. Each individual move forward is the result of a very private weighing of costs and benefits. Each assessment of the costs and benefits is grounded in individual circumstances and individual vision. The wide, and growing variation in women's life patterns places enormous weight on the personal decisions and responsibility of each woman. The variations in their lives frequently make them feel isolated, as each acts according to her own inner prompting and within the detailed circumstances in which she acts. But most women, however successful in their careers and professions, are aware that their advance through institutions and hierarchies and organizational cultures was partly accidental. However much their abilities and achievements warranted their success they knew that, as women, their histories might have been very different. There is a growing underground of women who, through the examples they set, are passing on patterns to other women who, like them, are still haunted by social and emotional determinants whose force they would rather resist. Their stories are not easy, and their choices and directions cannot provide simple blueprints for others. The women who come after them will also have to find their own ways; but there is much well-broken ground. The women whose stories contributed to this book showed that each sought a way to create flexibility and balance and high ideals without waiting for the world to change first. As they enact different patterns, their different choices will resonate with other women's and men's need to combine work and love in better ways. In resisting structures individually, they can join together in restructuring the time in which we live.

Notes

Introduction

1. Jane O'Reilly, *The Girl I Left Behind* (New York: Macmillan, 1982).

2. Judi Marshall, *Women Managers: Travellers in a Male World* (Chichester, UK: Wiley, 1984); Ann Oakley, *Sex, Gender and Society* (London: Temple Smith, 1972).

3. Virginia Woolf, *A Room of One's Own* (London: Virago, 1977).

4. Lillian Rubin, *Worlds of Pain: Life in the Working Class Family* (New York: Basic Books, 1976).

5. Arlie Russell Hochschild, with Anne Machung, *The Second Shift* (New York: Viking, 1989).

6. Judith Chaney, 'Social Networks and job information: the situation of women who return to work', EOC/SSRC Joint Panel of Equal Opportunities (June, 1981), p. 32.

7. Marilyn French, *The War Against Women* (Harmondsworth: Penguin, 1993).

8. Rosalind Coward, *Our Treacherous Hearts: Why women let men have their way* (London: Faber, 1992); Colette Dowling, *The Cinderella Complex* (New York: Summit Books, 1981); Matina Horner, 'Toward and Understanding of Achievement Related Conflicts in Women,' *Journal of Social Issues,* 28 (1972).

9. Rosalind Coward, 1992, as above.

10. Matina Horner, 1972, as above.

11. Judi Marshall, 'Re-visioning career concepts: a feminist invitation',

in M. B. Arthur, D. T. Hall and B. S. Lawrence (eds), *Handbook of Career Theory* (Cambridge: Cambridge University Press, 1989).

12. Judi Marshall, 1984, as above.

13. Carol Gilligan, 'Joining the Resistance: Psychology, politics, girls and women', *Michigan Quarterly Review*, Vol. XXIX, no. 4, 1990, pp. 501–36; and *In a Different Voice: Psychological theory and women's development* (Cambridge, Mass.: Harvard University Press, 1982).

14. Matina Horner, 1972, as above.

15. Georgia Sassen, 'Success Anxiety in Women: A constructivist interpretation of its source and significance', *Harvard Educational Review*, Vol. 50, no. 1 (1980) pp. 13–24.

16. Nancy Chodorow, *The Reproduction of Mothering* (Berkeley: University of California Press, 1978).

17. Colette Dowling, *The Cinderella Complex* (New York: Summit, 1981).

18. Matina Horner, 'Towards an understanding of achievement-related conflicts in women', *Journal of Social Issues*, 28, (1972) pp. 157–76.

19. Sylvia Ann Hewlett, *A Lesser Life: The Myth of Women's Liberation in America* (New York: Warner Books, 1986).

20. Sylvia Ann Hewlett, as above; Patricia Allat, Teresa Kiel, Alan Bryman and Bill Bytheway (eds), *Women in the Life Cycle: Transitions and turning points* (London: Macmillan, 1987).

21. P. Young and M. Wilmot, *The Symmetrical Family* (London: Routledge and Kegan Paul, 1973), cited in Elizabeth Garnsey, 'Working Hours and Workforce Divisions', in Roger Tarling (ed.), *Flexibility in Labour Markets* (London: Academic Press, 1987).

22. V. George and P. Wilding, *Motherless Families* (London: Routledge and Kegan Paul, 1972).

23. Elizabeth Garnsey, 'Women's Labour and Soviet Economic Growth', working paper, Department of Engineering, University of Cambridge (1982), p. 20.

24. In 1946 there were under 60 men per 100 women in the age group 35–49. 'The deficit of males is only just beginning to lose its impact on many features of Soviet society.' Elizabeth Garnsey, 1982, as above.

25. Monica Fong and Gillian Paul, 'The Changing Role of Women in Employment in Eastern Europe', World Bank Discussion Paper, no. 8213, February, 1992.

26. B. Holland (ed.), *Soviet Sisterhood* (Bloomington: University of Indiana Press, 1983), cited in B. A. Engel, 'Soviet Women', *Signs*, Vol. 12, no. 4, 1987, pp. 781–96.

27. B. A. Engel, 1987, as above.

28. For a fictional account of this fact which has been noted elsewhere, see Julia Voznesenskaya, *The Women's Decameron (Damskii dekameron)* (London: Methuen 1986).

29. Arlie Russell Hochschild, with Anne Machung, as above, 1989.

30. Elizabeth Badinther, *L'XY de la Masculinité* (Odile Jacob: Paris, 1992); Chodorow, 1978, as above.

31. Suzanne Gordon, *Prisoners of Men's Dreams* (Boston: Little, Brown, 1991), p. 16.

32. OECD, 1982; cited in Garnsey, 1987; and Juliet Schor, *The Overworked American: The unexpected decline of leisure* (New York: Basic Books, 1991).

33. Naomi Wolf, *The Beauty Myth* (London: Chatto, 1990).

34. Susan Faludi, *Backlash: The undeclared war against American Women* (New York: Crown, 1991).

35. Juliet Schor, as above.

36. Betty Friedan, *The Feminine Mystique* (New York: Summit Books, 1963).

37. Germaine Greer, *The Female Eunuch* (London: MacGibbon and Kee, 1970).

38. 'Working Mothers and Preserving Family Living Standards', Congress of the United States, Joint Economic Committee (9 May 1986); cited in Rosabeth Moss Kanter, *When Giants Learn to Dance* (New York: Simon and Schuster, 1989).

39. Terri Apter and Elizabeth Garnsey, 'The Social Enactment of Obstacles to Equal Opportunity' (forthcoming).

1 What Do Women Want?

1. Claudia Golden, *Understanding the Gender Gap* (New York: Oxford University Press, 1990), p. vii.

2. Goldin, 1990, as above, p. 4.

3. Goldin, 1990, as above, p. 4.

4. Goldin, 1990, as above, p. 170.

5. Goldin, 1990, as above, p. 176.

6. Goldin, 1990, as above, p. 179; 1957 Hussey Report: 8 October 1965; 24 August 1956.

7. Elizabeth Beardsley Butler, *Women and the Trades: Pittsburgh, 1907–1908* (Pittsburgh: University of Pittsburgh Press, 1984), p. 373; cited in Goldin, as above, p. 204.

8. Goldin, as above, p. 203.

9. Gilbert Brim, *Ambition* (New York: Basic Books, 1992).

10. E. Lee, *Export-processing Zones and Industrial Employment in Asia* (ILO, ARTEP, 1985), p. 40; cited in Elizabeth Garnsey and Liba Paukert, *Industrial Change and Women's Employment: Trends in the new international division of labour*, Research Series no. 86 (Geneva: International Institute for Labour Studies, 1987).

11. Garnsey and Paukert, as above, p. 28.

12. Kathleen Hirsch, 'A New Vision of Corporate America', *Boston Sunday Globe Magazine* (21 April 1992), p. 16.

13. Byron, *Don Juan*, 1, cxciv.

14. Inge Brovermann *et al.*, 'Sex Role Stereotypes and Clinical Judgements of Mental Health', *Journal of Consulting and Clinical Psychology*, 34 (February 1970).

15. Roger Philips and Faith Gubroy, 'Sex Role Stereotypes and Clinical Judgements of Mental Health: the Broverman's findings re-examined', *Sex Roles* 12 (1985) pp. 179–93.

16. Diane Ehrensaft, *Parenting Together: Men and women sharing the care of their children* (New York: Free Press, 1987).

17. Judi Marshall, *Women Managers: Travellers in a Male World* (Chichester: John Wiley, 1984).

18. Marilyn Heins, 'Current Status of Women Physicians', *International Journal of Women's Studies*, 1: 3 (1978), pp. 297–305.

19. Hochschild, 1989, as above.

20. Hochschild, 1989, as above.

21. Marshall, 1984, as above.

22. Liz Roman Gallese, *Women Like Us* (New York: Morrow, 1985).

23. James Duesenberry, 'Comment on "An Economic Analysis of Fertility," by Gary Becker', in *Demographic and Economic Change in Developed Countries* (Princeton: Universities–National Bureau Conferences series, 11, 1960).

24. *How to Complain about Goods and Services* (London: Consumer's Association, 1987).

25. Isabell Sawhill, 'Economic Perspectives on the Family', in Alice Amsden (ed.), *The Economics of Women and Work* (Harmondsworth: Penguin, 1980).

26. Isabell Sawhill, as above.

27. Claudia Goldin, Lois Shaw and David Shapiro, 'Women's Work Plans: Contrasting expectations and actual work experience,' *Monthly Labor Review*, 110 (November 1987), pp. 7–13.

2 Why do Women Mother?

1. For example, Nancy Friday, *My Mother My Self: The daughter's search for identity* (New York: Delacorte Press, 1977).

2. Colette Dowling, *The Cinderella Complex* (New York: Summit Books, 1981).

3. I refer to Nancy Chodorw, *The Reproduction of Mothering* (Berkeley: University of California Press, 1978) and Carol Gilligan, *In a Difference Voice* (Cambridge, Mass.: Harvard University Press, 1982).

4. See, for example, Freda Bright, *Futures* in which a high-powered business woman is transformed by the problems of child care and separation anxiety into a traditional woman who chooses a gender-conservative man. An ad for cable television, too, showed a woman who had decided to give up her job to spend more time with her daughter. She waits for her by the school bus stop and they go home together for cookies and milk and good television viewing in one another's company.

5. See, for example, Anita Shreve, *Women Together, Women Alone* (New York: Viking Penguin, 1989).

6. B. Pfau Effinger, *Erwerbsverlauf und Risiko.* Arbeitsmarktrisiken im Generationenvergleich Weinhem (1990); cited in Birgit Pfau-Effinger, 'Modernisation, Culture and Part-Time Employment', paper presented to the XIVth World Conference of the International Working Party on Labour Market Segmentation in Cambridge (16–21 July 1992).

7. Ann Oakley, *Housewife* (Harmondsworth: Pelican, 1976), p. 176.

8. Ann Oakley, *Subject Woman* (London: Faber, 1985), p. 167.

9. John Kenneth Galbraith, *Economics and the Public Purpose* (Andre Deutsch: London, 1974), p. 33.

10. Ann Oakley, *Housewife*, 1976, as above.

11. Betty Freidan, *The Feminine Mystique* (New York: Summit, 1963).

12. Reported in Ann Oakley, 1978, as above.

13. Ann Oakley, *Taking it Like a Woman* (London: Fontana, 1985), p. 85.

14. Nancy Chodorow, 1978 as above, p. 169.

15. Gary Becker, *Human Capital: A Theoretical and Empirical Analysis with Special Reference to Education* (New York, 1964).

16. Alice Rossi, 'A biosocial perspective on parenting', *Daedelus*, 106, no. 2 (1978), pp. 1–31.

17. V. George and P. Wilding, *Motherless Families* (London: Routledge and Kegan Paul, 1972).

18. Jane Humphries is currently involved in a Leverhulme-supported project to fill this gap.

19. Sylvia Ann Hewlett, 1986, as above.

20. Arlie Hochschild, *The Second Shift*, as above.

21. Sue Newell, 'What affects women's career decisions at the point when they enter motherhood?', paper presented to the Women and Psychology Conference (14 July 1990).

22. G. Friedrich, 'Sozialversicherungsfreie Beschaftigung' (Koln: Untersuchung im Auftrag des Bundesministers Fur Arbeits und Sozialordnung, 1989), and H. Stuck, *Die modern Angestellen* (Hamburg, 1991), cited in B. Pfau-Effinger, 1992.

23. Jouko Natti, 'Part-time employment in the Nordic countries: a trap for women?' paper delivered to the International Working Party on Labour Market Segmentation Conference in Cambridge (14 July 1992).

24. Thirty-eight per cent of female part-timers and 16 per cent of full-timers said that during their working history they had chosen part-time work for family reasons. (Other reasons are studying, health, age.) See Natti, 1992, as above.

25. Ursula Beer and Ursula Miller, 'Coping with a new reality: barriers and possibilities', paper presented to the XIVth World Conference of the International Working Party on Labour Market Segmentation in Cambridge (16–21 July 1992).

26. Margery Spring Rice, *Working Class Wives* (London: Virago, 1981).

27. Rosalind Coward, *Our Treacherous Hearts: Why women let men have their way* (London: Faber, 1992).

28. Valerie Grove, *The Compleat Woman: Marriage, motherhood, career* (London: Hogarth Press, 1987).

29. Ann Oakley, *Taking it Like a Woman* (London: Jonathan Cape, 1984).

30. Adrienne Rich, *Of Woman Born* (London: Virago, 1977).

3 What Do the Children Need?

1. Freda Bright, *Futures* (London: Collins, 1983), p. 244.

2. Ann Oakley, 1984, as above, p. 13.

3. Alice Walker, *In Search of Our Mothers' Gardens* (New York: Harcourt Brace, 1983).

4. The women in this sample were in this respect very different from the women executives studied by Margaret Hennig and Ann Jardim (see *The Managerial Woman* [London: Pan, 1979]). The earlier study showed women eschewing their traditional mothers and having benefited from a close

relationship to their fathers. Many of the women in my sample spoke admiringly of their fathers and appreciated his 'input' in their self-confidence and sense of direction, but they were no less, and more generally, supported by their mothers and influenced by them – albeit sometimes negatively – wanting to be what the mother had not become.

5. Arlie Hochschild, 1989, as above.

6. Telephone interview with Dr David Scarff, Washington, DC, 10 April 1983.

7. Arlie Hochschild, 1989, as above.

8. The remarkable studies on monkeys which showed that the monkey infant, offered two dummy mothers, one with exposed wires which provided food, and another which never provided food but which was wrapped with towels, ran to the soft dummy to seek comfort in distress. H. E. Harlow and M. K. Harlow, 'Learning to Love', *American Scientist*, 54(3), (1966), pp. 244–72.

9. Daniel Stern, *The Interpersonal World of the Infant: A view from psychoanalysis and developmental psychology* (New York: Basic Books, 1985).

10. Penelope Leach, *Who Cares? A New Deal for Mothers and their Small Children* (Harmondsworth: Penguin, 1979).

11. Michael Rutter, *Maternal Deprivation Reassessed* (Middlesex: C. Nicholls, 1972).

12. Margaret Bone, *Preschool Children and their Need for Day Care*, Office of Population Census and Surveys (London: HMSO, 1977).

13. For examples, see Sylvia Ann Hewlett, *When the Bough Breaks: The cost of neglecting our children* (New York: Basic Books, 1991), and Andree Aelion Brooks, *Children of Fast-Track Parents* (New York: Viking, 1989).

14. Sylvia Ann Hewlett, 1991, as above, p. 83.

15. Rosemary Jackson, *Mothers Who Leave Their Children* (Glastonbury: Gothic Image, in press).

16. Sylvia Plath, 1962, *Letters Home*, in A. S. Plath (ed.) (New York: Bantam, 1962), pp. 443–4.

17. Sylvia Plath, as above, p. 570.

18. Andrea Rock, 'Can you afford your kids?' *Money* (July 1990); Vivian Zelizer, *Pricing the Priceless Child: The changing social values of children* (New York: Basic Books, 1985).

19. Isabel Sawhill, 1980, as above.

20. Sylvia Ann Hewlett, as above.

21. Sylvia Ann Hewlett, as above, p. 26.

22. Gilbert Brim, 1992, as above, p. 80.

23. Gilbert Brim, 1992, as above, p. 81.

24. J. L. Richardson, *et al*, 'Substance Abuse Among Eighth-Grade Students Who Take Care of Themselves After School', *Pediatrics* 84, no. 3 (September, 1989) pp. 556–66.

25. Oliver Moles, National Institute of Education, paper presented to conference, Washington, DC (25 March 1983).

26. William H. Whyte, *The Organization Man* (New York: Simon and Schuster, 1956).

27. Sylvia Ann Hewlett, 1991, as above, p. 83; Walter Kiechel III, 'The Workaholic Generation,' *Fortune* (10 April 1989), p. 51.

28. Victor Fuchs, *Women's Quest for Economic Equality* (Cambridge, Mass.:

Harvard University Press 1988) p. 111; people now work an average of six hours more per week than in 1973. See Juliet Schor, *The Overworked American* (New York: Basic Books, 1991); Nancy Gibbs, 'Has America Run out of Time?' *Time* (24 April 1989); Sylvia Ann Hewlett, as above.

29. Sylvia Ann Hewlett, 1991, as above; see also, cited by Hewlett, Susan Cotts Watkins, Jane A. Menken and John Bongaarts, 'Demographic Foundations of Family Change,' *American Sociological Review* 52, no. 3 (1987); pp. 346–58.

30. Juliet Schor, 1991, as above.

31. William R. Mattox, Jr, 'The Family Time Famine', *Family Policy* 3, no. 1 (1990).

4 Having It All – New Options; New Myths

1. Erik H. Erikson, *Childhood and Society*, 2nd edn (New York: W. W. Norton, 1963).

2. Julia Brannen and Peter Moss, *Managing Mothers: Dual earner households after maternity leave* (London: Unwin Hyman, 1991).

3. *Beyond the Career Break*, IMS report no. 223 (IMS: University of Sussex, 1992), p. 2.

4. Julia Brannen and Peter Moss, 1991, as above.

5. Lillian Rubin, *Women of a Certain Age* (New York: Harper and Row, 1979).

5. The Wage Learners: Working as Necessity

1. Katherine Gerson, *Hard Choices* (Berkeley, California: University of California Press, 1985).

2. See Judith Chaney, 'Social networks and job information: the situation of women who return to work', a research project funded by the EOC/SSRC Joint Panel on Equal Opportunities (Equal Opportunities Commission, Manchester, 1981).

3. Arlie Hochschild, 'Foreword', in Terry Arendall, *Mothers and Divorce* (Berkeley: University of California Press, 1986).

4. Gary Becker, 'A theory of the allocation of time,' *Economic Journal* 75, no. 299 (1965), pp. 493–517; Talcott Parsons, 'The Social Structure of the Family,' in R. Anshen (ed.), *The Family, Its Functions and Destiny* (New York: Harper, 1949).

5. Clare Dyer, 'Single mothers lose child care claim' *Guardian* (30 July 1990), p. 4.

6. Judith Chaney, 1981, as above.

7. V. Beechy, 'Some notes on female wage labour in capitalist production,' *Capital and Class*, no. 3 (1977), pp. 45–66.

8. Jill Rubery (ed.) *Women and Recession* (London: Routledge and Kegan Paul, 1988).

9. Marcia Freedman, 'The Search for Shelters', in *Labour Markets: Segments and Shelters* (New York: Allanhead, Osman/Universal Books, 1976).

10. Jill Rubery, 'The Economics of Equal Value', Research Discussion Series No. 3 (Manchester, England: Equal Opportunities Commission, 1992).

11. Terri Apter and Elizabeth Garnsey, as above (forthcoming).

12. Monica Fong and Gillian Paul, 'The Changing Role of Women in Employment in Eastern Europe', World Bank Discussion Paper, no. 8213 (February 1992).

13. B. Holland, ed., *Soviet Sisterhood* (Bloomington: University of Indiana Press, 1983) cited in B. A. Engel, 'Soviet Women', *Signs*, Vol. 12, no. 4, (1987) pp. 781–96.

14. B. A. Engel, 1987, as above.

15. Ginni Morrow, 'Children's Work', paper presented to the Cambridge Social Stratification Seminar (9 September 1992).

16. Ginni Morrow, 1992, as above.

17. Jean Duncombe and Dennis Marsden, ' "Workaholics" and 'Whingeing Women": Gender Inequalities in the Performance of "Emotion Work"', Cambridge Social Stratification Seminar (9 September 1992); Diane Ehrensaft, 1987, as above.

18. Stephen Pudney and Jonathan Thomas, 'Unemployment benefit, incentives and the labour supply of wives of unemployed men: econometric estimates' (London: HMSO, May 1992); US figures from J. Micklewright and G. Giannelli, 1991, 'Why do women married to employed men have low participation rates?', Working paper, European University Institute, Florence; A. Dilnot and M. Kell, 'Male unemployment and women's work', in A. Dilnot and I. Walker (eds), *The Economics of Social Security* (Oxford: Oxford University Press, 1989).

19. Pudney and Thomas, 1992, as above.

20. Jay Ginn and Sara Arber, 'Class, caring and the life course', in S. Arber and M. Evandrou (eds), *Ageing, Independence and the Life Course* (London: Jessica Kingsley, forthcoming).

21. Juliet Schor, 1991, as above; Lotte Bailyn, 'Freeing Work from the Constraints of Location and Time', *New Tech. Work and Employment* 3, no. 2 (1988), pp. 143–52.

6   Why Women Fail

1. Lois Waldis Hoffman, 'Early Childhood Experiences and Women's Achievement Motives', *Journal of Social Issues*, 28, no. 2, (1972) pp. 129–55; L. M. Terman and M. N. Oden, *The Gifted Child Grows Up* (Stanford, CA: California University Press, 1947).

2. Liz Roman Gallese, *Women Like Us* (New York: Morrow, 1985).

3. Judi Marshall, 1984, as above.

4. Lyn Mikel Brown and Carol Gilligan, *Meeting at the Crossroads: Women's psychology and girls' development* (Cambridge, Mass.: Harvard University Press, 1992).

5. N. T. Feather and A. C. Raphelson, 'Fear of Success in Australian and American Student Groups: Motive or sex-role stereotype?', *Journal of Personality*, 42 (1974), pp. 190–201; L. Monahan, D. Kuhn and P. Shaver, 'Intrapsychic versus cultural explanations of the fear of success motive',

Journal of Personality and Social Psychology, 29 (1974), pp. 60–4; M. Hyland, 'There is no motive to avoid success: the compromise explanation for success-avoiding behavior, *Journal of Personality* 57, no. 7 (1989), pp. 665–91.

6. Mary Douglas, *The Home and the School* (London: MacGibbon and Kee, 1964), pp. 70–1.

7. D. Bem and S. Bem, 'We're all non-conscious sexists', *Psychology Today*, 4, no. 6 (November 1970).

8. S. V. Rosser, 'The Gender Equation', *The Sciences* (September–October 1992), pp. 42–7.

9. Lynn Mikel Brown and Carol Gilligan, 1992, as above.

10. Mary Douglas, *All Our Future* (London: MacGibbon and Kee, 1968).

11. Cited in S. V. Rosser, 'The Gender Equation', *The Sciences* (September–October 1992), p. 44.

12. Carolyn Heilbrun, *Writing a Woman's Life* (New York: Ballantine Books, 1989).

13. J. W. Atkinson, 'Motivational determinants of risk taking behavior', *Psychological Review*, 64 (1957) pp. 359–72; J. O. Raynor and E. E. Entin, 'Future orientation and achievement motivation', in J. O. Raynor and E. E. Entin (eds), *Motivation, Career, Striving and Aging* (New York: Hemisphere Books, 1982), pp. 13–82.

14. Matina Horner, 'Fail: Bright Women', *Psychology Today*, 3 (6) (1969) p. 36.

15. Matina Horner, 'Towards an understanding of achievement-related conflicts in women, *Journal of Social Issues*, 28 (1972), pp. 157–76.

16. Virginia Woolf, 'Professions for Women' in *The Death of the Mother and Other Essays* (New York: Harcourt Brace, 1942), pp. 236–8.

17. Georgia Sassen, 'Success Anxiety in Women: A Constructivist Interpretation of its Source and its Significance', *Harvard Educational Review*, Vol. 50, no. 1 (February 1980), pp. 13–24.

18. M. E. Hyland, C. Curtis, and D. Mason, 'Fear of Success: motive and cognition,' *Journal of Personality and Social Psychology*, 55 (1985), pp. 642–51.

19. 'Health Notes', *Harpers* (October 1992), p. 120.

20. Suzanne Gordon, *Prisoners of Men's Dreams* (Boston: Little, Brown, 1991), pp. 6–9.

21. Judi Marshall, 'Patterns of Cultural Awareness as Coping Strategies for Women Managers', in S. E. Kahm and B. C. Lang (eds), *Women, Work and Coping: A multidisciplinary approach to workplace stress* (Montreal: McGill–Queen's University Press, 1993).

22. This term is used to describe different perceptions of 'on time' and 'off time' events in R. Helson, V. Mitchell and G. Moane, 'Personality and Patterns of Adherence and Nonadherence to the Social Clock', *Journal of Personality and Social Psychology*, 26 (1984), pp. 1079–96.

23. Susan Faludi, *Backlash: The undeclared war against American women* (New York: Crown, 1991).

24. Judi Marshall, 1984, as above; K. Gerson, 1985, as above.

25. H. Zuckerman, J. R. Cole, and J. T. Bruer, *The Outer Circle: Women in the scientific community* (New York: W. W. Norton, 1992).

26. Vaclav Havel, 'The power of the powerless' in *Living in Truth* (London: Faber, 1986), p. 45.

27. Garnsey, 1987, as above.

28. Elizabeth Garnsey, 'Exploring a critical systems perspective', *Innovation in the Social Sciences* (forthcoming, 1993).

29. E. Garnsey, 1993, as above.

7 Depression: A Female Ailment?

1. Maggie Scarf, *Unfinished Business: Pressure points in the lives of women* (New York: Doubleday, 1981).

2. G. W. Brown and T. Harris, 1978, *Social Origins of Depression* (London: Tavistock, 1978).

3. Jane Ussher, *Women's Madness: Misogyny or mental illness* (Hemel Hemsptead, England: Harvester, 1991) p. 3.

4. Jane Ussher, 1991, as above, pp. 5–6.

5. Ann Oakley, *Women Confined: Towards a Sociology of Childbirth* (Oxford: Martin Robertson, 1980).

6. Michele Barrett and Helen Roberts, 'Doctors and their patients: the social control of women in general practice,' in C. Smart and B. Smart (eds), *Women, Sexuality and Social Control* (London: Routledge and Kegan Paul, 1978).

7. R. Cooperstock and H. L. Lennard, 'Some social meanings of tranquillizer use', *Sociology of Health and Illness*, I, no. 3, (1979), pp. 331–47.

8. M. Seligman, 'Learned Helplessness and Depression', in R. Friedrich and M. Katz (eds), *The Psychology of Depression: Contemporary Theory and Research* (Washington, DC: US Government Printing House, 1979); A. Beck, *Cognitive Therapy and Emotional Disorders* (New York: International Universities Press, 1976).

9. G. Baruch, R. Barnett, C. Rivers, *Lifeprints* (New York: Signet, 1983).

10. Dana Crawley Jack, *Silencing the Self* (Cambridge, Mass.: Harvard University Press, 1991).

11. Lyn Mikel Brown and Carol Gilligan, 1992, as above.

12. Seymour Epstein and Walter Fenz, in Gardner Linzey and Calvin Halls (eds), *Theories of Personality: Primary sources and research* (Ann Arbor: University of Michigan, 1979).

13. Ann Oakley, 1976, as above.

14. Jane Elliot and Felicia Huppert, 'In sickness and in health: associations between physical and mental well-being, employment and parental status in a British nationwide sample of married women', *Psychological Medicine*, 21 (1991), pp. 515–24.

15. P. D. Cleary and D. Mechanic, 'Sex Differences in psychological distress among married people', *Journal of Health and Social Behaviour*, 24 (1983), pp. 111–21; R. C. Kessler and J. A. McRae, 'The effects of wives' employment on the mental health of married men and married women', *American Sociological Review*, 47 (1982), pp. 216–227.

16. Jane Elliott and Felicia Huppert, 1991, as above.

17. C. E. Roass and J. Mirrowsky, 'Child care and emotional adjustment to wives' employment, *Journal of Health and Social Behaviour*, 29 (1988), pp. 127–38, found that among employed wives, psychological well-being is affected not by children *per se* but by the difficulty of arranging child care.

18. Arlie Hochschild, 1989, as above.

19. Arlie Hochschild, 1989, as above.

20. Dorothy Rowe, *The Depression Handbook: The way of understanding depression leads to wisdom and freedom* (London: Collins, 1991).

21. Jane Elliott and Felicia Huppert, 1991, as above.

22. Dorothy Rowe, 1991, as above.

23. Jane Ussher, 1991, as above; Janice Lieberman, 'Issues in the Psychoanalytic Treatment of Single Females Over Thirty', *Psychoanalytic Review*, 78 no. 2 (Summer 1991), pp. 178–98.

24. Ann Oakley, 1985, as above, p. 81.

8 Dressed for Success

1. Margaret Hennig and Ann Jardim, *The Managerial Woman* (London: Pan, 1979).

2. This term is taken from R. Helson, V. Mitchell and G. Moane, 1984, 'Personality and Patterns of Adherence and Nonadherence to the Social Clock', *Journal of Personality and Social Psychology*, 46, pp. 1079–96.

3. Rosabeth Moss Kanter, *When Giants Learn to Dance* (New York: Simon and Schuster, 1989), p. 62.

4. Rosabeth Moss Kanter, 1989, as above, p. 62.

5. Rosabeth Moss Kanter, 1989, as above, p. 63.

6. Rosabeth Moss Kanter, 1989, as above, p. 43.

7. Patricia Aburdeen and John Naisbett, *Megatrends for Women* (New York: Century, 1992).

8. Korn/Ferry International, *Profile of Women Senior Executives* (Washington, DC, 1982).

9. Betty Friedan, *The Second Stage* (New York: Summit, 1981).

10. Suzanne Gordon, 1991, as above.

11. Judi Marshall, 1993, as above.

12. *The Key to the Men's Club* (Bristol: Institute of Management Books, 1992).

13. S. V. Rosser, 1992, as above.

14. Deborah Tannen, *You Just Don't Understand* (New York: Morrow, 1990).

15. Carol Gilligan, 1982, as above.

16. Jessi Bernard, *The Female World* (New York: Free Press, 1981).

17. Judi Marshall, 1993, as above.

18. D. L. Sheppard, 'Organizations, power and sexuality: the image and self image of women managers', in J. Hearn, D. L. Sheppard, P. Tancred-Sheriff, G. Burrell (eds), *The Sexuality of Organizations* (London: Sage Publications, 1989).

19. H. Callaway, 'Women's perspectives: research as revision', in P. Reason and J. Rowan (eds), *Human Inquiry* (Chichester: Wiley, 1981).

20. Judi Marshall, 1993, as above, p. 8.

21. Judi Marshall, 1993, as above.

22. Judi Marshall, 1993, as above, p. 5.

23. Judi Marshall, 1993, as above.

24. Judi Marshall, 1984, as above; D. L. Sheppard, 1989, as above.

25. Faye Crosby, 'The denial of personal discrimination,' *American Behavioral Scientist*, 27, (1989), pp. 371–86.

26. Judi Marshall, 1993, as above.

27. Judi Marshall, 1993, as above.

28. Judi Marshall, 1993, as above.

29. Neil Lyndon, *No More Sex War* (London: Sinclair-Stevenson, 1992).

30. Judi Marshall, 1993, as above.

9 Looking Ahead

1. S. Prendergast and A. Prout, 'Education for Parenthood' (Cambridge: Child Care and Development Group, University of Cambridge, 1985).

2. Sylvia Ann Hewlett, 1991, as above, p. 110, cites 'The Alimony Myth: Does No-Fault Divorce Make a Difference?' *Family Law Quarterly*, 14 (Fall 1980), p. 185.

3. Betty Friedan, 1963, as above, p. 256.

4. Norman Bonney and Elizabeth Reinach, 'Full-time Homeworkers: Changing Roles and Diverging Experiences,' paper presented to Cambridge Social Stratification Seminar (10 September 1992).

5. Sylvia Ann Hewlett's telephone interviews with Bob Cleveland, US Bureau of the Census, 30 April 1990; 2 May 1990; 22 September 1990. (Cited in Sylvia Ann Hewlett, 1991, as above, p. 39.)

6. Sylvia Ann Hewlett, 1991, as above, p. 39.

7. Lotte Bailyn, 'Toward the Perfect Workplace?', *Social Aspects of Computing*, 34, no. 4 (April 1989), pp. 460–71.

8. Juliet Schor, 1991, as above.

9. Jane Elliott and Felicia Huppert, 1991, as above.

10. Pamela Schwartz, 'Working Mothers of Infants: Conflicts and Coping Strategies', in *Women's Lives* (Ann Arbor, Michigan: Center for Women's Studies, University of Michigan, 1979).

11. P. Wilmot and M. Young, *The Symmetrical Family* (London: Routledge and Kegan Paul, 1973).

12. Kathleen Hirsch, as above.

13. Juliet Schor, as above; Lotte Bailyn, as above.

14. See Kathleen Hirsch, as above.

15. Lotte Bailyn, quoted by Kathleen Hirsch, as above.

16. Quoted in S. V. Rosser, 1992, as above, p. 46.

References

P. Aburdene and J. Naisbitt, *Megatrends for Women* (New York: Century, 1992).

M. D. Ainsworth, *et al., Deprivation of Maternal Care: A reassessment of its effects* (New York: Schocken Books, 1966).

H. S. Akiskal and W. T. McKinney, 'Overview of Recent Research in Depression', *Archives of General Psychiatry*, 32 (March, 1975), pp. 285–95.

P. Allat, T. Kiel, A., Bryman and B. Bytheway (eds), *Women in the Life Cycle: Transitions and turning points* (London: Macmillan, 1987).

T. Apter, *Why Women Don't Have Wives* (London: Macmillan, 1985).

T. Apter and E. Garnsey, 'The Social Enactment of Obstacles to Equal Opportunity' (forthcoming).

J. W. Atkinson, 'Motivational determinants of risk taking behavior', *Psychological Review*, 64 (1957) pp. 359–72.

L. Bailyn, 'Freeing Work from the Constraints of Location and Time', *New Tech. Work and Employment* 3, no. 2 (1988), pp. 143–52.

L. Bailyn, 'Toward the Perfect Workplace?', *Social Aspects of Computing*, 34, no. 4 (April, 1989), pp. 460–71.

J. Bardwick, *Readings in the Psychology of Women* (New York: Harper and Row, 1972).

J. Bardwick, 'The Dynamics of Successful People', *New Research on Women* (Ann Arbor: University of Michigan Press, 1981).

M. Barrett and H. Roberts, 'Doctors and their patients: the social control of women in general practice', in C. Smart and B. Smart (eds), *Women, Sexuality and Social Control* (London: Routledge and Kegan Paul, 1978).

G. Baruch, R. Barnett, C. Rivers, *Lifeprints* (New York: Signet, 1983).

References

E. Beardsley Butler, *Women and the Trades: Pittsburgh, 1907–1908* (Pittsburgh: University of Pittsburgh Press, 1984).

A. Beck, *Cognitive Therapy and Emotional Disorders* (New York: International Universities Press, 1976).

G. Becker, *Human Capital: A Theoretical and Empirical Analysis with Special Reference to Education* (New York, 1964).

G. Becker, 'A theory of the allocation of time,' *Economic Journal*, 75, no. 299 (1965), pp. 493–517.

V. Beechy, 'Some notes on female wage labour in capitalist production,' *Capital and Class*, no. 3 (1977), pp. 45–66.

D. Bem and S. Bem, 'We're all non-conscious sexists', *Psychology Today*, 4, no. 6 (November 1970).

J. Bernard, *The Female World* (New York: Free Press, 1981).

Beyond the Career Break, IMS report no. 223 (IMS: University of Sussex, 1992).

M. Bone, *Preschool Children and their Need for Day Care*, Office of Population Census and Surveys (London: HMSO, 1977).

N. Bonney and E. Reinach, 'Full-time Houseworkers: Changing Roles and Diverging Experiences', paper presented to Cambridge Social Stratification Seminar (10 September 1992).

J. Bowlby, *Attachment and Loss*, Vol. 1 (London: Hogarth Press, 1969).

J. Bowlby, *Attachment and Loss*, Vol. 2 (New York: Basic Books, 1973).

J. Bowlby, *Attachment and Loss*, Vol. 3 (London: Hogarth Press and Institute of Psychoanalysis, 1980).

J. Brannen and P. Moss, *Managing Mothers: Dual earner households after maternity leave* (London: Unwin Hyman, 1991).

J. B. Braslow and M. Heins, 'Women in Medical Education', *New England Journal of Medicine*, 305 (May, 1981), pp. 1129–35.

F. Bright, *Futures* (London: Collins, 1983).

G. Brim, *Ambition* (New York: Basic Books, 1992).

A. A. Brooks, *Children of Fast-Track Parents* (New York: Viking, 1989).

I. Brovermann *et al.*, 'Sex Role Stereotypes and Clinical Judgements of Mental Health', *Journal of Consulting and Clinical Psychology*, 34 (February 1970).

L. M. Brown and C. Gilligan, *Meeting at the Crossroads: Women's psychology and girls' development* (Cambridge, Mass.: Harvard University Press, 1992).

G. W. Brown and T. Harris, *Social Origins of Depression* (London: Tavistock, 1978).

R. J. Burke, 'Women in management in Canada: past, present and future prospects', *Women in Management Review and Abstracts*, 6, (1991), pp. 11–16.

H. Callaway, 'Women's perspectives: research as revision', in P. Reason and J. Rowan (eds), *Human Inquiry* (Chichester: Wiley, 1981).

J. Chaney, 'Social networks and job information: the situation of women who return to work', a research project funded by the EOC/SSRC Joint Panel on Equal Opportunities (Equal Opportunities Commission, Manchester, 1981).

N. Chodorow, *The Reproduction of Mothering* (Berkeley: University of California Pres, 1978).

P. D. Cleary and D. Mechanic, 'Sex Differences in psychological distress among married people', *Journal of Health and Social Behaviour*, 24 (1983), pp. 111–21.

R. Cooperstock and H. L. Lennard, 'Some social meanings of tranquillizer use', *Sociology of Health and Illness*, I, no. 3, (1979), pp. 331–47.

R. Coward, *Our Treacherous Hearts: Why women let men have their way* (London: Faber, 1992).

F. Crosby, 'The denial of personal discrimination,' *American Behavioral Scientist*, 27, (1989), pp. 371–86.

A. Dally, *Inventing Motherhood* (New York: Schocken Books, 1981).

A. Dilnot and M. Kell, 'Male unemployment and women's work', in A. Dilnot and I. Walker (eds.) *The Economics of Social Security* (Oxford: Oxford University Press, 1989).

M. Douglas, *The Home and the School* (London: MacGibbon and Kee, 1964).

M. Douglas, *All Our Future* (London: MacGibbon and Kee, 1968).

C. Dowling, *The Cinderella Complex* (New York: Summit Books, 1981).

J. Duesenberry, 'Comment on "An Economic Analysis of Fertility," by Gary Becker', in *Demographic and Economic Change in Developed Countries* (Princeton: Universities–National Bureau Conference series, 11, 1960).

J. Duncombe and D. Marsden, '"Workaholics" and "Whingeing Women": Gender Inequalities in the Performance of "Emotion Work",' Cambridge Social Stratification Seminar (9 September 1992).

D. Ehrensaft, *Parenting Together: Men and women sharing the care of their children* (New York: Free Press, 1987).

J. Elliot and F. Huppert, 'In sickness and in health: associations between physical and mental well-being, employment and parental status in a British nationwide sample of married women', *Psychological Medicine*, 21 (1991), pp. 515–24.

B. A. Engel, 'Soviet Women', *Signs*, Vol. 12, no. 4, (1987), pp. 781–96.

C. F. Epstein, *Women's Place, Options and Limits in Professional Careers* (Berkeley: University of California Press, 1980).

S. Epstein and W. Fenz, in Gardner Linzey and Calvin Halls (eds), *Theories of Personality: Primary sources and research* (Ann Arbor: University of Michigan, 1979).

E. H. Erikson, *Childhood and Society*, 2nd edn (New York: W. W. Norton, 1963).

S. Faludi, *Backlash: The undeclared war against American women* (New York: Crown, 1991).

N. T. Feather and A. C. Raphelson, 'Fear of Success in Australian and American student groups: Motive or sex-role stereotype?', *Journal of Personality*, 42 (1974), pp. 190–201.

M. Fong and G. Paul, 'The Changing Role of Women in Employment in Eastern Europe', World Bank Discussion Paper, no. 8213 (February, 1992).

M. Freedman, 'The Search for Shelters', in *Labour Markets: Segments and Shelters* (New York: Allanhead, Osman/Universal Books, 1976).

A. Freud and D. Burlingham, *Young Children in Wartime* (London: Allen and Unwin, 1943).

S. Freud, 'Female Sexuality' in J. Strachey (ed.), *Standard Edition*, Vol. 21 (London: Hogarth Press, 1961), pp. 223–43.

S. Freud, 'Femininity', in J., Strachey (ed.), *Standard Edition*, Vol. 22 (London: Hogarth Press, 1964), pp. 112–35.

References

N. Friday, *My Mother My Self: The daughter's search for identity* (New York: Delacorte Press, 1977).

B. Friedan, *The Feminine Mystique* (New York: Summit Books, 1963).

B. Friedan, *The Second Stage* (New York: Summit, 1981).

V. Fuchs, *Women's Quest for Economic Equality* (Cambridge, Mass.: Harvard University Press, 1988).

J. K. Galbraith, *Economics and the Public Purpose* (Andre Deutsch: London, 1974).

L. R. Gallese, *Women Like Us* (New York: Morrow, 1985).

E. Garnsey, 'Women's Labour and Soviet Economic Growth', working paper, Department of Engineering, University of Cambridge (1982).

E. Garnsey, 'Working Hours and Workforce Divisions', in R. Tarling (ed.), *Flexibility in Labour Markets* (London: Academic Press, 1987).

E. Garnsey, 'Exploring a critical systems perspective', *Innovation in the Social Sciences* (forthcoming, 1993).

H. Gavron, *The Captive Wife* (Harmondsworth: Penguin, 1968).

V. George and P. Wilding, *Motherless Families* (London: Routledge and Kegan Paul, 1972).

K. Gerson, *Hard Choices* (Berkeley, California: University of California Press, 1985).

N. Gibbs, 'Has America Run out of Time?' *Time* (24 April 1989).

A. Giddens, 'Action, Structure, Power', in *Profiles and Critiques in Social Theory* (London: Macmillan, 1982), Ch. 3.

C. Gilligan, *In a Difference Voice* (Cambridge, Mass.: Harvard University Press, 1982).

C. Gilligan, *et al., Making Connections* (Cambridge, Mass.: Harvard University Press, 1989).

J. Ginn and S. Arber, 'Class, caring and the life course', in S. Arber and M. Evandrou (eds), *Ageing, Independence and the Life Course* (London: Jessica Kingsley, forthcoming).

C. Golden, *Understanding the Gender Gap* (New York: Oxford University Press, 1990).

C. Goldin, and Lois Shaw and David Shapiro, 'Women's Work Plans: Contrasting expectations and actual work experience', *Monthly Labor Review*, 110 (November 1987), pp. 7–13.

S. Gordon, *Prisoners of Men's Dreams* (Boston: Little, Brown, 1991).

G. Greer, *The Female Eunuch* (London: MacGibbon and Kee, 1970).

V. Grove, *The Compleat Woman: Marriage, motherhood, career* (London: Hogarth Press, 1987).

H. E. Harlow and M. K. Harlow. 'Learning to Love', *American Scientist*, 54 (3), (1966), pp. 244–72.

V. Havel, 'The power of the powerless' in *Living in Truth* (London: Faber, 1986).

C. Heilbrun, *Writing a Woman's Life* (New York: Ballantine Books, 1989).

M. Heins, *et al.*, 'Current Status of Women Physicians', *International Journal of Women's Studies*, 1: 3 (1978), pp. 297–305.

M. Heins and J. Thomas, 'Women Medical Students: A new appraisal', *Journal of the American Medical Association*, 34, no. 1 (1979) pp. 408–15.

M. Heins, *et al.*, 'The Importance of Extra-Family Support on Career Choices of Women', *Personnel and Guidance Journal* (April 1982).

References

R. Helson, V. Mitchell and G. Moane, 'Personality and Patterns of Adherence and Nonadherence to the Social Clock', *Journal of Personality and Social Psychology*, 26 (1984), pp. 1079–96.

M. Hennig and A. Jardim, *The Managerial Woman* (London: Pan, 1979).

S. A. Hewlett, *A Lesser Life: The Myth of Women's Liberation in America* (New York: Warner Books, 1986).

S. A. Hewlett, *When the Bough Breaks: The cost of neglecting our children* (New York: Basic Books, 1991).

K. Hirsch, 'A New Vision of Corporate America', *Boston Sunday Globe Magazine* (21 April 1992), p. 16.

A. Hochschild, 'Foreword', in T. Arendall, *Mothers and Divorce* (Berkeley: University of California Press, 1986).

A. Hochschild, with Anne Machung, *The Second Shift* (New York: Viking, 1989).

L. W. Hoffman, 'Early Childhood Experiences and Women's Achievement Motives', *Journal of Social Issues*, 28, no. 2, (1972), pp. 129–55.

L. W. Hoffman, 'The Effects of Maternal Employment on the Academic Attitudes and Performance of School-Aged Children', *School Psychology Review*, 9, (1980), pp. 319–35.

B. Holland (ed.), *Soviet Sisterhood* (Bloomington: University of Indiana Press, 1983).

M. Horner, 'Fail: Bright Women', *Psychology Today*, 3 (6) (1969), p. 36.

M. Horner, 'Towards an understanding of achievement-related conflicts in women', *Journal of Social Issues*, 28, (1972), pp. 157–76.

M. Horner, C. Nadelson and M. Notman (eds), *The Challenge of Change: Perspectives on family, work and education* (New York: Plenum, 1983).

K. Horney, *Feminine Psychology* (New York: Norton and Norton, 1976).

M. E. Hyland, C. Curtis, and D. Mason, 'Fear of Success: motive and cognition', *Journal of Personality and Social Psychology*, 55 (1985), pp. 642–51.

M. Hyland, 'There is no motive to avoid success: the compromise explanation for success-avoiding behavior, *Journal of Personality* 57, no. 7 (1989), pp. 665–91.

D. C. Jack, *Silencing the Self: Women and Depression* (Cambridge, Mass.: Harvard University Press, 1991).

R. M. Kanter, *When Giants Learn to Dance* (New York: Simon and Schuster, 1989).

R. C. Kessler and J. A. McRae, 'The effects of wives' employment on the mental health of married men and married women', *American Sociological Review*, 47 (1982), pp. 216–27.

W. Kiechel III, 'The Workaholic Generation,' *Fortune* (10 April 1989), p. 51.

Korn/Ferry International, *Profile of Women Senior Executives* (Washington, DC, 1982).

P. Leach, *Who Cares? A New Deal for Mothers and their Small Children* (Harmondsworth: Penguin, 1979).

E. Lee, *Export-processing Zones and Industrial Employment in Asia* (ILO, ARTEP, 1985), p. 40; cited in Elizabeth Garnsey and Liba Paukert, *Industrial Change and Women's Employment: Trends in the new international division of labour*, Research Series, no. 86 (Geneva: International Institute for Labour Studies, 1987).

References

J. Lieberman, 'Issues in the Psychoanalytic Treatment of Single Females Over Thirty', *Psychoanalytic Review*, 78, no. 2 (Summer 1991), pp. 178–98.

N. Lyndon, *No More Sex War* (London: Sinclair-Stevenson, 1992).

J. Marshall, *Women Managers: Travellers in a Male World* (Chichester: John Wiley, 1984).

J. Marshall, 'Patterns of Cultural Awareness as Coping Strategies for Women Managers', in S. E. Kahm and B. C. Lang (eds), *Women, Work and Coping: A multidisciplinary approach to workplace stress* (Montreal: McGill–Queen's University Press, 1993).

W. R. Mattox, Jr, 'The Family Time Famine', *Family Policy* 3, no. 1 (1990).

J. Micklewright and G. Giannelli, 'Why do women married to employed men have low participation rates?' Working paper, European University Institute, Florence (1991).

O. Moles, National Institute of Education, paper presented to conference, Washington, DC (25 March 1983).

L. Monahan, D. Kuhn and P. Shaver, 'Intrapsychic versus cultural explanations of the fear of success motive', *Journal of Personality and Social Psychology*, 29 (1974), pp. 60–4.

G. Morrow, 'Children's Work', paper presented to the Cambridge Social Stratification Seminar (9 September 1992).

C. Nadelson, C. *et al.*, 'Success or Failure: Psychotherapeutic Considerations for Women in Conflict, *American Journal of Psychiatry*, 135, no. 9 (1978), pp. 1092–6.

C. Nadelson, 'The Psychology of Women: An Overview', paper presented to the American Psychiatric Association Conference, Women's Studies in Psychiatric Education (San Francisco, 17 January 1983).

J. Natti, 'Part-time employment in the Nordic countries: a trap for women?', paper delivered to the International Working Party on Labour Market Segmentation Conference in Cambridge (14 July 1992).

S. Newell, 'What affects women's career decisions at the point when they enter motherhood?', paper presented to the Women and Psychology Conference (14 July 1990).

A. Oakley, *Housewife* (Harmondsworth: Pelican, 1976).

A. Oakley, *Women Confined: Towards a Sociology of Childbirth* (Oxford: Martin Robertson, 1980).

A. Oakley, *Taking it Like a Woman* (London: Jonathan Cape, 1984).

A. Oakley, *Subject Woman* (London: Faber, 1985).

J. O'Reilly, *The Girl I Left Behind* (New York: Macmillan, 1982).

T. Parsons, 'The Social Structure of the Family,' in R. Anshen (ed.), *The Family, Its Functions and Destiny* (New York: Harper, 1949).

B. Pfau Effinger, *Erwerbsverlauf und Risiko*. Arbeitsmarktrisiken im Generationenvergleich Weinhem (1990).

B. Pfau-Effinger, 'Modernisation, Culture and Part-Time Employment', paper presented to the XIVth World Conference of the International Working Party on Labour Market Segmentation in Cambridge (16–21 July 1992).

R. Philips and F. Gubroy, 'Sex Role Stereotypes and Clinical Judgements of Mental Health: The Broverman's findings re-examined', *Sex Roles* 12 (1985), pp. 179–93.

S. Plath, *Letters Home*, in A. S. Plath (ed.) (New York: Bantam, 1962).

L. Pollock, *Forgotten Children: Parent–Child Relationships from 1500 to 1900* (Cambridge: Cambridge University Press, 1983).

S. Prendergast and A. Prout, 'Education for Parenthood' (Cambridge: Child Care and Development Group, University of Cambridge, 1985).

S. Pudney and J. Thomas, 'Unemployment benefit, incentives and the labour supply of wives of unemployed men: econometric estimates' (London: HMSO, May 1992).

L. Radloff, 'Sex Differences in Depression', *Sex Roles*, 1, no. 3 (1975), pp. 249–65.

R. Rapoport and R. N. Rapoport, *Dual Career Families Re-examined* (London: Martin Robertson, 1976).

J. O. Raynor and E. E. Entin, 'Future orientation and achievement motivation', in J. O. Rayor and E. E. Entin (eds) *Motivation, Career, Striving and Aging* (New York: Hemisphere Books, 1982), pp. 13–82.

M. S. Rice, *Working Class Wives* (London: Virago, 1981).

A. Rich, *Of Woman Born* (London: Virago, 1977).

J. L. Richardson, *et al.*, 'Substance Abuse Among Eighth-Grade Students Who Take care of Themselves After School', *Pediatrics* 84, no. 3 (September 1989), pp. 556–66.

C. E. Roass and J. Mirrowsky, 'Child care and emotional adjustment to wives' employment, *Journal of Health and Social Behaviour*, 29 (1988), pp. 127–38.

A. Rock, 'Can you afford your kids?' *Money* (July 1990).

S. V. Rosser, 'The Gender Equation', *The Sciences* (September–October 1992), pp. 42–7.

A. Rossi, 'A biosocial perspective on parenting', *Daedelus*, 106, no. 2 (1978), pp. 1–31.

D. Rowe, *The Depression Handbook: The way of understanding depression leads to wisdom and freedom* (London: Collins, 1991).

J. Rubery, 'The Economics of Equal Value', Research Discussion Series No. 3 (Manchester, England: Equal Opportunities Commission, 1992).

J. Rubery (ed.), *Women and Recession* (London: Routledge and Kegan Paul, 1988).

L. Rubin, *Women of a Certain Age* (New York: Harper and Row, 1979).

M. Rutter, *Maternal Deprivation Reassessed* (Middlesex: C. Nicholls, 1972).

G. Sassen, 'Success Anxiety in Women: A Constructivist Interpretation of its Source and its Significance', *Harvard Educational Review*, Vol. 50, no. 1 (February 1980), pp. 13–24.

I. Sawhill, 'Economic Perspectives on the Family', in Alice Amsden (ed.), *The Economics of Women and Work* (Harmondsworth: Penguin, 1980).

M. Scarf, *Unfinished Business: Pressure points in the lives of women* (New York: Doubleday, 1981).

J. Schor, *The Overworked American: The unexpected decline of leisure* (New York: Basic Books, 1991).

F. N. Schwartz, 'Management women and the new facts of life', *Harvard Business Review* (January–February 1989), pp. 65–76.

P. Schwartz, 'Working Mothers of Infants: Conflicts and Coping Strategies', in *Women's Lives* (Ann Arbor, Michigan: Center for Women's Studies, University of Michigan, 1979).

References

M. Seligman, 'Learned Helplessness and Depression', in R. Friedrich and M. Katz (eds), *The Psychology of Depression: Contemporary Theory and Research* (Washington, DC: US Government Printing House, 1979).

D. L. Sheppard, 'Organizations, power and sexuality: the image and self image of women managers', in J. Hearn, D. L. Sheppard, P. Tancred-Sheriff, G. Burrell (eds), *The Sexuality of Organizations* (London: Sage Publications, 1989).

A. Shreve, *Women Together, Women Alone: The legacy of the consciousness-raising movement* (New York: Viking Penguin, 1989).

M. Stanworth, *Gender and Schooling* (London: Women's Research and Resource Center, 1981).

D. Stern, *The Interpersonal World of the Infant: A view from psychoanalysis and developmental psychology* (New York: Basic Books, 1985).

A. Symonds, 'The Liberated Woman: Healthy and Neurotic', *American Journal of Psychoanalysis*, 34 (1974), pp. 177–83.

A. Symonds, 'A Neurotic Dependency in Successful Women', *Journal of the American Academy of Psychoanalysis*, 38 (1978), pp. 195–205.

D. Tannen, *You Just Don't Understand* (New York: Morrow, 1990).

L. M. Terman and M. N. Oden, *The Gifted Child Grows Up* (Stanford, CA: California University Press, 1947).

J. Ussher, *Women's Madness: Misogyny or mental illness* (Hemel Hemsptead, England: Harvester, 1991).

A. Walker, *In Search of Our Mother's Gardens* (New York: Harcourt Brace Jovanovich, 1983).

M. Weissman and G. Klerman, 'Sex Differences and the Epidemiology of Depression', *Archives of General Psychiatry*, 34 (1977), pp. 98–111.

W. H. Whyte, *The Organization Man* (New York: Simon and Schuster, 1956).

S. C. Watkins, Jane A. Menken and John Bongaarts, 'Demographic Foundations of Family Change', *American Sociological Review* 52, no. 3 (1987), pp. 346–58.

P. Wilmot and M. Young, *The Symmetrical Family* (London: Routledge and Kegan Paul, 1973).

N. Wolf, *The Beauty Myth* (London: Chatto, 1990).

V. Woolf, 'Professions for Women' in *The Death of the Mother and Other Essays* (New York: Harcourt Brace, 1942), pp. 236–8.

'Working Mothers and Preserving Family Living Standards', Congress of the United States, Joint Economic Committee (9 May 1986).

T. Vilkinas, 'Australian women in management', *Women in Management Review and Abstracts*, 6 (1991), pp. 17–25.

V. Zelizer, *Pricing the Priceless Child: The changing social values of children* (New York: Basic Books, 1985).

H. Zuckerman, J. R. Cole and J. T. Bruer, *The Outer Circle: Women in the scientific community* (New York: W. W. Norton, 1992).

Index